By the same Author

★

NO EASY WAY

FOUR GUINEAS
(A Journey Through West Africa)

THE SORCERER'S APPRENTICE
(A Journey Through East Africa)

RACE AND POLITICS IN KENYA
With Margery Perham

EAST AFRICA
(Commonwealth in Pictures)

ATLANTIC ORDEAL

WHITE MAN'S COUNTRY:
LORD DELAMERE AND THE MAKING OF KENYA

Novels

THE RED ROCK WILDERNESS

A THING TO LOVE

I DON'T MIND IF I DO

THE WALLED CITY

RED STRANGERS
(A Story of Kenya)

DEATH OF AN ARYAN

MURDER ON SAFARI

MURDER AT GOVERNMENT HOUSE

Kinsey

THE FLAME TREES OF THIKA

Memories of an African Childhood

Elspeth Huxley

WILLIAM MORROW AND COMPANY
NEW YORK

To the images
of whom Robin and Tilly are reflections,
and the ghosts who sleep at Thika

Printed in the United States of America.

Library of Congress Catalog Card Number 59-13894

Chapter One

WE set off in an open cart drawn by four whip-scarred little oxen and piled high with equipment and provisions. No medieval knight could have been more closely armoured than were Tilly and I, against the rays of the sun. A mushroom-brimmed hat, built of two thicknesses of heavy felt and lined with red flannel, protected her creamy complexion, a long-sleeved white blouse clasped her by the neck and a heavy skirt of khaki drill fell to her booted ankles.

I sat beside my mother, only a little less fortified in a pith helmet and a starched cotton dress. The oxen looked very thin and small for such a task but moved off with resignation, if not with speed, from the Norfolk hotel. Everything was dusty; one's feet descended with little plops into a soft, warm, red carpet, a red plume followed every wagon down the street, the dust had filmed over each brittle eucalyptus leaf and stained the seats and backs of rickshaws waiting under the trees.

We were going to Thika, a name on a map where two rivers joined. Thika in those days—the year was 1913—was a favourite camp for big-game hunters and beyond it there was only bush and plain. If you went on long enough you would come to mountains and forests no one had mapped and tribes whose languages no one could understand. We were not going as far as that, only two days' journey in the ox-cart to a bit of El Dorado my father had been fortunate enough to buy in the bar of the Norfolk hotel from a man wearing an Old Etonian tie.

While everyone else strode about Nairobi's dusty cart-tracks in bush shirts and khaki shorts or riding breeches, Roger Stilbeck was always neatly dressed in a light worsted suit of perfect cut, and wore gold cuff-links and dark brogue shoes. No bishop could have appeared more respectable, and his wife, who looked very elegant, was said to be related to the Duke of Montrose. Roger Stilbeck had met us at the station when we arrived and Mrs. Stilbeck came to see us off, a mark of grace by no means conferred on every buyer of her husband's land.

Tilly, eager as always to extract from every moment its last drop of interest or pleasure, had ridden out early on the plains to see the game, and had returned peppered with tiny red ticks. These she was picking off her clothes while she supervised the loading of the cart. Wearing a look of immense concentration, as when at work on her embroidery, she popped them one by one with finger and thumb. Mrs. Stilbeck watched with fascinated horror. Then she put a pale, soft-skinned hand to her eyes.

"Roger," she said, "I don't feel very well. You must take me home."

Tilly went on squashing ticks while a great many Africans in red blankets, with a good deal of shouting and noise, stowed our household goods in the cart. There was a mountain of boxes, bundles and packages. On top was perched a sewing machine, a crate of five Speckled Sussex pullets and a lavatory seat. The pullets had come with us in the ship from Tilbury and Tilly had fed them every day and let them out on the deck for exercise.

Robin, my father, did not come with us in the cart. He was there already, locating the land and, Tilly hoped, building a house to receive us. A simple grass hut could be built in a couple of days, but this needed organization, and Tilly was not counting on its being there.

"I only hope that if he builds one, he will do so on the right farm," she said.

Farm was of course the wrong word. My father had picked out on a map five hundred acres of blank space with a wriggling line, presumed to be a river, on each side.

"Best coffee land in the country," Stilbeck had remarked.

"Has anyone planted any yet?"

"My dear fellow, there's no need to *plant* coffee to make sure of that. Experts have analysed the soil. Altitude and rainfall are exactly right. Fortunes are being made already out at Kiambu. You've only got to *look* at the place to see how well everything grows. The trouble is to keep the vegetation down."

"It's untried land?" Robin ventured.

Roger Stilbeck rolled up the map. "You're right, of course, about that. If you're in any doubt, my dear fellow, I shouldn't look at it. Between ourselves, I'm rather glad. Buck Ponsonby has bought a thousand acres a bit farther out and he was keen as mustard to get the whole block. I told him I couldn't let him have it as I'd given my word to another fellow. This leaves the way clear. What about a ranching proposition down near Voi? Or there's a syndicate starting to buy up cheap land in Uganda. . . ."

Robin bought the five hundred acres between the wriggling lines at Thika. He paid four pounds an acre, a fabulous price in those days. As this was much more than he could afford, he also bought a share in the syndicate in Uganda, which Roger Stilbeck said was certain to make a great deal of money in a very short while and which would therefore enable him to finance the coffee enterprise at Thika. On paper, the logic was inescapable. The Uganda syndicate made nothing at all for fifteen years; Robin received the annual accounts, which nearly always started with the item: "To manager's funeral expenses, six rupees." After that it went into liquidation.

Robin got a map from the Land Office with a lot of lines ruled on it, from which the position of our holding could be deduced. Nothing had been properly surveyed. The boundary between the land earmarked for settlement and land reserved for the Kikuyu was about a mile away.

"Any amount of labour," Roger Stilbeck had said. "You've only got to lift your finger and in they come. Friendly enough, if a bit raw. Wonderfully healthy climate, splendid neighbours, magnificent sport, thousands of years of untapped fertility locked up in the soil. I congratulate you, my dear fellow, I really do. You've been lucky to get this opportunity. Buck Ponsonby was bitterly disappointed. Best of luck, and look us up when you come in for the races. Keep in touch, old man."

When our oxen had plodded over Ainsworth bridge, just beyond the Norfolk, we were out of the town. The dusty road ran through a mixture of bush and native shambas, where shaven-headed women in beads and leather aprons weeded, dug, and drew water from the swampy stream that gave the town its name in gourds or in *debes*, those four-gallon paraffin tins that had become a universal water-vessel, measure and roofing material. The road was not a thing that had been made, it had simply arisen from the passage of wagons. For the most part it ran across a plain whose soil was largely murram, a coarse red gravel that baked hard and supported only thin, wiry grass, sad-looking thorn trees and tortured-branched erythrinas, with flowers the colour of red sealing wax.

It became very hot in our ox-cart, or on it rather, as we had no covering. Tilly hoisted a parasol with black and white stripes which helped a little, but it had not been made for tropic suns. I was fortunate; being only six or seven, I wore no stays or stockings, but Tilly was tightly laced in, her waist was wasp-like, her skirt voluminous and the whole *ensemble* might have been designed to prevent the circulation of air. In a very short while the dust and sweat combined to make us both look like Red Indians, with strange white rings around our eyes.

Once out of the town the oxen flagged, and no wonder, and the driver shouted less. He fell into a kind of shuffle beside the beasts, who were coated now with flies. We had to keep flapping flies off our own faces. When we encountered a span of sixteen oxen drawing a long, low wagon we were immersed in a thick red fog which made us choke and smart and settled over everything. The stunted thorn-trees and shrubs beside the road were coated with it and we travelled always with its sharp, dry, peculiar smell tickling our nostrils.

One cannot describe a smell because there are no words to do so in the English language, apart from those that place it in a very general category, like sweet or pungent. So I cannot characterize this, nor compare it with any other, but it was the smell of travel in those days, in fact the smell of Africa—dry, peppery yet rich and deep, with an undertone of native body smeared with fat and red ochre and giving out a ripe, partly rancid odour which nauseated some Europeans when they first encountered it but which I, for one, grew to enjoy. This was the smell of the Kikuyu, who were mainly vegetarian. The smell of tribes from the Victoria Nyanza basin, who were meat-eaters and sometimes cannibals, was quite different: much stronger and more musky, almost acrid, and, to me, much less pleasant. No doubt we smelt just as strong and odd to Africans, but of course we were fewer in numbers, and more spread out.

All day long we passed through flat country with distant ranges of hills and one abrupt round bump, Donyo Sabuk, standing out from the plain. This was where a rich, benign and enormously fat American sportsman lived on a large buffalo-infested ranch called Juja, dispensing hospitality that, even in those hospitable days, was legendary, when he was not riding about on a mule that could barely be seen beneath him—he weighed over eighteen stone—shooting animals. All day long we saw game of many different kinds. The animals were still there in unsuspecting millions, they did not know that they were doomed. Tommies with their broad black insignia wagged their tails as if the world belonged to them, giraffe bent their patch-work necks towards the small spreading acacias. No one has ever seen a thin zebra, although they are stuffed with parasites; these were no exception. They looked like highly varnished animated toys. It would be tedious to list all the kinds of animal we passed.

"We might see a lion," Tilly said, "if we keep a sharp look-out." Lions were often observed to stroll about in broad day-light among their potential dinners, who displayed no alarm. But we did not see any lions; Tilly said they were asleep in the patches of reed and papyrus we passed from time to time. She longed to stop the cart and get out to look for them, as people sometimes stopped the train from Mombasa if they saw a fine specimen. We jolted on, getting hotter and hotter, and more and more irritable and sore. At last we reached Ruiru, about half-way. We were to stop there for the night. About fifteen miles a day was all that oxen could be expected to manage, or porters either, when they carried sixty-pound loads. It was quite enough, too.

Ruiru was just a few dukas kept by Indians and a river cross-ing, not even a bridge: a causeway made by shovelling murram into the swampy stream and putting up some white posts. In the rains it was awash or under water and wagons often stuck, some-times for days. Tufted papyrus grew all around, like a forest of feather dusters standing on end. A small dam had been built at Ruiru, and a flume to carry water to a turbine which made Nairobi's electricity. Once an inquisitive hippo, unable either to advance or reverse, had got wedged in the flume, and all Nairobi's lights had failed.

Our host for the night was a large-framed, flat-faced, beefy South African called Oram, a hard-bitten man in his late fifties who seemed to me immensely old, I suppose because most of the white people one met then were young, like my parents. Henry Oram was the kind of man who never settled down. He had left a prosperous farm in the Transvaal, and before that in the Free State, and before that in the Cape, to come to B.E.A. (as everyone then called it), and bully into productiveness another patch of bush and veld. He had a little bougainvillea-covered house of corrugated iron, full of sons. A number of green, shiny coffee bushes grew in rows all round it and were expected soon to make him rich, but now he could see signs of a neighbour's cultivation on the opposite ridge.

"It's getting overcrowded," he said in a South African voice, flat and strong like himself. "It's time I moved on."

"Where to?" Tilly inquired.

"They're opening up new land beyond the Plateau. Splendid country, they say. No settlers yet, no natives, lots of game and centuries of untapped fertility. I'm off to have a look at it soon."

"But your coffee's only just coming into bearing."

"This place will be a suburb of Nairobi in a few years. There's talk of a railway to Thika, soon there'll be a horde of Indians, someone will start a club. . . ."

"I don't see anything wrong about a club. And now your wife has made a home. . . ."

"With a wagon, a fire and a pound of coffee any true woman can make a home," Henry Oram replied. Tilly thought him pompous, but he may have been pulling her leg. They had quite a comfortable house at Ruiru and, as Robin pointed out, would probably sell the place for a nice profit and get a lot of good land farther out for next to nothing.

Tilly, who had the home-making instinct, remarked to Mrs. Oram: "You will be sorry to leave, now that you have made a garden."

"Oh, but the whole country is a garden; a garden God has planted. Look what He has provided—streams to drink from, trees for shade, wild fruits and honey, birds and beasts for company. How can any of His creatures improve on that? Isn't it a waste of time to plant a border when the rain coaxes up a dozen different kinds of wild flower? There's nothing I love better than to walk in the wilds and return with my hands full of the bright jewels of veld and forest—the shy creepers, pink storm lilies, humble forget-me-nots."

"They die quickly in water," Tilly said coldly. She reacted like a clam to this sort of thing, and when she summed up Mrs. Oram as a gushing woman, Mrs. Oram was condemned. Yet the Orams were hard workers, their hospitality was always unstinted and their craving for the wilder places of the earth was genuine. But everything had to be twice as big as life size.

"They are romantics," Robin suggested later.

"They are fools," Tilly replied. She disapproved of romantics, but of course was one herself, though she concealed it like a guilty secret. It is always our own qualities that most appal us when we find them in others, and for this reason Mrs. Oram entered into her bad books. Nevertheless she was grateful, and later on sent Mrs. Oram a turkey and several packets of English seeds.

Chapter Two

BEFORE the sun was really hot next morning the little weather-beaten oxen with their humps and sagging dewlaps were inspanned and we set off again down the wagon track.

On our right the tawny plain stretched away, a bowl of sunlight, to the Tana river and beyond: you felt that you could walk straight on across it to the rim of the world. On our left rose a long, dark-crested mountain range from which sprang rivers that watered a great part of Kikuyuland. These rivers, no larger than streams, had dug down through soil red as a fox and rich as chocolate to form steep valleys whose sides were now green with young millet and maize. So numerous were these streams that on a map they looked like veins and arteries in a diagram of anatomy. Our track crossed them at the point where the intervening ridges flattened out into the great plain, so we had to ford several streams; but their banks were no longer steep, and their water was becoming sluggish. Instead of mossy rocks and ferns and trees bending over rushing water, we traversed incipient swamps with papyrus and reeds.

Sometimes we passed or encountered Kikuyu travellers, the backs of the women always bent low under enormous burdens suspended by leather straps that bit into their sloping foreheads. They wore pointed leather aprons and trudged along looking like big brown snails. As a result, no doubt, of this pack-animal existence you never saw a good figure, except among the young girls; once married, the women's breasts sagged like empty purses and their legs moved in a quick, shuffling gait.

The men, on the other hand, were slim and upright and often had a remarkable look of fragility; their bodies were hairless, shining and light. The young warriors wore their locks embellished with sheep's fat and red ochre and plaited into a large number of short pigtails to hang down all round, like the fleece of a long-haired sheep; they walked with a loping stride quite different from the women's plod. By now the influence of missionaries and government combined had put them into blankets, which they wore like togas, knotted over one shoulder.

Most of the blankets were red with black stripes and looked well against coppery skins and gay red and blue ornaments. Ear-lobes were pierced, and the hole enlarged to take plugs of wood, coils of wire or bead necklaces that hung down to their shoulders; the young bloods wore a beaded belt from which depended a slim sword in a leather scabbard dyed vermilion with an extract from the root of a creeper.

We had with us in the cart a cook-cum-houseboy called Juma lent to us, as a great favour, by Roger Stilbeck to see us in. He was used to grander ways and, the farther we travelled from Nairobi, the more disapproving he became of the local inhabitants, who to me looked as wild and exciting as the gazelles and antelopes.

"They are small like pigeons," he said loftily. "They eat chickens, which make them cowardly. Look at their legs! Thin like a bustard. And their women are like donkeys, with heads as smooth as eggs. They are not to be trusted. Why do you wish to live amongst such stupid people? Here your crops will not prosper, your cattle will die. . . ."

Juma was a Swahili from the Coast, or said he was: Swahilis were fashionable, and quite a lot of people who were nothing of the sort appointed themselves as members of this race, with its Arab affinities. He also claimed to be a Muslim, though it was hard to say in what this consisted. We never saw him at his prayers and doubted if he knew the direction of Mecca. His only strict observance was his refusal to eat meat unless the throat of the animal providing it had been cut. So when Robin shot a buck, a knife would materialize in Juma's hand, he would gird his long white *kanzu* round his waist (he wore nothing underneath) and sprint like a flash to the stricken antelope. He was a great meat-lover.

He was also a magician. With three stones, a few sticks and one old, black cooking-pot he would produce a four-course meal a great deal better than anything to be had in most restaurants or hotels. He had the secret, known only to Africans, of serving food hot and promptly, and yet not dry and burnt, at any hour of the day or night. Cooks were men of substance and authority, respected and well-paid. Juma made the most of his superior position. In fact he was a bully—large, strong and black-skinned.

"We are coming now to the country of the cannibals," he

said facetiously, and quite untruthfully. "These Kikuyu, they scavenge like hyenas, they will dig up corpses and eat them. Sometimes their women give birth to snakes and lizards. They have never heard of Allah. They eat the intestines of goats and circumcise their women. They——"

"Silence, Juma!" Tilly commanded. She was hot, tired, dusty and in no mood for anatomical gossip, and her understanding of the Swahili tongue was still shaky. Although she had studied it with her usual energy and grasp on the voyage out, her phrase-book, acquired from the Society for the Propagation of the Gospel, had not always suggested sentences most helpful to intending settlers. "The idle slaves are scratching themselves" . . . "Six drunken Europeans have killed the cook" . . . turning these over in her mind, on top of the ox-cart in the sun, she doubted if their recital, even in the best Swahili, would impress Juma favourably.

After his remarks I stared at the passing Kikuyu with a new interest. They looked harmless, but that was evidently a pose. We passed a woman carrying a baby in a sling on her back, as well as a load. I could see the infant's shiny head, like a polished skittle ball, bobbing about between the mother's bent shoulders, and looked hopefully for the glimpse of a snake or lizard. But no doubt the mothers would leave these at home.

"These oxen," Juma grumbled, "they are as old as great-grandmothers, their legs are like broken sticks, this driver is the son of a hyena and lacks the brains of a frog. When the new moon has come we shall still be travelling in this worthless cart."

"No more words," Tilly said snappily. Juma had a patronizing air that she resented, and she doubted if he was showing enough respect. Those were the days when to lack respect was a more serious crime than to neglect a child, bewitch a man or steal a cow, and was generally punishable by beating. Indeed respect was the only protection available to Europeans who lived singly, or in scattered families, among thousands of Africans accustomed to constant warfare and armed with spears and poisoned arrows, but had themselves no barricades, and went about unarmed. This respect preserved them like an invisible coat of mail, or a form of magic, and seldom failed; but it had to be very carefully guarded. The least rent or puncture might, if not immediately checked and repaired, split the whole garment asunder and expose its wearer in all his human vulnerability. Kept intact, it was a thousand times stronger than all the guns and locks and metal in the world; challenged, it could be brushed aside like a spider's web. So Tilly was a little sensitive about respect, and Juma was silenced.

We came at last to a stone bridge over the Chania river, newly built, and considered to be a great achievement of the P.W.D.'s. Just below it, the river plunged over a waterfall into a pool with slimy rocks and thick-trunked trees all round it, and a little farther on it joined the Thika. This meeting-place of rivers was a famous hunting-ground; not long before, Winston Churchill had slain a lion there, and many others came to camp and shoot. The game, like the soil's fertility, seemed inexhaustible; no one could imagine the disappearance of either.

A hotel had been started just below the falls. It consisted of a low-roofed, thatched grass hut whose veranda posts were painted blue and gave the place its name; of three or four whitewashed rondavels to sleep in, and a row of stables. The manager was a lean, military-looking, sprucely-dressed man with a bald head and a long moustache, who had the misfortune to be very deaf. One day a safari visitor, admiring his host's neat attire, rashly asked: "Who made your breeches?" After he had bawled this question several times, growing more and more embarrassed, the deaf man seized his hand and shook it warmly, saying: "Ah, yes, Major Breeches, delighted to see you, hope you will enjoy your stay." After that the innkeeper was always called Major Breeches, and I never knew his real name at all. The owner was a rich young man called Harry Penton whose best-known exploit (if it could be called that) was to be found stark naked astride the roof of the Norfolk hotel proclaiming himself to be a mushroom, and holding a tin bath over his head.

Robin rode down on a mule to meet us at the Blue Posts.

"Is the house built?" Tilly asked hopefully.

"Not exactly," Robin answered. "I've picked out a splendid site, only there doesn't seem to be any labour to build it with."

"But Roger Stilbeck said there was any amount."

"Perhaps he was thinking of ticks and white ants; there are plenty of those."

"Well, we've got tents," Tilly said. I think she was glad,

really; already she had fallen in love with camp life and was in no hurry to become civilized again.

"There are said to be some chiefs in the reserve," Robin added. "I shall go and see them. The bush is much heavier than Stilbeck led me to believe. I shall have to do a lot of clearing before I can plough any land."

All the clearing had to be done by hand, by young men with pangas. They started off in blankets but soon laid these aside and glistened in the sun like red fish, jingling with charms and ornaments. They did not work hard, and rested often, and their wages were very low. Generally speaking they could earn the price of a goat in thirty days. This was about four rupees. The goat would be added to a flock being slowly assembled to pay for a bride.

"I can only find one river," Robin added. "The other seems to be just a sort of gully with no water in it. And there are several *vleis* which won't be much use."

"Mr. Stilbeck doesn't seem to have been particularly truthful."

"Perhaps he didn't know himself," suggested Robin, who always found excuses, when he could, for his fellow-men, and indeed for himself where necessary. "There's a lot of red oat grass, which everyone says means high fertility. The stream that *is* there has a nice fall and we shall be able to put in a ram. Later on perhaps a little turbine might be possible. . . . There's building stone by the river bank. And lots of duiker and guinea-fowl; we oughtn't to go hungry, anyway."

It all sounded wonderful, except the ticks. I had already found a lot crawling up my legs and had learnt to pluck them off and squash them in my fingers. They were red and active, and itched like mad when they dug into the skin. They left an itchy little bump and, if you scratched it, you soon developed a sore.

There were also jiggas. These burrowed under your toe-nails, laid their eggs and created a swollen, red, tormenting place on your toe. To extract it, you had to wait until the jigga was ripe. Juma was an expert at this. He would seize a needle, which you first held in a match-flame, grip your toe with thumb and forefinger and plunge the needle in with such skill and dispatch that in a few moments he had cleared a pathway to the jigga and extracted on the end of his weapon the neatest little white bag, about as large as an onion seed, containing the eggs.

It was the female who caused all the trouble; male jiggas either leapt about at large, or displayed the masculine habit of clustering together, in this case round the eyes or ears of dogs and chickens, evidently the clubs, lodges and messes of the jigga world. I soon learnt never to go barefoot, or, if I had mislaid my slippers, to walk with my toes curled up off the ground, a habit that persisted for years after jiggas had passed out of my life.

We had reached, now, the end of the road: or, rather, the road continued to Fort Hall, where perhaps a quarter of a million Kikuyus were ruled by a solitary District Commissioner, and we had to make our way through roadless country to our piece of land. This lay uphill, towards the Kikuyu reserve.

"I don't know how the cart will get there," Robin mused. "For one thing, there are no bridges."

"Then we must get some built," Tilly replied. She never dwelt for long on difficulties.

Robin borrowed a mule for each of us from Major Breeches and we set out early next morning, before the heat of the day. A steepish hill immediately confronted us. Dry, wiry-stalked brown grass—hay, as it were, on the hoof—reached up to the mules' shoulders and wrapped itself round my legs and knees. There were trees, but this was not forest; each tree grew on its own. Most of these were erythrinas, about the size of apple-trees, with rough bark and twisted boughs—rather tortured-looking, not calm and dignified like cedars; they bore their brilliant red flowers on bare branches, and only when these were over turned their attention to leaves. Tapering ant-hills like spires, or the ruins of castles, thrust themselves above the grass and bush; they were hard as sandstone, and the same colour. These were the craft of termites and underneath each one, if you dug, and if it was still in use, you would find a big, fat, slug-like white queen, large as a sausage, manufacturing egg after egg for years on end.

It soon grew very hot. The erythrinas were in bloom, and glowed like torches: Tilly called them sealing-wax trees. Small doves with self-important breasts cooed from the branches. The country undulated like the waves of the sea.

We followed a native path that corkscrewed about like a demented snake. There was not a straight stretch in it, and one could not see why, it did not seem to be avoiding anything, or even linking up dwellings. Its convolutions must have made the journey three times as long. Our attempts at short cuts were unsuccessful. The first time we tried it, we came to an unexpected stream with boggy edges which we failed to cross, and had to rejoin the path. Our second attempt led to the sudden disappearance of Robin. At one moment he was there, or at least the top part of him was, sheltering under a dirty, battered, broad-brimmed felt hat, with a dreamy look on his finely-cut, amiable features—the bottom part was hidden by long grass; at the next, he had completely vanished. A swaying and rustling in the grass betrayed the mule, as a disturbance in the ocean will suggest the passage of a school of fish just below the surface.

"Robin," Tilly called in alarm. "What's happened?"

Had we indeed reached the land of magicians? I looked round, half-expecting to see him transformed into a tree. The grass writhed, his head slowly rose, hatless, followed by his shoulders.

"The mule has got my theodolite," he said. This object, folded up, was strapped to the saddle; he had gone to great trouble to borrow it, for he thought it would help him to install a ram and other mechanical devices.

The mule had fallen into a hole made by ant-bears or by wild pigs. The ground was perforated by such cavities, and thenceforward we stuck to the path. Even that was not fool-proof, but at least you could see the holes, or the mule could. The mules were tiny, and walked with very short tripping steps, like dancers. When they decided to stop for a breather no amount of belabouring and kicking would budge them an inch. It seemed a very long five miles, and the heat stifled us like a heavy blanket. Cicadas kept up a shrill, continuous chorus that quivered like the heat in the air, and the heads of the grasses. It seemed that everything was quivering—air, heat, grass, even the mules twitching their hides to dislodge flies who paid no attention; the strident insect falsetto seemed like the voice of air itself, chattering through all eternity to earth and grass. The light was blinding and everything was on a high note, intensified, concentrated: heat, light, sound, all blended into a substance as hard and bright and indestructible as quicksilver.

I had never before seen heat, as you can see smoke or rain. But there it was, jigging and quavering above brown grasses and spiky thorn-trees and flaring erythrinas. If I could have stretched my hand out far enough I could surely have grasped it, a kind of colourless jelly. But it danced away as I rode uncomfortably towards it, my mule's feet now and then tripping off tufts and hummocks.

Once or twice, on rounding a hairpin bend, we found ourselves face to face with a Kikuyu who stood transfixed, just like an antelope pierced by the instinct to bolt, and then stepped aside to let us pass. But the women uttered high-pitched squeals like those of piglets, and scattered into the grass as if they had been partridges, their loads and babies swaying on their backs. We could see their heads turned towards us at a safe distance in startled alarm, while the men shouted at them not to be fools. But they would not approach. They chattered in excited voices, like a flock of starlings, the wire coils on their arms winking in the sun.

"You see," Robin remarked with a certain glum satisfaction, "it scarcely looks as if they're longing to come out to work."

This ride through sun and heat, jolted by the sluggish mules, prickling with sweat, seemed to go on forever. We crossed a treeless *vlei* whose grass was short and wiry and where a duiker leapt away from under the mules' feet. Robin pulled up and said, "Here we are." We did not seem to be anywhere. Everything was just the same, biscuit-brown, quivering with heat and grasshoppers. There was not even an erythrina tree.

"You mean this is the farm?" Tilly asked. Her voice suggested that her feelings were much the same as mine. Even Robin did not sound very confident when he replied that it was.

None of us quite knew what to say, so Robin began to praise our surroundings in a rather hearty voice he always used when bolstering-up was needed.

"This grass and stuff will burn off easily, we ought to be able to start our ploughing before the rains. There's not a lot of clearing to be done in places, for instance round here."

"This is a swamp," Tilly objected. It did not look like one, in fact it was hard as rock; but we had been told that rain would flood these bits of open *vlei*, and we could see that nothing seemed anxious to grow there.

"Not at all," Robin replied, rather hurt. "Roger said *all* the land was ploughable. Except of course the river bank, which is just over there."

"I can't see a river," Tilly said.

"Of course you can't, if you don't look." Robin's testiness was a sign of disappointment; he had hoped for Tilly's enthusiasm. He himself had already furnished the site with a large mansion equipped with running water and electric light, with a garden, an avenue of flame trees and several hundred acres of fruiting coffee trees.

"This is where I thought we'd put the house," he added, leading the way up a slight rise to command a prospect of more brown grass, dark-green spiky bush and scattered trees. "There's a good view towards Mount Kenya, and we can ram the water to a reservoir on top of the hill and feed it down by gravity to the house and factory. The pulping place will be down there, and the first plantation over to the left; we might irrigate a vegetable garden, too, and start a small dairy. Lots of people will be settling here soon, we can sell them milk and butter and make a bit that way. Then we can plant an avenue, and an orchard, and make a feeder road of course down to Thika. I've heard that the Italian Mission has some coffee seedlings; if I can buy them there, we'll save at least a year, and make a nursery by the river for the next plantation, over towards the other boundary. . . ."

Robin talked on; the whole place was thriving and making several thousand pounds a year before Tilly had managed to dismount and sit down on an old eroded ant-heap to wipe her face, coated with sweat and red dust as all our faces were, and start to pull ticks off her ankles.

"And in the meantime," she said, "it would be nice to have a grass hut to sleep in, or even a few square yards cleared to pitch the tent."

"Oh, that won't take long. But just for the next night or two, perhaps we'd better put up at the Blue Posts."

So we all rode back again, rather silently, though Robin rallied once or twice to tell us of the neighbours who would soon hem us in on every side. Tilly said he made it sound like Wimbledon, to which Robin complacently replied:

"One of them *is* a stockbroker, as a matter of fact." All the land had been sold, he added, though the only settler actually to arrive was a South African who was living in a tent somewhere by the river and spent all his time shooting animals;

Robin had tried to find him, but he was never there. He had some oxen, however, and Robin hoped for help over the ploughing.

Robin had never ploughed anything in his life before. He had been in other parts of Africa, but had spent his time prospecting, and going into partnership with men who knew infallible ways to make money quickly without having any capital. By a series of extraordinary mischances, something invariably went wrong, and it was always Robin's little bit of cash that vanished, together with the partner. Unfortunately his father, dying young, had left him some money, so instead of learning how to make it in the ordinary humdrum manner, after an unproductive period in the Army he had indulged a passion for inventing things that never quite worked (though perhaps they might have done, had he been able to persevere) and starting companies to exploit them.

These companies involved partners, who seemed to have the same traits wherever Robin went; there came a gloomy day when everyone went about as if there had been a death in the family—as I suppose, in a sense, there had—and preparations were made to evacuate the house and sell most of our possessions. On the first occasion my nanny—to start with we had enjoyed such luxuries—replied sepulchrally to my inquiries: "Daddy has a hole in his pocket." I demanded why it could not be mended, and received no answer; I could only suppose, correctly in a sense, that all the golden sovereigns had fallen out before Robin had noticed the hole. So he had vanished to seek a new fortune in the colonies, as they then were, and I had attached myself to Tilly, instead of to a nanny, at the home of relatives.

Robin's mind ran to precious stones and metals; he sought diamonds unsuccessfully, and moved on to some remote, lethal and obscure region inhabited by Portuguese and cannibals, where he actually did acquire a gold mine. I do not think it was a large one, and all its previous owners had died very quickly of drink or malaria, so that it had never had a chance to show its metal (as he wrote to Tilly, being fond of puns). Robin was tougher than one might have expected, and managed to get the mine into production, as he put it, though I think that consisted only of persuading some of the cannibals to hack at a hillside with picks and wash the resulting rock in a stream. In a romantic moment he sent Tilly a ring made of gold from his own mine and a diamond from a digging in which he had owned a share; looking at it sadly some years later, he remarked that it represented the total output of his mining career.

This cannot have been quite true, for he managed to sell his portion of the interior of Mozambique at a profit, which would have been larger had the buyers paid more in cash and less in shares in a syndicate which went broke soon afterwards. But the cash payment was enough to take him on a dubious cargo boat to British East Africa. All the good reports he had heard about the country seemed to him more than justified. Letters that might have been penned by Roger Stilbeck himself fired Tilly, also, with a longing for this land of splendour and promise that offered sunshine, sport and adventure, with the prospect of independence and the rebuilding of lost fortunes; and here we now were, again united, and the owners of a ninety-nine-year lease of five hundred acres of land.

If it was not quite all that Tilly, at any rate, had expected, it was nevertheless there, under all that coat of grass and bush. With hard work and patience, the vision could become real: a house could arise, coffee bushes put down their roots and bloom and fruit, shady trees grow up around a tidy lawn; there was order waiting to be created out of wilderness, a home out of bush, a future from a blank and savage history, a fortune from raw materials that were, as they then existed, of no conceivable value at all.

All this would take, perhaps, longer than Tilly and Robin had at first counted on, it would need more money than they had, it would be a harder struggle than they had anticipated; but they were young, hopeful and healthy, and what others had done before them could be done again. Their spirits had rallied by the time they got back to the Blue Posts, and although we were sore, hot, exhausted and bitten, although no cool grass hut awaited us, no span of oxen ready for the plough, by the time I was sent off to bed they had already harvested their first crop, bought a motor-car, built a stone house and booked their passages for a holiday trip home, when they would stand their relations expensive meals and take a grouse-moor in Scotland for the rest of the summer.

Chapter Three

ROBIN'S plan to take the Scotch cart to the new land had to be abandoned because of all the pig and ant-bear holes, and the unbridged rivers. Everything was unpacked and made into loads for porters to carry on their heads. Robin was to make a camp, enrol some labour and start to clear land, and we would follow in a few days when tents were pitched and everything in order.

Robin rode off on a mule at the head of a peculiar cavalcade. Bedding, tents, chairs, tables and boxes of stores made loads that were conventional if uncomfortable; as well as these, we seemed to have a lot of oddments, like a side-saddle, a grindstone, an accordion, the Speckled Sussex pullets, an amateur taxidermist's outfit, a pile of enamel basins, a light plough with yokes and chains, rolls of barbed wire and a dressmaker's dummy which a friend of Tilly's had given her, assuring her it was indispensable for a woman in the wilder parts of Africa.

"I wonder what the porters think about it all," Tilly speculated, watching one of them stagger off underneath a tin bath containing a sewing machine and a second-hand gramophone.

"They don't *think*," said Major Breeches, dismissing the notion as absurd. They sang, however, and marched off in fine style, though they were only what Major Breeches called a scratch lot, and did not get far before various loads fell off, or got tangled in trees, and several of the carriers grew disheartened, dumped their burdens and fled. But the distance was only five miles, so the safari did not have to be highly organized.

The gramophone had been suggested to Robin as a convenient way of breaking the ice with the natives. It enticed them, as a light attracts insects; once, as it were, captured, the advantages of signing on for work could be explained, and some would feel bold enough to try the experiment. So Robin took the gramophone and, when we were installed in tents, hopefully played "The Bluebells of Scotland" and "The Lost Chord" over and over again. As the records were scratched and the gramophone an old one, extraordinary sounds emerged from its trumpet to be lost very quickly in the surrounding bush and long grass. Its only effect was to deflect Juma from his labours; he listened entranced; and one of the mules was found gazing pensively down the trumpet.

The local inhabitants, however, remained aloof. No one seemed to live anywhere near. But the reserve was said to hold a great supply of able-bodied young men who did nothing all day but grease their limbs and plait their pigtails while their mothers and sisters toiled in shambas, and who would be a great deal better employed (according to their prospective employers) in useful work like clearing bush, ploughing land and building houses. These young men were not to be lured, it seemed, even by the magic of sound coming out of a trumpet, which was generally held, by those unfamiliar with the invention, to issue from a familiar spirit held captive in the box.

Before we left the Blue Posts, a young Irishman arrived one day on a bicycle, with a broken fly-wheel strapped to his back. He paused for a drink, which he must indeed have needed; the sun was vicious, the fly-wheel must have weighed at least fifty pounds and pedalling along a wagon track deep in dust and ruts, and full of holes and tree-roots, cannot have been easy.

He came, he said, from Punda Milia, a stretch of country about fifteen miles farther on and called after the zebra that infested it, and he was taking the fly-wheel to Nairobi to be repaired. He was not much larger than a well-grown jockey, but as tough as hippo hide, and he had the quick, gay smile and bright eyes of many Irishmen, with a trace of the brogue, but not enough to make him sound as if he was putting it on, which is often the effect created by the genuine article.

The bicycle, he said, was shared between himself and his partner. If both young men wanted to visit the town together, they took it in turns to walk and ride. One went ahead on the bicycle, left it ten miles along the road and proceeded on foot. The second walked the first ten miles, found the bicycle and caught up his friend. In this way they reached Nairobi, a distance of fifty miles, in one day. No one ever molested the bicycle, which they had bought second-hand for ten rupees.

His name was Randall Swift, and he found life so entertaining that he was very seldom without a laugh and a smile, so that he endeared himself to everyone, and became one of my parents' closest friends. Moreover he was now an old hand, having arrived in the country in 1904, so they looked upon him as a kind of oracle.

"All the same, he's been here eight years and his only form of transport is a ten-rupee bicycle," Tilly mused when he had gone. "He hasn't made *his* fortune very quickly."

"He's a splendid fellow, but he hasn't stuck to one thing," Robin explained. "All his trial trips were no good. But now he's settled on sisal, he's sure to do well. There's big money in sisal."

Randall Swift had told us how he and his partner had secured the last consignment of bulbils (the young sisal plants) to leave German East Africa the day before the Germans put an embargo on their export. Now they would be able to supply other aspiring sisal planters with bulbils at a profit, and they had built a factory to extract fibre from the long, tough, prickly-tipped leaves.

"It needs a lot of capital," Robin said wistfully. "How do you manage about that?"

"The bank, of course," Randall replied, roaring with laughter. "At first we shot game and dried the meat and sent it to the coast. Then we got hold of a tractor weighing eight tons. When it came it broke all the P.W.D. bridges and we got a contract hauling sand to build new ones."

The tractor's fastest speed was four miles an hour and he and his partner, Ernest Rutherfoord, had taken turns to haul sand, day and day about, from Punda Milia to the bridge by the Blue Posts. It consumed prodigious quantities of wood, and at intervals the driver would dismount with a hatchet and hack more fuel from the bush. Once the tractor ran out on a treeless stretch; at the opportune moment, there came into sight a column of porters, each of whom carried a pole. Waving his axe, Randall halted the safari, commandeered the poles, chopped them up and proceeded on his tractor. A few days later, an angry official arrived at Punda Milia demanding restitution for the telegraph poles that had been on their way to establish a new line. Both partners had brewed beer at Mortlake before they came to Africa. Randall was like a robin, with a bright eye and friendly manner and a habit of cocking his head on one side.

He gave us some good advice about labour.

"Get hold of the local chief," he said. "Meanwhile, I'll give you a tip. Put a safari lamp up on a pole outside your tent at night. These people have never seen lamps before. Once they get over thinking it's a spirit, they can't resist a closer look at such a remarkable thing."

When the gramophone failed him, Robin remembered this. For the first two or three nights nothing happened, except that droves of insects beat and scorched themselves to death against the glass. It was always dark by half past six or seven and, after I was sent to bed, I lay awake and watched people moving about by lantern-light and the flickering of the camp fire, a small speck of warmth and comfort amid a great encircling continent where cities, friends and civilized ways were not to be found, not for thousands and thousands of miles across plain and bush and forest.

At such times, when all the furtive noises of the night beyond that speck of firelight crept unasked like maggots into your ears, you could feel very isolated and lonely. At such times, I think, Robin and Tilly, although they did not say so, wondered why they had come, and what they were doing, and whether they had set their hands to a hopeless task. For until you actually saw it and travelled across it on foot or on horseback or in a wagon, you could not possibly grasp the enormous vastness of Africa. It seemed to go on for ever and ever; beyond each range of hills lay another far horizon; always it was the same, pale-brown grass and bush and thorn-trees, rocky mountains, dark valleys, sunlit plain; there was no break and no order, no road and no town, no places even: just marks on a map which, when you got there, turned out to be merely an expanse of bush or plain exactly like the rest of the landscape.

And here they were, on all sides only blankness, committed to the task of somehow shaving off a patch of bush in the middle of nowhere and ploughing it up and getting little plants put in, and a house built in the wilderness: surely a daunting task for two people not at all well equipped to tackle it. Like rusty hinges, frogs croaked from surrounding *vleis*, the air was pierced by the ceaseless cry of cicadas: how many between here and the Indian Ocean? More, perhaps, even in the few miles around us, than stars that prickled in such millions overhead, clear, transcerulean and indifferent, each the centre of an unbelievably remote universe of its own.

On the third night, a new sound came from beyond the golden circle, something to mingle with the queer whispers and stirrings and insect calls that came out of the darkness and seemed to hesitate upon the edge of light. I lay in bed and listened with a thumping heart. Often I used to imagine our camp to be beleaguered by creeping unseen beasts with red fiery eyes and ripping jaws and fangs who crouched just outside the fragile bubble of light, or by savage spearmen with naked limbs gliding towards us like eels. The first sound was a cough which did not sound at all savage but human; then something moved and it was as if the darkness parted for an instant to reveal an inner core—as if the night were a great lake of black water and in it fishes and monsters moved about, and troubled the water, breaking the surface with a coil or fin.

"They've come after all!" Robin exclaimed; he had not really believed in the lamp trick, as he called it.

"We mustn't frighten them." Tilly spoke as if they had been shy antelopes or birds.

"I wonder what we do next?"

They waited, and Robin smoked a small cheroot. Tilly was struggling with some tapestry work under the indifferent light. She was talented at this, and at embroidery, and never liked to sit still with nothing to do.

"Juma will deal with them," she said.

Juma had faithfully maintained his contempt and indifference towards the local inhabitants. It appeared that he, whose forbears had no doubt been slaves of the Arabs, felt that the sooner these people were enslaved the better; it might even make them into Muslims, and therefore into human beings.

"Tell them we are friends, and if they come back in the morning they can have some meat," Robin suggested. Juma had dressed up not only in his white *kanzu,* which he always wore on duty, with a red fez, but also in his scarlet sash kept normally for best occasions. Robin wore pyjamas and a dressing-gown and high mosquito-boots; he remarked that the tradition of dressing for dinner in the jungle was safe in Juma's hands.

"They do not eat meat," Juma pointed out.

"Oh, well. What do you suppose they'd like? Of course there are beads, and calico and copper wire. . . . Unfortunately we haven't any of those. Or have you any beads you can spare, Tilly?"

"The only beads I had went long ago to Uncle's," she replied, referring to her pearls which had not survived Robin's unhappy partnerships. Almost the only relic of her jewel-case was a pair of ear-rings to which, for some reason, she was devoted, and often wore on the most unsuitable occasions because she was afraid they would be stolen if she left them behind. She had them on now.

"Tell them they can have whatever it is they like to eat," Robin suggested, "and that if they come to work I will give them all a rupee to start off with."

"They are too stupid to understand rupees," Juma said with even greater scorn than before.

"For heaven's sake think of *something*, Juma!"

The invisible spectators kept just beyond the firelight, as a buck will edge its way out of rifle range. They knew no language but their own, and of this Juma was ignorant. He had, however, attached to himself at some point a child, known simply as the *toto*, a fetcher and carrier. The *toto* was now summoned and appeared, large-headed, skinny-limbed, velvet-eyed and rather pathetic. He stood by Juma, looking as if he expected to be cooked and eaten, and addressed a few quavering sentences to the unseen crowd. At least, one felt it to be a crowd, but it may have been only two or three young men.

The *toto's* voice brought forth one of them almost into the open. He was young and oiled and red, with twists of ochred hair dangling all over his head and down to his eyes, like a Yorkshire terrier. He carried a spear and wore a short cloak of leather, and a belt with a throwing-club tucked into it, and the usual red scabbard. His speech was soft, liquid, musical, almost whining, like water over rocks, with underneath a plaintiveness, a nervous tremor.

"He asks, what is this light," said Juma in his mixture of English and Swahili. "He says, is it a bit that has fallen from a star."

"Show it to him," Robin instructed.

But the young man retreated as Juma advanced with the lantern in his hand. The darkness gave way before Juma and he moved in a golden glow. The light slid down a limb, caught the flash of a spear-head, flickered across a startled eye, and then all trace of the young man and his companions evaporated. Juma called. No answer. The huge and silent night closed in like an infinite sea over all traces of our visitors.

Robin swore with disappointment.

"No matter," Juma said. He used a kind of basic child's Swahili for our benefit. "They will come back tomorrow, and the next night. And then by day."

On the following night, the young men were bolder and edged more closely into the circle of light. They were like bronze statues endowed with life and moved tautly, as if on springs, ready to bound forward or back. One felt that just as they vanished into the void like antelopes when alarmed, they might spring forward when angered and thrust with spears; they were triggered men.

The *toto* spoke to them for longer this time and the lantern itself was taken from its pole and displayed at close quarters. They touched it boldly, and one burnt his hand against the glass.

Although we were astonished at their ignorance even of lamps, devices known to the Romans and indeed to others long before that, the sight of a tongue of flame imprisoned in a bubble, independent and mobile, must have appeared altogether miraculous to those confronted with it for the first time. It was these very inventions that to us appeared so obvious and simple, like lamps and matches and wheels, and putting water into pipes, that struck these people with the force of wonder and amazement. Later, when Europeans displayed the inventions in which they themselves took so much pride, like aeroplanes and radios, they were often disappointed at the Africans' attitude of indifferent acceptance. But if you had lived for many centuries without control over the elements, quite at their mercy, it would be the realization that fire and water, your daily companions, could be mastered, that would come as a revelation to you, not the ingenuity of some more refined device for enabling you to do something you had never thought of doing, like travelling through the air.

Robin had a bright idea. "Tell them," he instructed Juma, "that to every man who comes to work for me for one month, I will give a lamp like this."

Juma, the *toto* and the Kikuyu conversed in their curious mixture of tongues for some time.

"They say," Juma reported in his tone of contempt for the aborigines, "that this lamp contains a spirit which obeys Europeans. They do not believe it would stay inside and serve them."

"Tell them not to be such idiots," Robin said briskly. "Explain about paraffin."

"Is there a word for paraffin?" Tilly inquired.

"It is called fat," Juma replied.

His exposition caused a stir among the young men. They uttered startled exclamations and drew back a little, poised for flight. Juma almost shook the *toto* in his vehemence, and the *toto* wound up his speech to a higher pitch. He was a very slender, fragile link between two worlds, and seemed at times about to snap like a piece of thread.

"I have told them," Juma reported with disgust. "They think it is human fat, and we are cannibals."

"I could cheerfully become one," Robin said, "if this goes on. Tell them it is fat that comes out of the ground."

"They will not believe it," said Juma.

"It seems unlikely, if you look at it that way," Tilly agreed, "that there should be wells of fat in the ground."

"We shall be here all night," Robin protested, "if Juma is going to put them through a course in economic geography. Tell them that they can take this lamp away and examine it. But explain that it will die when its food is finished and if they bring it back tomorrow, they shall have some more."

No one could be found brave enough to grasp the lantern. The young men backed away, and Juma left it, with the flame turned low, in the grass at a short distance from our tents. It stayed there till everyone had gone to sleep, but in the morning it had gone.

"Those savages will come back," Juma prophesied.

They did come back, two days later, and in the hours of daylight, and they brought with them several older men who did not wear a lot of little pigtails but merely black curls, and bright bead ornaments in their ears, and snuff-horns hanging by thin chains from their necks, and a good many amulets and coils of copper wire. One or two wore red blankets and the others cloaks of monkey-skin, beautifully sewn together and edged with beads.

These men carried no weapons, but one had a polished staff in his hand. He was thickset for a Kikuyu, though among a less slender race he would not have seemed so; his skin was light, his eyes keen, his voice quiet and he was clearly accustomed to authority. This man was called chief Kupanya. It was only much later that we discovered he was wrongly labelled because the Kikuyu did not have chiefs in their hierarchy. They had elders of various grades, and he was a spokesman for his particular set of elders. But the policy of the Government was to appoint local chiefs where they did not exist already, and his polished staff indicated that he had been selected as ruler of the district closest to our land.

The chief and his companions sat down under a tree near our camp, and took snuff.

"I suppose I ought to give them something," Robin remarked. "I wonder what?"

"They would like beer," Juma informed him. "And a fat sheep."

"We haven't any beer or fat sheep."

Yet to leave them under the tree without any refreshment did not seem a propitious start.

"We've got some soda-water siphons," Tilly suggested. In those days no camp, house or safari was complete without these useful devices, and a box of sparklets to recharge them.

Juma fetched all our tin mugs and handed them to the Kikuyu, who examined them with interest. For themselves they used calabashes, made from the gourds we saw growing everywhere, often clambering up the roofs of huts. Robin produced a siphon and squirted the frothing water into one of the mugs. This created a sensation; here was water obviously possessed of a most ebullient and irrepressible spirit, who might well be displaying anger. Or perhaps they thought a spirit lived inside the bottle and was blowing out a kind of steam. At any rate it said much for their courage that they did not run away. As elders, they had their dignity to preserve. Juma drank some of the soda-water as a demonstration, but this was too much even for chief Kupanya. They held the mugs gingerly, and after a while poured the soda-water respectfully into the ground.

"I want some strong young men to clear the bush," Robin explained. "I will pay them in rupees." Kupanya spoke a little Swahili, so Juma was able to act as interpreter.

Robin had thought it would be easy to explain his needs, but it was not. Kupanya asked a great many questions. Why had Robin come, where was the shamba to be, what was he going to grow in it, who was to plant the crop and harvest it? Was he a relation of the Italians at the Mission? (This made Robin smile; he had an ear-to-ear grin, and when amused he beamed like a sun.) Or was he a relation of the District Commissioner? Had he a shamba in his own country? Had he seen King George? Had he any of the powerful European medicines against coughs and against worms?

"We shall go on for ever at this rate," Robin said impatiently. "He doesn't seem to realize that this is my land and I'm offering his young men a chance to work." The whole thing was as mysterious to Kupanya, as his attitude was baffling and dense to Robin, and no doubt the chief would have considered two or three days' conversation under the tree well spent, had it led to clarification. But in Robin's opinion this meeting was not intended as a leisurely exchange of views, it was a simple matter that could be dealt with in a quarter of an hour.

"You might get on quicker," Tilly suggested, "if you offered the chief baksheesh of some kind."

So Kupanya was told he would receive a goat for every ten young men who came to work and stayed a month. There would be no payment for those who left in less than thirty days. After that, negotiations did seem to proceed more swiftly. When the elders left, they took the tin mugs, which they clearly looked on as a present. Robin did not like to stop them, so after that we had nothing to drink out of but half a dozen very precious Irish cut-glass tumblers, salvaged from what was always referred to as the Crash, until Robin rode down to Thika and borrowed some more mugs from the Blue Posts.

Chapter Four

THE young men arrived about a week later. Robin remarked ruefully that he appeared to have summoned up a sort of Zulu *impi* rather than a labour force. They were painted as for war, or perhaps a dance, with chalk and red ochre and feathers tucked into their freshly decorated hair, and they arrived in a column stamping and chanting and waving spears. At the first sight of them Tilly and Robin were somewhat alarmed, but it soon became apparent that this was all in fun, so to speak, and to show that they were ready for anything. With them were some of the elders and, at a safe distance, a party of shy and giggling young women heavily greased and ochred and covered with beads.

When they had calmed down and communication had been established, each man who wished to work was given a small square of cardboard ruled into thirty squares and called his ticket. One square was crossed off for each day on which he worked. When he completed the ticket, which might take him several months, he was paid. When it came to accepting tickets, only a small proportion of the impi proved to be stayers; the rest had come to see what was going to happen, and to join in the fun.

The young men's first task was to build themselves sleeping quarters, which they did in an amazingly short time merely by felling trees, driving branches into the ground and tying together bundles of long, dry grass to make walls. But they would not thatch the huts themselves, as this was against their custom.

Everything except the thatch was prepared on the first day. On the second, the house was assembled. The young men had erected the walls and the skeleton of the roof by midday. Then a file of young ladies arrived, each one bearing on her back a bundle of reeds cut from a river-bed and previously dried in the sun. These maidens, clad in short leather aprons, clambered up to the skeleton roof and tied the thatch in place with twine made from forest creepers. It was very well organized and, in two days, the huts were done. The Kikuyu had a strict rule that every building must be completed between sunrise and sunset; if a hut were to be left unroofed overnight, evil spirits would move in and nothing, apparently, could be done to dislodge them. This was a most fortunate belief, from a European point of view.

After they had completed their own houses, Robin put them on to building one for us. It was to have a single living-room flanked by two bedrooms, all in a straight row like a stable—not, perhaps, inspired architecturally, but this was to be a temporary arrangement, until a proper stone residence went up. He stuck some pegs in the ground to indicate the corners and cut a little trench between, to make the shape quite clear.

A young man called Njombo had emerged as the spokesman of the labourers, who were always called boys. How this name for grown men first originated I do not know, but everyone used it. Njombo, with several friends, looked incredulously at the trench and the pegs.

"We cannot build a house like that," he said.

"Why not?"

Njombo shook his head. He knew very little Swahili. "Not good," was all he could say.

"It is good for me," Robin retorted, "and I am to live in it."

Njombo and the others engaged in a long conversation in Kikuyu that sounded full of outraged alarm.

"It will fall down," he said finally to Robin.

"Not if you build it properly."

"Why do you not have a house like that?" he asked, pointing to one of the round Kikuyu huts built by the young men.

"Because I am not a Kikuyu, I am a European," Robin explained with what he thought was patience. "Europeans have houses like this, with straight lines and corners. So do not argue any more."

Njombo clearly thought Robin's insistence not merely peculiar, but sinister. Goodness knows how many evil spirits would not find shelter in a house with corners. He had been as far as Thika and had therefore seen the Indians' houses, which were rectangular, so the whole idea, although strange, was not unheard-of, but he had never been asked to take part in the actual building of such a monstrosity.

"Are rectangular buildings a sign of civilization?" Robin wondered. "I can't think why they should be, but it seems to be so."

"The Colosseum was round," Tilly reminded him. "And the Pantheon."

"They were public buildings. Roman houses had corners like ours. I can't think of anything round in England, except Martello towers. Even the Saxons had square dwellings. There must be a connection, though I don't know what it is."

"Perhaps it's the furniture," Tilly suggested. "It doesn't fit very well into round houses. Natives have scarcely any furniture at all."

This was indeed true, at the time; all they had were three-legged stools, round also, and beds made of sticks lashed together on posts high enough for goats to sleep underneath. They kept a fire burning in the middle of the hut and had no windows; you could not call it hygienic, but it was warm. The smoke was said to kill lice, and the goats' urine to keep down jiggas, so in a way it was all well-planned; but the smoke also gave children eye troubles, and the fug led to chest complaints, so perhaps what the Kikuyu gained on the roundabouts they lost on the swings.

To build a rectangular house naturally took longer. Its roof was a major difficulty: the structure of rafters, purlins and a ridge-beam was a total novelty and Robin's explanations got nowhere, although when he clambered up—we had no ladder—and, with the aid of many willing but unpractised hands, secured the main poles in position, much interest was shown. We started off with nails, but after the first day all the long ones vanished; we had no safe or store to lock things in and these handy little lengths of iron, just right for turning into ornaments, proved irresistible to the Kikuyu. Robin cursed and swore and made up his mind to ride to Nairobi on a mule to get a fresh supply, but Njombo considered this quite unnecessary.

"Those things," he said (the Swahili word for things came in for heavy use), "they are useful, but it is wrong to put iron in houses. Iron is for weapons and for ornament. Let us build the house according to our custom and keep the iron for bigger things."

"The house will fall down without nails," Robin said.

"Why should it fall down? Our houses do not. And if it does, you can build another."

So Robin agreed to let them try, and they bound the poles together with twine in their customary fashion. The house was standing when we left the farm fifteen years later and never caused us any trouble, and the roof withstood many storms and gales. Njombo's young men did not thatch it in a day, however, so no doubt all sorts of devils got in, but these never caused us trouble either, or at least no more trouble than it was reasonable to expect.

After the grass walls had been tied in position, the house was lined with reed matting. The floor was made of earth rammed into a hard red clay which could be swept as if it had been tiled, and it was soon covered, at least partially, with skins of leopards, reedbuck, Grant's gazelle and brown-haired sheep. Its only disadvantage was the shelter it offered to jiggas, and at some later stage, though not for several years, we put down a layer of cement. This was the only material that did not come from the farm, or from the bush round about.

The house was airy, comfortable, cool and most companionable, for a great many creatures soon joined us in the roof and walls. The nicest were the lizards, who would stay for hours spread-eagled on a wall quite motionless, clinging to the surface with small scaly hands, like a very old woman's, whose claws looked like long finger-nails. They would cock their heads a little on one side and then scuttle off suddenly in a tremendous hurry, or vanish into the thatch.

This thatch was always full of sounds, little rustling, secretive noises from unseen fellow-residents meaning no harm—except for white ants, those termites who will destroy anything with their tiny but ferocious jaws, and betray themselves by little tunnels, like long blisters, marking their passage across walls and beams. A constant war was waged against termites and it must have been largely successful, as our house did not get eaten away. The whole house took about a fortnight to build and its cost, which no one ever worked out, could not have been above £10. Our light came first from safari lanterns, but later we acquired a pressure lamp that had to be pumped up at frequent intervals, emitted a faintly sinister hissing like a snake, made the room too hot and leaked paraffin.

"On the whole, modern improvements seem to be expensive, temperamental and smelly," Robin once remarked pensively. "I sometimes wonder whether civilization is all that it's made out to be."

"The bits that reach us here are rather part-worn," Tilly said. But she liked to have reminders of it round her, so far as she could. Although we ate, for the most part, what the country offered, apart from flour, tea, sugar and a few things out of tins, the evening meal always ended with black coffee drunk from tiny lustre cups of very thin china—Coalport, I think they were. They dwindled rapidly in number, but I remember loving their lightness and thinness and graceful shape, and the fascinating blend of tones like shot silk or mother-of-pearl. Also we had the cut glass I have mentioned, the few bits of jewellery Tilly had salvaged from the Crash and, later on, one or two pieces of furniture which came out from England and must have looked incongruous in our earthen-floored grass hut.

Most of our furniture was made out of the packing-cases that had sheltered our few salvaged possessions, such as a French bureau with ornate, curly legs, used by Tilly as a writing-desk and adorned always by two tall, embossed silver flower-vases. She also had a delicate little work-table where she kept her embroidery, and a fat-bellied commode used as a medicine-chest, full of queer brews of turpentine, ether, linseed oil, camphor and other strong-smelling liquids, together with calomel, castor-oil, iodine and that sovereign remedy for almost everything, Epsom salts. No more unsuitable tenants could possibly have been found for the commode. Robin noticed this one day—he was not at all observant, as a rule, about his immediate surroundings, generally having his mind on distant, greater matters, always much more promising and congenial than those closer at hand—and grew rather angry, for the commode had come from his side of the family.

"It's a shame to treat good things in that way," he said.

"How else can we treat it?" Tilly asked. "This isn't the Victoria and Albert Museum."

"It's sometimes very like the Natural History, with all these insects and reptiles everywhere. I should have thought the commode could have had a little more respect shown to it, that's all."

Tilly looked deeply hurt, and also riled by the injustice, as she felt it to be; for Robin would have been the first to have stuffed anything that came to hand into the commode. He respected most theories, a few great men of history and Tilly, but not possessions, governments, nor the practical necessities of everyday life.

"I wish I'd never come to this rotten country," she exclaimed when he had gone, with tears in her eyes. Sometimes she spoke aloud in my presence without exactly speaking to me; I was a kind of safety valve, helpful to her feelings even in a passive role.

"Everything is raw and crude and savage and I hate it!" she cried. "The place is full of horrible diseases and crawling with insects, no one knows how to do anything properly and there's nobody to talk to for hundreds of miles!"

Tilly had already been upset that morning by one of those gruesome little tragedies in which Africa abounds; tragedies that happen in a thousand places, and many times a day, that no one hears of, that do not matter, and yet for someone like Tilly, brought up to believe that life could be, and ought to be, full of joy and happiness for all creatures, capable of wounding the spirit and wringing the heart. It concerned the Speckled Sussex pullets she had brought from England, with a fine young cockerel, to start a new line of poultry. One of the pullets, now a hen, had been sitting and the chicks had just emerged: fluffy yellow balls, like animated chrysanthemum buds, that darted about, cheeping, full of life and charm. They had hatched the day before; in the night a column of *siafu,* those black, purposeful, implacable and horribly sinister warrior ants, had marched through the nest. In the morning the yellow chicks were limp, bedraggled, soiled little corpses with their insides eaten out, lying in the nest. The hen was alive, and that was the worst part of it, for the ants had swarmed over her and eaten half her flesh away and her eyes, and she lay there twitching now and then, as if to demonstrate that unreasoning persistence of life that is the very core of cruelty. The hen was released from her pain and Tilly stood with a wisp of yellow fluff in her hand, herself white with misery, appalled by thoughts of the helpless chicks' last moments of agony, and by her own failure to prevent the tragedy.

"They were just hatched," she said. "Why did this have to happen? What *good* do *siafu* do?"

"When they march, rain will come," Juma said, removing the corpses. He was quite unmoved; *siafu* were a natural hazard, and had done many worse things than that. They liked to swarm over living creatures and eat into their soft parts, especially the eyes.

Later that morning, a woman brought along a baby that, several days before, had fallen into the fire. The burns had suppurated, and the pus been set upon by flies; the baby, like the hen, still persisted in living in spite of every discouragement, including pain that could never have relented, and that only death could relieve. The contents of the commode were quite inadequate to deal with this situation, as was Tilly's knowledge of first aid. It was remarkable how soon the news had spread that white folk possessed healing medicines, and how women who had refused even to approach us a few weeks ago were already anxious to hand over their children for treatment. Tilly was doubly horrified, by the baby's ghastly injuries and by her own inability to justify its mother's faith.

"She must take it to hospital," Tilly said. Robin was out with the greased warriors, trying to persuade them to cut down bush.

Everyone looked blank. Juma pointed out that the nearest hospital was in Nairobi which was two days' journey, and that in two days the baby would certainly be dead.

"Then we must take it in at once," Tilly insisted.

"How. memsabu?"

"In the mule cart, of course."

"One of the mules has a bad stomach."

"It must go all the same."

"The other one is lame. And a wheel of the cart is broken."

"You are telling lies," Tilly cried.

Juma shrugged his shoulders and relapsed into a sulk, and Tilly was left to deal with the sick baby without support, advice or co-operation. Its mother held it silently, regarding it with an impassive face that revealed no feeling. When Juma had so resolutely resisted all attempts to help her, she had not attempted to intervene. Probably she did not understand; if she had, she would not have argued; she accepted uncomplainingly the authority of men. Tilly was sure that Juma was lying, but she failed to find the mule-boy or even the mules. It was useless to fight the battle single-handed. She did what she could, which was very little, to treat the baby, and the operation nearly made her sick, the stinking sores were so rotten and the baby so silent, as if even at that stage of its existence it accepted disaster, pain and death as its natural lot.

So that was why she was upset by Robin's rebuke about the commode. He did not know the reason, and went off thinking her careless and touchy. He was having his troubles too. He had bought some native oxen, and was trying to train them to the plough. They were quite unfamiliar with this implement; they were strangers even to yokes and chains.

The difficulty of teaching them was all the greater in that none of the Kikuyu had an idea how to train them either. In South Africa, Robin had often walked beside a wagon and watched the Boers control their teams by the inflexion of their voices and the cracking of their long whips. It looked easy enough for any fool to do; but it was not. The Boers had developed a remarkable affinity for oxen, an almost magical authority. They could command them as a circus trainer can command his ponies, or a shepherd his dog. But they had never taught Robin—they never would teach anyone who was not a fellow Boer—and, when he tried it, the oxen did not behave at all according to plan. Not only did they refuse point-blank to draw the plough but they broke chains and skeys and yokes, they cavorted all over the place like a herd of buffaloes, they tangled themselves up in the gear and finally most of them escaped altogether. The Kikuyu ran about just as wildly, with no idea of the correct response.

It was fortunate that after tea, when both Tilly and Robin were exhausted and on edge, Randall Swift arrived to see how things were going. He had to push his bicycle most of the way from Thika, and he was always anxious to get back quickly to Punda Milia, but I think the inexperience and general unpreparedness of Robin and Tilly worried him, and as we had no neighbours (excepting the Dutchman, Mr. Roos, who was still away somewhere hunting animals) he made it his business to see if he could help.

Robin explained his difficulties about the oxen. "I can't even get them yoked," he said. "They won't stand still long enough."

"I can give you a tip about that," said Randall, who had a

large store of useful wrinkles. "First of all you climb a thorn-tree with the yoke, then you get a boy to drive the creature underneath you and then you drop the yoke down on its neck. Provided the boy doesn't let go of the traces you've got your bullock properly caught."

"It *sounds* all right," said Robin, who was beginning to discover that the gap between promise and performance was not, as he had so confidently hoped, any less wide in Africa than elsewhere.

"You can often trip up a man from behind where you can't knock him down to his face," Randall said cheerfully. "But I'll tell you what I'll do. You need a headman here who knows a bit about these Kikuyu fellows. I think I can find a man for you, and I'll send him along."

Robin accepted the offer gratefully, and resolved to build a house for him next morning. Everyone got on better at building houses than at yoking oxen to the plough.

Chapter Five

THE prospect of a party, even if it consisted only of one guest with nothing beyond a clean pair of socks in his saddle-bag, always gave Tilly's eye a sparkle and her laugh a new contagious gaiety. Life could stab her to the heart, but her powers of resilience were great. She could write off her failures, not because she did not mind about them but because she minded too much; the next venture was sure to succeed, life would be unbearable if it did not.

Having lost her cherished hen in such distressing circumstances, Tilly instructed Juma to wring the neck of one of its valuable companions in order to provide a meal worthy of the occasion. I was allowed to stay up for the party, the first we had enjoyed in the grass hut. I picked some wild flowers and Tilly arranged them in one of the cut-glass tumblers, but we were still eating off a packing-case, over which a damask tablecloth was spread. A hollow silver cow that held (or should have held) sweets of some kind, occupied the centre of the table, but we ate with kitchen knives and forks, the rest of the silver having been swept away in the Crash. In Tilly's bedroom the packing-case which did duty as a dressing-table bore a number of cut-glass bottles and jars with silver tops on which her initials were elaborately engraved, and which belonged to a handsome dressing-case that she had managed to retain.

By now Tilly's attempts to preserve an appearance of leisured elegance, never perhaps very determined, had gone by the board. She was by nature a participator, and had a dozen enterprises under way. While Juma took care of the domestic chores, she was abroad in the sunshine laying out a garden, supervising the planting of coffee seedlings, marking out a citrus plantation, paying labour in a corner of the store that served as an office, rendering first-aid, and in many other ways filling her day with occupations that made her hot, dirty and tired. Now she had a chance for once to dress up like a lady, and she took it. She wore grey, a kind and gentle background for her corn-gold hair and milky skin and wild-rose complexion, and her emerald ear-rings shone with the radiance of a sunlit beach-leaf in spring. I was allowed to squeeze the scent-spray, encased in a coat of mesh, that lived among her bottles, a simple pleasure rarely indulged. She looked at her hands with a frown.

"I haven't any white gloves; anyway, that would be overdoing it. My hands are like a navvy's, dirt won't come out of the cracks and as for my nails. . . ." She had been attacking them with a file, long, thin scissors, a buffer and some polish from a tiny flat jar, but the result was discouraging. Tilly was downcast; as with all perfectionists, it was the detail others might not notice that destroyed for her the pleasure of achievement. I doubt if she was ever fully satisfied with anything she did. But she breasted each failure as a dinghy rides a choppy sea, and faced the next with confidence and gaiety. So she frowned at her nails, remarked: "Well, they're clean anyway, and there's nothing I can do about it," and proceeded to arrange her hair in a new fashion she had noticed in an illustrated magazine.

Randall was entranced, as indeed he might have been, for she was a handsome woman in the fullness of youth and she had besides that flame of animation without which all beauty is petrified. I think he fell in love with her a little that night and never lost his admiration afterwards. He was himself at heart also a romantic, drawn to Africa less by a dream of fortune than by a wish for freedom and the danger to be found in sport. His Sundays were spent walking about the plains and hills in search of lions and buffaloes.

"When we make our fortune out of sisal," he said, "I shall go home every winter to hunt the fox in County Meath, and in the summer I shall come back here to hunt the elephant. Ah, what a grand life that will be! And when the coffee's made a fortune for you, what will you do with it?"

"I don't know what comes first," Tilly answered. "Robin wants a castle in Scotland, and I should like a safari across the Northern Frontier into Abyssinia and home by the Nile. And then I'd like to own a balloon, and to breed New Forest ponies, and to get to China on the trans-Siberian railway, and to have a model poultry farm, and buy a Daimler, and fish in Norway—oh, and lots of other things."

When the same question was put to Robin, he replied that he

meant to buy the most expensive luxury in the world. The others tried to guess its nature: running a yacht, shooting tigers, owning a racing stable, buying jewels for Tilly. Robin beamed genially, and said:

"Doing absolutely nothing. A very expensive affair." He quoted a favourite West Highland song:

"Oh that the peats would cut themselves
And all the little fishes would leap upon the shore,
That I might lie upon my back
And rest for ever more. Oich! Oich!"

Then Randall turned to me and asked me the same question. Not only was I acutely embarrassed by this sudden attention, but the question baffled me. I had no money and it did not seem to be a thing one needed for any purpose at all.

"He means, what would you like best in all the world if you could choose?" Tilly explained.

I knew that a quick, decisive answer was expected and my thoughts fled like a herd of kongoni when a shot is fired. Of course I wanted a lot of things, but no one great need overtopped the others. A sharper knife, a mule of my own, one of the lustre coffee cups to keep, a guinea-pig, mice made of pink and white sugar? What I wanted most of all was perhaps a companion, but I knew this did not fall within Randall's meaning, so I answered at random, "a chameleon". Indeed these creatures with their air of patient, knowing and obstinate complacency fascinated me. I admired the way they swivelled their deep and watchful eyes in big, baggy purple sockets that enabled them to see in any direction they pleased, and loved to feel the dry, cold, burr-like pluck of their agile little fingers on my flesh, and to observe them sway backwards and forwards, like a man about to take a tremendous leap, when they contemplated a sudden, darting, forward waddle.

My reply caused the sort of laughter any child dislikes, because it has a ring of patronage; but Juma had made a meringue-crusted pudding with which I was able to console myself, while my elders returned to a topic that never bored them, that of sport. Although Tilly and Robin then believed as firmly as their friends did that to shoot animals was one of life's richest pleasures, I do not believe their hearts were ever wholly in it. Safaris they loved, and Robin would enjoy a walk with his gun in the cool of the evening to bang away at a red-legged francolin or a fat guinea-fowl, but as a rule he left the antelope alone, and he was not always hoping, as most others were, for a trip to the game-abounding plains along the Athi river. He preferred to plan irrigation works, dams and furrows, forestry projects and sites for little factories to treat the coffee, citrus and other crops that were not even planted; and, of an evening, to sit by the hissing lamp with any reading matter he could lay his hands on, even out-of-date copies of motoring journals or *The Field*, and to cover scraps of paper with detailed, complicated calculations which invariably proved, beyond all question, the brilliant success of whatever plan he was hatching.

Once, when clearing up some of these abandoned bits of paper, Tilly noticed, at the bottom of a long column of very high figures, the terse conclusion: "Therefore, small sums do not matter." It was on this robust principle that Robin conducted his affairs.

Randall kept his word about a headman, and in due course Sammy arrived. He was a tall, beak-nosed individual with fine, almost Asiatic features and thin bones; instead of the usual blanket he wore a shirt and shorts and a pair of leather sandals. He brought a chit from Randall which said: "You will find this boy reliable and clever, so long as you keep him off the drink. He is half a Masai, so despises the Kikuyu, but the other half is Kikuyu so he understands them. If you give him grazing for his cattle, he will think you a king."

I became friends with Sammy. To the Kikuyu he was stern and often arrogant, but to us he was always polite and dignified. The Kikuyu, as a rule, were not much interested in their surroundings. Although they had a name for all the shrubs and trees and birds, they walked about their country without appearing to possess it—or perhaps I mean, without leaving any mark. To us, that was remarkable: they had not aspired to re-create or change or tame the country and to bring it under their control. A terraced Italian landscape or an English farming county is a very different matter from the stretch of boggy forest first provided as the raw material; it is the joint creation of nature and man. The natives of Africa had accepted what

God, or nature, had given them without apparently wishing to improve upon it in any significant way. If water flowed down a valley they fetched what they wanted in a large hollow gourd; they did not push it into pipes or flumes, or harass it with pumps. Consequently when they left a piece of land and abandoned their huts (as eventually they always did, since they practised shifting cultivation), the bush and vegetation grew up again and obliterated every trace of them, just as the sea at each high tide wipes out footprints and children's sand-castles, and leaves the beach once more smooth and glistening.

Sammy took more note of things. He showed me nests of the small golden weavers that built in swamps; neatly-woven purses, lined with seed-heads, depending from bent-topped reeds and giving them a look of pipes with long, thin, curved stems; he followed the yellow-throated francolin whose clutch of speckled eggs, laid under a grass-tuft, was as hidden as the weavers' nests were plain.

Also he introduced about half a dozen of his little native cattle to graze on our land.

"This is a bad place for cows," he said, "so I shall bring only a few, enough to keep me from hunger."

"Where are the rest?"

"My father herds them for me with his own."

It was his father who was the Masai. "My father's cattle are as many as gazelle on the plain. When he moves them, it is like droves of zebra who seek water in the dry season. My father's cattle are fat as lice. These Kikuyu cattle, they are thin as grasshoppers."

Unlike the Kikuyu, he always made the most of his wealth and importance. If you asked a Kikuyu how many goats he had, he would shake his head and answer: "How should I own any goats? I am a poor man." The Kikuyu looked in others for the cunning they possessed themselves. If you believed a man to be well-off in goats and cattle, it was ten to one you were thinking of taxes, or levies of some kind. The poor, thought the Kikuyu, were like lizards who could take refuge under stones and exist even if they lost their tails. To the Masai, this attitude was contemptible. A man's glory resided in his herds and flocks, and if he had no glory, what sort of man was he? As for risking the loss of them, any Masai felt himself able to defend his own against all comers, even against the Government. They would do as no man told them, only as their own sense of fitness prescribed.

Sammy did not at first bring a wife with him, but a boy, some kind of relation: a red, greased boy who had exactly the look of a buck that pauses for an instant to await some infinitesimal movement or sound that will send him flying like a spear from the hand. This boy prepared his master's food and acted the part of page to a medieval knight, and Sammy stalked about like a squire, creating around himself an aura of feudal authority.

One day he showed me how he bled his cattle. A Kikuyu seized the head of a brindled bull and twisted it over his thigh, gripping its neck with one hand so as to swell the jugular vein. Sammy took a bow from his boy's hand and, from a few yards' range, fired an arrow straight into the jugular. The arrowhead was ringed with a little block of wood so that its point could not penetrate more than about half an inch. Still with a casual air, Sammy plucked out the arrow and the blood spurted into a calabash held by the boy. Then Sammy closed the arrow-prick with finger and thumb and, to my surprise, it stayed closed and the bleeding stopped. The bull, released, strolled off and started to graze. I suppose this was no more harmful to it than bleeding human patients used to be—less so, in fact, as the bull was in good health. Sammy did not drink the blood in the calabash. The boy mixed it with milk and other ingredients, of which cows' urine was one, and let the brew ferment for a day or two. When it was ready to eat, its consistency was like that of soft cheese.

Work on the farm proceeded much more smoothly after Sammy came. He and Robin between them organized a system of piece-work and gave each man a daily task. Most people finished by noon and had the afternoon free for rest and talk. and the evening for eating and, if occasion offered, for dancing and making merry. But none of the young men drank beer. That was for the elders, who made up for what they had missed in their youth, when warriors had to keep themselves fit and ready to spring to arms when the horn of war sounded.

Sammy was a proud man, but this pride was so instinctive, and so unselfconscious, that it imposed upon others the obligation to respect it, and no European used to him the bullying tones often adopted towards the Kikuyu. Robin and Tilly spoke to Sammy as they would speak to a fellow European. In return, Sammy gave them his complete loyalty. African society was feudal then, and Europeans who were used to the system fitted in without any trouble. This feudal relationship, however, was a subtle thing and not the same as the relation of an employer to a hired man.

Our ploughing got on better under Sammy's care, but the oxen were still wild. They broke away quite often and had to be chased through long grass until they were rounded up and yoked again. The furrows wove a tortuous way across charred, black stubble, avoiding craters from which had been slowly and painfully extracted the roots of trees.

"I believe these fellows would give anything on earth *not* to walk or plough in a straight line," Robin complained.

A straight line was perhaps unlucky; at any rate it was never risked. The ploughing looked very odd by English standards; there seemed to be no furrows, just a sea of lumps and clods, and a tangle of roots.

"I don't see how anything can be expected to grow," Robin said gloomily.

Tilly pointed out that things grew without much encouragement. "The veranda posts are beginning to sprout," she added.

Robin liked to think that we were the first to settle in this particular district, but in fact our Boer neighbour, Mr. Roos, had arrived before us. Several weeks after we started our struggle with the oxen he returned from his shooting expedition and rode over to see us on his mule. Robin thought he would resent our presence, because Boers notoriously disliked having close neighbours, and also because we were British *rooineks*, and as such to be despised. However, he seemed quite friendly, and when Robin addressed to him a few simple words of Afrikaans he immediately offered to demonstrate how oxen ought to be trained. He was a middle-aged, brown, leathery man with many wrinkles, a short but tangled beard, very blue eyes and a slow, flat, halting way of speaking our unfamiliar tongue.

Like most Dutchmen, when it came to handling oxen there was a touch of genius about him. It was as if he spoke their language. He was not rough or violent with them as the Kikuyu were, he did not shout, and although the long whip he cracked continually above their backs stung them like a hornet when he so intended, he did not use it with cruelty.

"You've got those oxen eating out of your hand," Robin commented with admiration.

"Your boys know nothing, man," our neighbour replied with contempt.

"We are all amateurs," Robin admitted. "But Sammy is a good boy."

"He is a stuck-up nigger and he will not speak to me again like that."

"He doesn't mean to be rude."

Robin spoke apologetically; as a matter of fact, he was not at all sure that he was right. Mr. Roos made no distinction between Sammy and the Kikuyu; to him, they were all niggers; and Sammy's pride had been touched. Mr. Roos was not going to stand for insubordination and decided to put the matter to the test. They were on the shamba, ploughing the last furrow before outspanning for the rest of the day. The Dutchman rasped out an order; Sammy ignored it, and walked away. Whereupon Mr. Roos threw down his whip, took a run at Sammy and kicked him on the backside. There was a Kikuyu youth standing by with a light spear in his hand. Sammy stumbled, wrested the spear from the startled youth and turned to face the Dutchman with murder in his eye.

Robin acted quickly. He brought Sammy down with a sort of rugger tackle and the spear was knocked away harmlessly. The Kikuyu came and picked it up and Sammy stood there quaking with rage. He was not just trembling, he was shaking all over like molten lava in a live volcano; his head was thrown back and there was foam on his lips. Mr. Roos shouted at him, demanding that he should be flogged then and there. Robin refused, if only because the Dutchman's arrogance annoyed him; Mr. Roos had bullied and blustered and behaved, Robin said afterwards, as if Sammy had been intent on starting a new Zulu war.

"You let a nigger strike a white man," the Dutchman cried, himself quivering with rage, "and next they will kill you in your bed."

"That would be much more comfortable than in the open," Robin replied. The more Mr. Roos stormed, the more stubborn Robin became. It was this attitude among the British that all the Boers loathed and feared. Theirs was simple. White men were few in a savage black land and only by standing together and stamping on the least sign of resistance could they hope to survive. The British feudal spirit that prompted them to protect their own men against, as it were, rival barons, appeared to the Dutch as a base betrayal. The British were concerned with personal status, the Dutch with racial survival. Each of the two peoples feared, distrusted and even detested the other's point of view.

Our neighbour went angrily away and did not let the matter rest there. In his view it should all have been settled, as these matters generally were, with twenty strokes of the hippo-hide whip, but as *rooinek* obstinacy prevented this, he still had the right of appeal to the law. He rode off to see the District Commissioner at Fort Hall, between thirty and forty miles away. A few days later a pink-faced young man sheltering beneath a very large topee arrived on a pony to say that a summons for assault had been taken out against Sammy. Robin was angry, Tilly alarmed, Sammy, when summoned, coldly contemptuous and the young official confused.

"I understood that he was violent and you wanted him arrested," he said. He had brought two large uniformed askaris, who arrived later on foot.

"I can't have him taken away or I shan't get the land ready before the rains," Robin said. "It was all Roos's fault anyway."

"I'm afraid he means to press the charge. We'd heard rumours that your boy was a bad hat who'd been stirring up trouble among the Kikuyu. In fact I had orders to bring your wife and daughter to Fort Hall if there was any sign of unrest."

The young man sounded disappointed. He had evidently hoped to bring a dangerous situation under control with two askaris and his own cool judgment and presence of mind. He stayed for lunch and then rode off on his pony.

The case against Sammy cost everyone a great deal of time, trouble and expense. When finally it came before the District Commissioner, Sammy went to Fort Hall and did not return for nearly a month. Fearing he had gone to jail, Robin sent a chit to the District Commissioner and learnt that the case had fizzled out owing to contradictory evidence, and Sammy had left a free, unfined man.

When at last he returned, sleek and smiling, Robin asked angrily what had detained him.

"I had to go to my father's *manyatta* to fetch some cattle," he replied.

"You did not have to pay a fine. Why did you need more cattle?"

"To pay the witnesses."

So it ended happily. All Europeans, in those days, received a native name derived from some peculiar characteristic, quality or habit. Soon we learnt that Mr. Roos's name was Meat of the Wild Pig.

Robin's name was bwana Kofia Mbaya, or Bad Hat. When, Tilly heard this she exclaimed: "But how extraordinary! That was the name the natives gave you in Rhodesia before we were married."

"It's not really so strange," Robin explained. "You see, it's the same hat."

Chapter Six

WITHIN a few months of our arrival, several neighbours had settled nearby.

The first was a shy but determined young man called Alec Wilson who had started life as an office boy in some drab Midland city and quickly risen, by means of excessive work and resolution, to become a solicitor's clerk. His was the sort of life and character that Arnold Bennett might have described. Then his health broke down and he was told to seek a dry and sunny climate if he was to survive. He came out with, I think, two hundred pounds of scraped-together capital, and was lucky enough to meet in the ship a man with somewhat larger resources, who became a sleeping partner, and the two between them bought a block of bush next to ours.

Alec Wilson knew even less than Robin did about the business in hand. But people who knew nothing at all were more likely to learn than those who knew a little, and mistook this for a great deal. Alec Wilson thought that he could learn from books. In this he was mistaken, for at that time little, if anything, that was useful had been recorded, and most of what had been recorded was wrong. But the grass hut he built for himself, one like ours, was soon filled with Government reports and pamphlets, manuals of engineering, text-books on plantation industries and works of that kind. When he came over to see us he would generally start the conversation with some such remark as: "According to my calculations, the volume of water in the river has fallen by point o five of a cusec, which would suggest that a furrow . . ." Or: "I have been giving some thought to the question of windbreaks; in Brazil the species *gravilea robusta* . . ."

This was a bore, yet his enthusiasm was touching. He was like a bird that has become the embodiment of a single intention, to migrate over thousands of miles of ocean and desert, so that nothing on earth will deflect it—no lure of food, no need for rest, no weariness and no temptation. It will get there or perish. No doubt he had a family in Wolverhampton or wherever it was, but he seldom mentioned them, although he corresponded with a married sister in Wales. Naturally enough, he counted every cent of his money. The only reason we knew about his married sister was that he would sometimes give us an unstamped letter to post next time we sent to Thika, and he never repaid us for the stamp. Robin helped him in a great many ways: lent him oxen to start his ploughing, chains to pull out tree-stumps, tools, all sorts of things, and even lent him Sammy for a week to organize his labour. When Alec Wilson paid Robin for some things bought on his behalf in Nairobi, he deducted one rupee for Sammy's keep.

When Sammy got back, he remarked: "That bwana should get a wife to make him comfortable. Now he is like a man who is always being bitten by *siafu.*" Soon he was called bwana *bado kwisha*, which means: not yet finished—a phrase that he was fond of using when the Kikuyu showed signs of knocking off for the day.

I thought him very old, as he was over thirty. He was not bad looking, although at first he seemed to us under-nourished and pasty-faced, with a stupid toothbrush moustache. But he had good, dog-like brown eyes and thick, wavy, chestnut hair, and when the sun had cooked him he lost the under-done appearance he had started with, his shoulders grew wider and even his moustache became more impressive.

On our other side was the Dutchman, Mr. Roos. The land immediately across the river was taken up by a Scot called Jock Nimmo who was always away shooting elephants. After a while he dumped a wife there to make a show of development. The regulations required every settler to spend a certain sum on his land within, I think, the first five years, and to do a certain amount in the way of clearing bush, fencing, cultivating and putting up buildings. Anyone who failed to do this lost his land. As Mr. Nimmo was a hunter, not a farmer, he left all this to his wife. Tilly thought that was why he married her. Why had she married him? It can hardly have been for security or for companionship, and must have been a disappointment if it was for love. She was a nursing sister from Edinburgh who had come out to the Nairobi hospital, and that was where Jock Nimmo had met her. Soon after their marriage he had left her in the bush with a drunken headman, a few unreliable Kikuyu, and some implements and untrained oxen, and had gone off to poach ivory in the Belgian Congo, with a promise that he would take her to the races on his return.

Mrs. Nimmo was not much interested in coffee-planting, and was shocked by what she called the "heathen immorality" of the natives. When Tilly inquired what she meant, she could hardly bring herself to speak of the sights she had seen. Tilly, hoping for some spicy revelations, sent me away. Afterwards she said to Robin:

"The woman's off her head. All she's worried about is that the boys don't wear trousers. And she a nurse! Besides, what about kilts?"

"Not in Edinburgh," Robin said with a flash of Highland snobbery.

Mrs. Nimmo had hoped to put nursing behind her, and disliked references to her former profession. She asked Tilly and myself to tea and produced a silver-plated teapot, fluted teacups decorated with rosebud-chains, thin bread-and-butter and many sweet and puffy little cakes which I greatly enjoyed. Each plate sat on a lace doily. Conversation was difficult. Mrs. Nimmo wanted to talk about Edinburgh society, the new Governor's pretty daughters and a controversy then splitting the world of fashion in regard to sleeves, as to whether they should be open, or gathered in at the wrist; whereas Tilly's mind was running on such topics as pleuro-pneumonia among oxen, twisted taproots in coffee seedlings and rumours of an outbreak of bubonic plague.

"I'm afraid I was a great disappointment," Tilly admitted regretfully afterwards. "The only other white woman for twenty miles and absolutely ignorant about the latest fashion in sleeves."

Early one morning a panting messenger arrived with a chit which said: "Please come at once. I have a loose murderer." Robin collected a mule and crossed the river by a new footbridge he had made. When he came back several hours later he remarked:

"She's an extraordinary woman. She goes on as if anything below a man's neck gives her the vapours, and there she was gaily strapping up a sliced buttock and a gashed tummy as if she thoroughly enjoyed it, as I think she did. Really it was a ghastly sight—the fellow had his skull laid open and one eye half chopped out as well—and when I remarked about it she said: 'Ah, weel, I've seen worse at the Infirmary on a Saturday night.' "

The drunken headman, it seemed, had got rather too drunk and attacked one of the Kikuyu, whose friends and relatives had promptly rounded on him and left very little of him intact. This was during the night. By dawn everyone had vanished, leaving the headman alone in the hut to bleed to death, as by all the rules he should have done. But when Mrs. Nimmo had discovered him in the morning he was still alive.

"He has no chance, poor fellow," she said, drawing on a good deal of experience; but she had not reckoned with African toughness. The headman was angry and wished very much to live, and so he did. On the other hand men who appeared to be quite healthy would sometimes die because they wanted to. This did not happen so much in Edinburgh, and Mrs. Nimmo never quite recovered from her amazement at the headman's survival. She wanted to call the police, but Robin dissuaded her. Even if the police did come, after a long delay, they could only ask a lot of questions, and as nobody would have admitted even to seeing the headman before, and as the relatives of anyone suspected of complicity would provide a complete alibi, we should not be any further forward at the end.

"I'll go and see Kupanya about it when your headman's fit to tell his story," Robin promised.

I suppose this incident made Mrs. Nimmo pack away her hopes with the silver-plated teapot. After that, she found herself reverting more and more to her profession, but now without a doctor's direction and certainly without pay. People came to her at all hours and from miles away and it was very hard to refuse them, yet she lacked the medicines to treat them with, or money to buy the necessary drugs, for Mr. Nimmo had left her with scarcely any cash. It was no good trying to charge the natives, for they had nothing either. Robin and Tilly used to buy supplies when they visited Nairobi, and a doctor Mrs. Nimmo had served under sometimes sent her things. For the rest, she worked by faith and Epsom salts. The clearing of the bush made slow progress. "I expect Nimmo will beat her for that when he reappears," Robin said.

The land next to the Nimmos' was taken up by an Australian called Victor Patterson. I believe he was some relation of the Patterson who wrote *The Man from Snowy River*, which became one of my favourite works. He was a self-taught prospector who had come to seek gold, and rumour had it that the block of land he now possessed had come to him in payment for a poker debt. What I remember most about him was his set of very badly fitting false teeth. They seemed to have a life of their own, jumping up and down without relation to the words emerging from his mouth, rather as, in the early days of sound-tracks, the voices often failed to synchronize with the actors' lips. I always believed them to be kept in with elastic, and sometimes it was a near thing that they stayed in at all. His face was lean and cadaverous, he spoke with a strong Australian twang and now and then gave a long, impressive hoicking in his throat that ended in a bold spit like the crack of a stock-whip.

About twice a week we sent a syce down to the post at Thika on a mule. Not much, as a rule, came back, except on those exciting occasions when an English mail-boat had arrived. But one day Robin received a letter from Roger Stilbeck that ran:

"Some people you will like have just bought a block of Thika land. His name is Hereward Palmer, you may have heard of him. He was in the 9th. She was a Pinckney, and is a dear. They are new to the game and I told them I was sure you'd give them a helping hand. She will be a friend for Tilly. I expect you have seen that good coffee land is now fetching up to £10 an acre. You got yours cheap. When are you coming in for the races? Look us up when you do. There is talk of starting a country club and I daresay I could put you up for it if anything comes of the idea."

This letter infuriated Tilly.

"He thinks he can dictate whom I'm to make friends with, just because he's sold us some land at a disgusting profit. Now he's gloating over having found more mugs. And I suppose the country club is another ramp of his. If the Palmers are friends of his I shall have nothing to do with them."

"They won't be friends after they discover how much he's stung them," Robin said soothingly. He did not like to admit it, but he looked forward eagerly to the Palmers' arrival.

Hereward Palmer was a Captain. Although no one could have disliked the Army more than Robin had when he was in it, now that he was not, it had acquired in his mind a certain enchantment. At times he thought of himself as a great soldier *manqué*, and after prolonged struggles with reluctant oxen, broken implements, weather that refused to do what was expected of it and Kikuyu who had very little idea of what they were expected to be doing at all, he yearned for the prospect of communication with more orderly minds. He hoped Tilly would not take against the Palmers. Like a spaniel, he always wanted to make friends.

Tilly ran into them at the Blue Posts hotel. We had ridden down to the *dukas* and looked in on our way back to leave a pair of socks Tilly had knitted for Randall, and some guava jelly she had made. We were hot, dusty and dishevelled, and saw on the veranda two tidy figures who had clearly stayed the night and not yet set forth on the day's journey. Tilly guessed at once who they were and tried to bolt, but Major Breeches came hurrying out to introduce them, so there was nothing for it but to face the Palmers as we were.

Although it is so long ago, and afterwards she changed so much, I can still remember Lettice Palmer as I saw her then for the first time: friendly, eager and above all handsome in a stylish, natural and entirely unselfconscious manner. Her skin was the finest I have ever seen, as fresh and translucent as the petal of a columbine. Her eyes were amber-brown and her hair an unusual colour, like a dark sherry; she had the spring and cleanliness of health about her, and a trick of tilting her head back and arching her nostrils, almost wrinkling them, when attentive or amused. Major Breeches practically fawned on her, like an ecstatic dog.

"What a journey!" she cried. "The grass is brown, the trees have huge flowers but no leaves, it's the women who carry everything. . . . And do you really live here? You've got a house, and a garden, and know how to speak to the boys? I hope that you'll help me, at present I feel like a lost sheep on a mountain full of wolves."

"A year ago I shouldn't have called it a house or garden," Tilly replied. "But I suppose we have both in a sense. Of course we'll help; Robin will come over, and lend you some boys."

"One doesn't know where to begin; I haven't felt so helpless since my small brother fell off a rocking horse when I was seven and filled the nursery with blood and no one came when I shouted. And Hereward thinks I should not have brought Chang and Zena, but I couldn't leave them behind. I love them dearly and they have the hearts of lions. Do you think it wrong?"

Chang and Zena were Pekinese, and lay at her feet looking disdainful and hot. Certainly on this bare veranda, beside a bougainvillea whose concentrated purple almost screamed aloud, and surrounded by tawny vegetation much the same colour as the Pekes' silky coats, the embroidered sleeve of an emperor's kimono seemed a long way off.

"They feel the heat," Tilly suggested. She invited them to make friends, but they stared at her indifferently from their huge myopic eyes and wiped their small pug-noses with enormous pink tongues.

Captain Palmer had jumped to his feet when Tilly appeared, bowed slightly over her hand and now stood as stiffly upright as one of the posts, surveying the scene with an air of male superiority and contempt for women's prattlings, combined with a touch of pasha-like complacency. He was a good-looking man: fair, with hair brushed straight back off a high forehead, a long bony face, strong features and a vigorous moustache. He could have been nothing on earth but an English officer and the observant might have placed him in the cavalry, perhaps from his heron-like legs and his walk. Whether they could have specified the regiment, I am not sure.

"Not fair on the dogs," he said.

Tilly disagreed with him. "They'll be all right if you're careful. You'll have to dress their coats every day with paraffin against the ticks, and boil their meat because of worms."

"What dreadful perils!" Lettice cried. "And the worst of it is, Hereward is powerless to protect them; he has five different kinds of gun, but all of them useless against ticks and worms."

"Plenty of game, I suppose?" inquired the Captain, feeling the bristles of his moustache with the tips of his fingers. He smelt faintly, and pleasantly, of bay rum.

"The only beautiful things in this country, so far as I can see, are the wild animals, and everyone thirsts to slaughter them," Lettice Palmer said. "When they have succeeded there'll be nothing left but ticks and dust and those pathetic little oxen with their humps and welts on their hides. And the children! Why have they all got such big tummies, as if they'd been blown up by a bicycle pump?"

"Eat too much," suggested the Captain.

"No, no, the wrong things," Tilly amended, "and at all hours of the night and day. But the doctors say it's partly an enlarged spleen from malaria."

Lettice Palmer impulsively covered her face with her hands, which were fine and white with long fingers. The gesture was theatrical but to her natural; she moved her hands and head a great deal, and yet nothing that she did struck one as false or affected. "How dreadful! There must be *something* we can do! All those children half-deformed and the women going along like toads under those enormous burdens and the babies with flies all over their eyes! Shall we ever be able to make an impression? Will it ever be changed?"

"My wife is very sensitive," Captain Palmer said with some pride. "These things always upset her. But she'll get used to it in time."

"That's just the trouble! One gets used to it in time and then one takes it for granted and then it all goes on as before. I should be a reformer out with nourishing soups and Keatinge's powder, instead of that I luxuriate at concerts or the ballet or lie in bed reading a novel. How dreadful it is!"

"It's impossible here," Tilly said.

"Yes, I'm sure this will do me a great deal of good. Layers of virtue will gradually be added to my stupid nature until at last I shall become a pearl for Hereward and adorn his establishment, like his record blackbuck he shot in Kashmir. How many inches was it, Hereward, from one end of its horns to the other?"

"Nepal," Hereward amended. "It was twenty-eight."

"Twenty-eight inches! How proud it must have been of its masculine glory, like a man with a magnificent moustache, or those narrow hips that look so well in uniform! And now those horns are in a crate in Nairobi. They're too precious to venture into the wilds until we have a house ready for them. They're kept with the uniform cases and the silver, and when we are ready to receive them, they will be sent for and arrive in state."

Hereward looked at her and smiled astringently. He had a curious trick, in smiling; he moved his whole scalp and slid the skin back across his forehead. When he laughed he looked aggressive, although we found that he was not.

"My wife's grandmother was a Russian," he said, as if that explained everything.

"The ship was full of people who thought they would very soon make a fortune, but now I've seen a little of the country I cannot think why. The natives have been here for thousands of years and all they have is a few beads. What is there to make a fortune out of? Of course there are ostriches. One man on the ship was going to rob the wild birds of their eggs and have a ranch full of ostriches. Then he would pluck the tail feathers of the cocks and sell them for enormous sums. That would be quite an easy way to grow rich and really quite respectable, too. But Hereward won't have it. He wants to own a plantation. . . ."

"I'd never bank on ladies' fashions," Hereward explained. "With respect"—he bowed to Tilly—"I know the sex too well. But a plantation—look at the fortunes made in India and Ceylon. A slow business, admittedly. Nothing back for five years."

"Five years!" Lettice looked as if he had stabbed her to the heart. "In five years my youth will be over, I shall be fat and middle-aged and letting out my dresses and Hereward will be feeling twinges of gout. Five years! And all that time we shall watch the sun rise and set and keep out of its way in between, and I shall make a garden and Hereward will watch the coffee bushes grow up very, very, slowly; and in five years Hugh will be nine years old and perhaps he'll have forgotten that he ever had parents at all. We have a son, you know," she added, "and of course he has to stay at home, and while I suppose that this is necessary, and Hereward says so, I find it hard to bear. But what a lot I am talking about myself, and how foolish this is, because I am not at all interesting; now you must tell us how we are to start setting about things on our piece of land."

Tilly gave advice, most of which dismayed Captain Palmer even more than his wife, for it sounded very haphazard and untidy to a military mind. They had with them two handsome ponies they had bought in Nairobi for a large sum, as things went in those days. Tilly told Captain Palmer that he ought not to take these ponies to his new farm until he had built a stable to accommodate them.

"But *we* shall be living in tents," Lettice protested. "Must they have something better?"

"They'll die of horse-sickness within a few months," Tilly warned her, "unless you shut them in before dark and keep them in a mosquito-proof stable."

"Roger Stilbeck said there was no horse-sickness here," the Captain remarked. "He said there was a move to start a polo club."

"He's a great talker," Tilly cautiously remarked.

"At least the altitude makes it healthy for human beings," Lettice suggested.

"Well, in a way; of course bubonic plague and smallpox are endemic, and the natives are riddled with yaws and parasites, so you must be very careful to boil the water. There's typhoid about, a lot of elephantiasis, and a man died of blackwater the other day. And you must be very careful of those dear little Pekes; it's terribly important to de-tick them every day, there's a form of tick-fever in this district that affects dogs. And of course there's rabies, so if you see a native dog behaving in a suspicious way you must quickly shoot it. As you know, rabies is quite incurable."

"Thank you," Lettice said. "You have been a great help to us."

"I shall come and call on your husband," the Captain added. He was looking displeased. "I'm sure he will take pity on a green-horn and put me on the right lines."

"If you can reach him through a sea of germs," Lettice remarked. She had taken up the two Pekineses in her arms and was playing with their silky ears as if to reassure herself that something in the world was still soft and desirable. Her skin was so thin that you could see the veins under it, like a leaf in spring. When she smiled good-bye, there seemed to be a warmth coming from her as from a peach on a wall in high summer, or from a bird cupped in the hand.

Tilly rode back a little guiltily, for she had liked Lettice, but never could resist the urge to deflate pomposity. She said to Robin:

"She'll be a fish out of water, I'm afraid."

"He has plenty of money. He can dig her a pool where she can shelter under water-lilies."

"I wonder why they came," Tilly speculated. "It doesn't seem their sort of life, and if they have money . . ."

"Sport, I suppose."

"Yes, but sport-lovers have a big safari and then go away until the next time; they don't settle. There's something queer about it, I think."

Tilly had a great capacity to scent mysteries. She leapt to conclusions with the unpredictability of a frog and, guided by a combination of alertness and sensitivity, sometimes landed much nearer to the truth than one would have expected. Robin merely said:

"There's something queer about anyone who comes to this country."

"It might have been some kind of scandal. And now I think of it, I vaguely remember hearing something of the kind connected with the name. Perhaps she ran away with him. He's quite attractive, but a type. She does the helpless female act, but underneath it all is probably as tough as old boots."

"A fellow like that will want a stone house," Robin meditated. "There's some stone that looks just right for building near the river bank, on our land. I wonder if he'd like to go into partnership over a small quarry?"

Chapter Seven

ONCE kindled, the notion of a quarry quickly gathered strength; soon, in Robin's mind, houses had sprung up all along our ridge, cut stone was being sold in large quantities and he, with Hereward Palmer as a sleeping partner, was a stone magnate of no mean degree. He returned from his first visit to the Palmers' camp only temporarily discouraged. Captain Palmer intended to employ a building contractor in Nairobi to put up his house.

"He must be very rich indeed," Robin said wistfully.

"Not for long, if he goes on like that."

"I warned him he'd waste hundreds of pounds. I think the idea sank in; he may change his mind, and decide to develop the quarry. . . ."

Tilly asked his opinion of Mrs. Palmer. He was unexpectedly cautious.

"I think she'll get fat in a few years' time."

"She isn't fat *now*; what does it matter what she'll be like in future?"

"I seemed to hear the clash of castanets," Robin said obscurely.

He added that their head-boy was defrauding them at every turn, their labour was nothing but a collection of scallywags and that Captain Palmer thought of little but shooting. He rode over to their camp quite often and much enjoyed, as Tilly put it, doing the heavy settler. It was surprising what a lot of difference half a year's experience made, and a knowledge, however rudimentary, of Swahili. This was just as much a foreign tongue to the Kikuyu as to us, but they picked it up quickly and, although it led to many acrimonious conversations conducted at cross-purposes, it did provide a means of communication a little more explicit than shouts and gestures.

"It's curious how many people think they can make foreigners or natives understand merely by shouting at them," Robin once remarked. He was quite right. On station platforms, in rickshaws and especially in hotels one often heard baffled Englishmen bellowing angrily at mute, uncomprehending Africans such phrases as: "Where—is—my—bedding" or "This—bacon—is—cold", as if hammering a nail into a stone wall.

After they had settled into their grass huts—larger and better ones than ours—the Palmers rode over on their superior ponies to lunch, and in the afternoon Robin showed Captain Palmer his development. There was not much to see, but what there was had been won hardly. The clearing of the bush was slow and difficult, especially the digging out of tree stumps. When you came to do it, there were more trees than you thought, and their roots were remarkably tough and prolific. The Kikuyu had never wielded picks before and used them rather as if they had been toothpicks, prodding gently round the stump as if afraid of touching a nerve. Eventually, when all the roots were freed, the ox-boys lashed a chain to the stump and their team, with luck, hauled it away. But the chain often snapped or slipped, and the oxen were apt to pull in several directions at once; and the more the Kikuyu shouted and flapped, the more confused and stubborn the oxen became.

However, at last the stumps had been drawn from a level piece of ground near our camp, and the land had been ploughed and worked down to a seed-bed that would have appalled any English farmer, but that was adequate for coffee, which was planted as seedlings ten or twelve inches high. In the dry weather before the long rains, a hot and dusty period, Robin had spent many sweaty and frustrating hours holding one end of a chain composed of thin steel rods, each three feet long. A Kikuyu warrior held the other end and Sammy went down the chain putting a stick into the ground at each joint, to mark the site of a future seedling. This was complicated by the spacing of the seedlings in triangles, and the forest of sticks which soon arose sometimes grew confused, and had to be uprooted to enable everyone to start again.

Eventually, however, the Kikuyu dug holes for the seedlings. This task was supposed to be finished before the rains, but of course was not, and then came a crisis when the seedlings Robin had bought arrived before the ground was ready for them. In future years the plantation would be supplied from a nursery beside the river, under Tilly's care, where coffee berries were planted in long mounds, like asparagus beds, and thatched with banana fronds to prevent the sun from drying out the moist riverine soil.

By now the first rains, which were torrential and cold and stopped the progress of all wagons and carts, had come and gone, and our seedlings had been planted in the freshly broken land. Already they had vanished beneath a carpet of weeds, which was rapidly becoming a jungle; the warriors had been set to work with pangas to demolish it, and give the precious seedlings a chance to find light and air.

After the first day of this, Sammy came to Robin to report that the warriors refused to demolish weeds any longer.

"But it is not such hard work as the clearing," Robin protested, "and they are paid the same."

"It is not that," Sammy said.

"Then what is the trouble?"

"Their pride would be injured if they were seen cutting weeds."

"What is the difference between clearing the grass away before the land is ploughed, and clearing the weeds away afterwards?"

"This is women's work," Sammy explained.

Robin was indignant. He thought that the warriors were making an excuse and, if they were not, that work like this should not be done by women, but by otherwise idle young men.

His anger did not make any difference. The young men downed pangas and said that they were going home.

"I know what our Dutch friend would do," Robin mused. "Put them down and give them twenty-five."

This was a sovereign remedy in those days, but Robin did not like it, and he dodged the necessity whenever he could. "If it's women's work," he added, "perhaps we had better get some women. We can't reform their customs overnight."

He consulted Sammy, and Sammy went to see chief Kupanya, and in due course a number of young women came swinging gaily down the path from the reserve chanting a song which, to judge from the laughter it aroused among the warriors, was ribald and obscene. Their heads were clean-shaven except for a patch on top, about as large round as an egg-cup, which showed them to be unmarried, although probably they were all bespoken, and awaited only the settlement of the bride-price before being claimed. They were bare to the waist and had shapely breasts, not yet spoilt by prolonged suckling, and wore a triangular leather apron in front and behind. They also wore beads and brass or copper ornaments, such as bangles and anklets, and objects dangling from their ears.

The young men were delighted to yield up their pangas, which the girls seized with strong wrists and practised holds, and went into action against the weeds with great gusto and dash. They sang all the time, and did three times as much work as the men. In the afternoon they marched up the hill again to their reserve. Their fathers were not letting them stay away at nights, and there was plenty waiting for them to do when they got home. Their wages they would pay over to their fathers, with no doubt a large cut for Kupanya on the side.

When Captain Palmer rode over he saw these young women at work with mingled disapproval and envy.

"Hardly seems quite the thing, does it," he suggested, "with all those idle young bloods eating their heads off and not lifting a finger."

"You know what tribal customs are," Robin answered knowingly, although it was unlikely that either of them had much information on this subject. Anthropologists had not yet made it respectable.

Tilly took Lettice to see her own activities, of which there were many, including hens and turkeys, a young orchard, an embryonic garden and rows of pegs where everyone hoped a house would one day arise in its glory. Lettice was deeply impressed.

"How do you find the *energy* to do so much?" she asked. "This country's full of sloth, the air distils it; the essence of a thousand generations of doing no more than is necessary to exist, of leaving things as they are, has settled into the ground. And it's become too strong for me to resist; I'm not very good at resisting things, I'm afraid. Or do you think I am just making excuses?"

Tilly did think so, but she smiled, and exchanged a sitting of turkey's eggs for a pair of tumbler pigeons, which were very soon eaten by hawks. In theory, Tilly disapproved, at least in Africa, of everything that Lettice was or represented, but in practice she could not help being entertained by Lettice and enjoying her company. Tilly was on her guard against anything laid on, as she expressed it, with a trowel, but Lettice did not lay on her charm at all, she simply exuded it as a rose its scent, and just as unwittingly. That afternoon she sat on our narrow lean-to veranda playing with the silky ears of her Pekinese and smiling a little forlornly at this glimpse into her own future. When to remedy a cold you take a lump of sugar soaked in eucalyptus oil, you taste the sharp, astringent flavour of the essence and the sweetness of the sugar at the same time. That is the kind of impression Lettice gave. The Pekinese looked out upon the world with an expression of lofty disdain probably due to their myopia, but which accorded well with their imperial origins and their bold, baroque design.

"This country frightens me," Lettice continued. "I don't mean the insects and the *idea* of snakes (I haven't actually seen one), or even the lions and rhinos—why people should be so much more nervous about wild animals, who nearly always run away except when provoked, than about other human beings, who are so much more dangerous and vindictive, I've never been able to understand. No, it isn't that which alarms me. It's a sort of quiet, smiling, destructive ferocity. Doesn't it strike you as strange that nothing people have created here has survived? Not even a few traces? No ruins of cities or temples—no ancient over-grown roads—no legends of past empires—no statues hidden in the ground—no tombs or burial mounds? No sign that generations of people have lived here, lived and died. Do you realize that quite soon *we* shall be the past? And what will there be to show that we have ever existed? We shall be swallowed up like everything else into a dreadful, sunny limbo."

"You're being morbid," Tilly said. "It's true the natives have done nothing yet with the country, but we shall."

"How confident you are! How do you keep your energy on the boil? When I start some simple task, a hundred distractions spring up to prevent me from completing it."

"I know just what you mean," Tilly agreed. "The other day I started to write to my sister and I counted twelve interruptions before I gave up. It wasn't so much the interruptions I minded but every one of them was trivial and unnecessary, like a hornets' nest in the larder, or a quarrel between Juma and the garden-boy, or a hawk taking a chicken. I never did finish the letter, and as for reading a book . . ."

"Ah! That's it. Since I've been here I find I cannot concentrate on French novels, and the other day I couldn't for the life of me remember the words of one of my songs. We've got a small grand piano on the way out. Do you think we shall ever get it here? First of all the railway and then an ox-wagon, I suppose. I tremble for its safety. . . ."

"It will be touch and go. And you will have to build a house for it before it arrives."

"And then I shall practise, practise, practise every day! I love the sun, I revel in the warmth, everything is bright and gay, there are wonderful birds and butterflies, and boys to do the donkey-work, everything combines to lull and please: and yet I'm not quite lulled. I can't understand why."

Lettice removed her hat, which involved the extraction of several long pins with heads of mother-of-pearl; her silky hair, wound over a frame called a sausage (I knew because Tilly used one) sat on her shapely head like a kind of plate, and threw a faint shadow over the top part of her face. The rolls of hair shone like polished mahogany, and the scent she used reminded me of heliotrope. It was rather like having seats at a play, she carried round a sense of drama as her own particular element.

"Last night," she said, "I dreamt I was back in Norway, the country that I like best in all the world. We spent one summer fishing in the fjords, and Hereward hunted elk in forests which smelt of moss and resin. The fjords, how wonderful they were! The black forest was like a bear's furry pelt coming right down to the edge of the dark, still water, and from the house we stayed in we could watch the fishing boats come in with their catch, and see the men wave to wives and friends in little white toy-like houses, so clean, so neat and somehow brave, pressed in by all those mountains and forests. . . . Once we saw the aurora borealis, it lit the sky like some tremendous ghostly signal for the end of the world, and everything was silent, even the dogs. . . . Well, there's plenty of beauty here, and splendour, but it doesn't make your heart swell and almost burst, it seems to compress it into a little button and make it hard and tight. Now I think I'm talking gibberish; you must try to forgive me, it's such a treat to have someone to talk to about something besides dead animals and crops and how dreadfully inefficient the natives are at everything, which I'm sure is true."

"It all comes as a bit of a shock at first," Tilly remarked. "But you'll get used to it. One sort of grows into the life."

Hereward and Robin came back from their tour almost as brothers. Although Robin had served only for a short while in the Yeomanry, he had managed to recall one or two slight acquaintances in the Ninth; and, once that had been established, Hereward had fallen into line very satisfactorily about the quarry. He would engage a mason to cut and dress enough stone for Robin's house as well as for his own. Robin would contribute the raw materials, which luckily did not need any wages.

"Now we shall be able to build some stables," Tilly said delightedly.

"And one for my piano," Lettice suggested.

Captain Palmer stroked his moustache and smiled at Tilly. "My wife is musical," he said, as if enlisting sympathy for some distressing ailment. "I can foresee difficulties in getting it here."

"It is with your trophies, Hereward," she reminded him. "They will need a stable too."

Hereward laughed good-humouredly. "They will share ours. Perhaps it is bringing coals to Newcastle, but they have been in store for so long that I'm anxious to rescue them before they get weevily. Though I say it as shouldn't, I have some fine specimens."

"I suppose you will add to them here," Tilly said.

"Well, of course, when we've settled in. . . . They tell me the ladies are as keen on safari as the men. Perhaps we could persuade you to join up with us and show us the ropes; I know your husband is an old hand."

Robin looked guilty and would not meet Tilly's eye. Hereward was a treat for him, and he was making the most of it.

And so the Palmers, by and large, were a success. Lettice even paid some attention to me. I had at this time a hospital for sick animals, which included a lame hen, a baby duiker and a pigeon with a broken leg. This I had bandaged with tape and set in splints made of two matches, and to everyone's surprise the bird had not yet died. (A hospital for sick animals has a quick turnover, since very few wild creatures that are both injured and in captivity will survive.) Lettice helped me to rearrange the pigeon's splints and to feed the duiker from a bottle; I do not think it was sick, it was merely small and deprived of its mother.

"I once knew a woman," Lettice said, "who wore a live snake instead of a necklace at dinner parties; she said it kept her neck cool. That sounds a very tall story, but it's true."

"There's a python in the river," I suggested hopefully.

"It would be more a question of the python wearing the woman, I'm afraid. . . . Which is your favourite animal, among all that you have seen since you arrived?"

Even Lettice, I thought sadly—even Lettice who fascinated me like some brilliant-plumaged flashing bird, or like a clown on a magic bicycle—even she did not avoid that distressing adult habit of asking enormous questions to which there could be no sensible reply. Cornered, however—I did not want to disappoint her—I fell back on my chameleons. She looked surprised, and stroked the ruffled pigeon with slender fingers on which there sparkled several rings.

"You should keep one as a pet," she said. "No, two; you must always have animals in pairs. Most people keep only one, and try to suck all the love out of it like a vampire, but that's cruel. . . . Look at this bird's eye, it's like a ruby in a certain light; why are pigeons' eyes red, I wonder? Yours are blue. So are Hugh's; he is much younger than you, and I've no idea whether he's fond of animals and birds, or whether he's musical, or what his likes and dislikes are, except that someone told me he was fond of Gentleman's Relish. . . . We must be going, Hereward; if we are away too long we shall find the headman drunk again and trying to murder someone, or perhaps successful, and everyone fled."

After they had left Robin said with satisfaction: "That was a good day's work about the quarry. I could never have afforded an Indian *fundi*. I hope he's got as much money as he seems to have. One can never be sure."

"There's something queer about them," Tilly said. "At least, about their being here."

"He's a pompous sort of cuss, but there's nothing very queer about that."

"Why did they come? They're not the type," Tilly insisted. "My guess is they ran off together and have to live abroad; anyway, I bet there's a scandal mixed up in it somewhere."

"A fine woman," Robin said appreciatively, looking after their departing ponies.

"Emotional," concluded Tilly. This was a word of condemnation, because Tilly was a devotee of reason; she came of a Liberal family and believed that powers of intellect should prevail. In fact, no one was a greater victim of emotions, at least of the more generous kind, but she felt that to give way to them was rather disgraceful, and hoped by frowning upon them, whether they were at work in herself or in others, to drive them away.

"The Palmers are too civilized for this life," Robin said. "Or, at least, she is; and he is too stupid. I fear she's thrown herself away."

"At least on to a comfortable rubbish-heap," Tilly remarked.

Chapter Eight

ONE day a syce arrived with a note scrawled on sky-blue writing paper in Lettice's large and sloping hand. "Please come at once," it said. "There has been a terrible disaster." Tilly sent for Robin, who was out on the farm. He returned reluctantly, some critical situation having arisen, and inquired of the syce:

"What is this bad news?"

"*Sijui*," said the syce, using that useful, universal word that covered almost every form of ignorance or indifference, and that had given its name to many rivers, districts and ranges of hills.

"It can't be anything much," Robin suggested.

"All the same, you ought to go over."

"I thought perhaps you might . . ."

"Robin!" cried Tilly. "Are you a man or a mouse?"

Robin paused for some time in thought, and lit one of the small cheroots he favoured.

"Well," he concluded, "I'm never quite sure." But with reluctance he climbed on to his mule and trotted off to the Palmers'.

A note came back about an hour later. "You had better come, there has been a fight, and bring iodine, bandages and a sharp pair of scissors." Tilly collected the equipment and set out, taking me with her. Outwardly, all seemed unruffled at the Palmers'; the sun shone, a man in a red blanket swung a sickle-ended stick very slowly to and fro decapitating grass-heads on what would one day be a lawn, several others drooped about in various attitudes of indolence and supple meditation among the foundations of the future house, which stood on a knoll commanding a wide view of grass, bush and scattered trees. A dire event needs a crowd to endow it with reality; it is the murmuring, nudging people, the peering heads, the avid eyes that give it drama; without these, it is insignificant, and might be part of a dream.

We asked for Lettice, who was not in the lime-washed rondavel that was their living-room; a houseboy led us to the Kikuyu huts a little way off and Lettice emerged from one of them looking white and shaky, with blood on her hands.

"Thank God you've come," she cried. "A wretched man inside has been cut to ribbons. I've done what I can but I'm not good at it; it's dark and everything is filthy and they've all run away. . . ." She staggered a little, dived for the back of the hut and I think was sick, and when she came back Tilly took her arm and told her to go in and lie down. "First aid is not my strong point either," Tilly said, "but I'm getting used to it; where has Robin gone?"

"He and Hereward have ridden off to catch the man who did it. Or perhaps there were several; half the boys seem to have run away."

"I had better send for Sammy," Tilly decided. She vanished into the dark little hut with its horrors, while I returned to the house with Lettice, who helped herself to brandy and then lay on a sofa with her eyes closed, white and limp. Her eyelids had little blue veins on them and looked like rice-paper, they were so thin.

"Perhaps I could have saved him," she said, opening her eyes, "if I had known enough about it; but this happened in the night and they never told us till the morning; and all that time the wretched man. . . ."

"Is he dead?" I inquired.

"Not quite, although I can't imagine why; if we could only have got him to a hospital. . . . As it is I don't know what we can do."

Lettice looked lovely and incongruous on the sofa in the rough hut. Or rather, the sofa was incongruous; the Palmers' furniture had arrived before their house was built and some of it was in the mud-floored rondavel, not at all at home. The sofa was covered in green velvet, and its ends were looped together by golden cords; it stood upon a floor of puddled clay, a low stool beside it on whose cushions, worked in *petit point*, Chang and Zena lay. It was very quiet in the rondavel, which smelt of lavender and had a vase of wild flowers on a French table with curved bandy legs and a fascinating surface of marquetry. Although there was much to look at in this room unfamiliar and queer, I wished I had been riding with Robin and Captain

Palmer up the paths into the reserve, in pursuit of murderers.

"I only hope that Hereward will keep his temper," Lettice murmured. "If he doesn't, there will be another murder on our hands. That man had a gash right through his skull; part of his scalp was hanging down over his cheek and there was nothing but pulp where one eye . . . What a conversation for a child! Get that box from the table in the corner and I will teach you how to play chess, if you don't already know; perhaps you are too young, but they say children start at four or five in China."

The carved pieces with their pennants and mitres and prancing horses fascinated me so much that the rules of the game hardly seemed to matter, but Lettice was very patient and showed me what to do. After a while Tilly came in and took off her heavy hat, made of two thicknesses of felt lined with red and worn all day; she was flushed and hot, and her hands trembled when she laid the hat aside.

"He's still alive," she said, "but I don't think he will be much longer. Only a surgeon could save his life. I wonder if we ought to put him in a cart even now, and take him to Fort Hall; but I don't see how he could possibly survive the journey."

"I am fiddling while Rome burns," Lettice said, "but there's nothing I can do to put out the fire. That poor creature, his eye haunts me. . . . Do you play chess?"

"They have all deserted him, which means they think it's hopeless; they won't sit with a dying person. Usually, you know, they make a hole in the side of the hut and drag the sick person out to die; that saves the hut. If someone dies inside it, they have to burn it down. I couldn't stand the fug any longer; there's still a fire in the middle of the hut and the smoke stung my eyes and throat and I kept coughing. . . . I've found someone to sit with him, a boy who isn't a Kikuyu, and there's no more to be done. . . ."

"Let's have a game of chess," Lettice suggested. Tilly glanced at her and started to speak, but then changed her mind, for she saw that Lettice was very pale and her hands were shaking.

"If you are a good player, you had better give me a castle," Tilly remarked. "I haven't played since I was at school."

But Lettice had only half her mind, or less than that, on the game.

"I am glad that Robin is with Hereward," she said. "He will have a calming influence. When Hereward is angry he doesn't bluster and shout, which gets it out of the system, he goes hard and cold as an icicle, and I'm always afraid that he will kill someone. In the days of duels he would have called people out almost every day."

"He may find life here difficult, it consists so much of petty irritations."

"Life has been difficult for Hereward everywhere in the last few years. But now I know he intends to stay, because he has sent for his heads."

"And you for your piano," Tilly reminded her.

"Yes; but how am I to keep it tuned?" Her voice was full of melancholy, so Tilly said:

"I daresay one could learn piano-tuning quite easily." Tilly was a great believer in learning things out of books, and was always writing to her sister for manuals on various subjects and skills. She had just sent for books on accountancy, plumbing, grafting trees and palmistry, and would no doubt put piano-tuning on her next list.

"I never trust the things I do myself," Lettice said sadly. "I know from experience that they are very seldom properly done. I would rather piano-tuning remained the mystery to me that it is and always would be, even if someone revealed its secrets."

This was what Tilly called doing the helpless female act, and she did not approve. Perhaps Lettice felt her reservations, for she added: "I know it's a luxury one can't afford, to be so useless at practical things. I shall try to reform. This appears to be a country where women do all the hard work while the men look fierce and decorative, like cock birds. That might suit Hereward, but I have a long way to go before I can be as useful as a Kikuyu woman. . . . That wretched, battered boy. If we could only do something. . . . I'm sorry, I'm afraid I must take your queen."

Alec Wilson arrived while they were still playing, a rifle slung over his shoulder.

"I heard there'd been trouble," he said, striding into the room in a purposeful manner, rather red in the face. "I thought a native rising might have started."

"It's scarcely that," Lettice said.

"Well, if there's anything I can do, here I am. Where's Captain Palmer?"

Lettice explained, and Alec looked relieved. "In that case, it's just as well I came; I can hold the fort while you two ladies are left on your own. One never knows what a spark may do; I sometimes wonder if we're sitting on a powder magazine."

"It's very thoughtful of you, Mr. Wilson," Lettice said.

"It's a privilege to feel I'm any use at all to someone as—to a lady of your—oh, well, you know what I mean." Poor Alec grew redder than ever and wiped his neck with a large, bright bandana handkerchief. When he looked at her his eyes went moist and soft, like a calf's, and his lips opened slightly. One could see that to a solitary, hard-working bachelor, who seldom went even so far as Nairobi, Lettice would seem as marvellous, magical and unexpected as, to a Cytherean fisherman, Aphrodite emerging from the foam must once have done.

Presently he escorted Tilly to the injured man's hut, and they returned, subdued and shaken, to say that he appeared at last to be dead.

"It's hard to tell for certain," Tilly said. "It's so hot in there and one's eyes water. We took a torch and I think . . ."

"No doubt about it," Alec added, with an emphasis suggesting some uncertainty. "It's a shame that you ladies should have been exposed to such a . . . well, it's a horrid experience for anyone, but for Mrs. Palmer . . ."

"I backed out and left it all to Tilly," Lettice said truthfully. "And now, of course, to you, Mr. Wilson; it is a great comfort to have your help and support."

Alec blushed and looked like a small boy presented with a new bicycle. His rôle as a protective male, however, was short-lived, for Hereward and Robin soon returned. They had not caught the murderer, but had seen the chief.

"There seems to have been a fight," Robin explained, "so probably it isn't murder but manslaughter, and no one knows who was to blame. Anyway Kupanya says he'll produce the culprit and then we can send him to the D.C."

"How will you know he *is* the culprit?" Lettice inquired. "I suppose the chief could produce almost anyone, and say he was the man."

"That will be for the D.C. to unravel," Captain Palmer said.

"Meanwhile, half my labour force has run away and I must get the fellow buried, and I'm told these Kikuyu won't touch a corpse."

This was true; but the contractor who was going to build the Palmers' house had sent out half a dozen men of another tribe, who would not mix with the Kikuyu. They were large and very black and liked to work stark naked, and came from the Kavirondo Gulf on Lake Victoria, so they were called Kavirondo, although this was not the name of a tribe. They did not object to handling corpses—in fact, rather the reverse. When at length we reached home on our mules, Sammy observed:

"Why does the bwana want to bury the dead man? They will only dig him up again."

"Who will?" demanded Robin.

"The Kavirondo."

"But why?"

"To eat, of course. The Kavirondo much enjoy corpses."

"Then they are *shenzis,*" Tilly said. *Shenzi* was another very useful word, meaning anything from savage to merely down-at-heel or untidy.

"Yes, indeed, they are *shenzis,*" Sammy agreed complacently. "The Kavirondo are like hyenas, not like men, not like Masai or Kikuyu."

"I wonder if I should warn Palmer," Robin remarked.

"Let sleeping dogs lie," advised Tilly.

We had a mule called Margaret, very tame and good-natured; she would come into the veranda and eat sugar out of Tilly's hand. I was allowed to ride her, and sometimes Sammy would escort me on his bicycle along the twisting paths; I think he liked the pretext for a ride, and besides he was fond of children. That afternoon, I got permission to take Margaret out, and went to find Njombo, who had taken over the duties of a syce, to ask him to saddle her. But Njombo had vanished. When I found Sammy, he said: "Njombo will come back in a few days. Kupanya has sent for him."

I felt an uneasy foreboding. "Is it because of the dead man?"

"Perhaps," Sammy said vaguely.

"Was it Njombo who killed him?"

"Why should you ask that?" replied Sammy. "Kimani—that

is the dead man—was at bwana Palmer's shamba, but Njombo works here."

"If you tell me, I will not say anything to my father."

Sammy looked at me and smiled. He had a rather wolfish smile, but I trusted him.

"These affairs are not for children."

"If Kupanya catches him, will Njombo be sent to the D.C.?"

"Njombo will not go to the D.C.," Sammy said firmly.

"Bwana Palmer will send him."

"It is nothing to do with bwana Palmer. Njombo's father, who is dead, was Kupanya's brother, children of the same belly. This man Kimani, he was drunk, and insulted Njombo. There was trouble between them about a woman, and Njombo hit him with a panga. And no doubt some enemy of Njombo's used medicine to make that fool Kimani die."

"But you said Njombo killed him with a panga."

"Njombo hit him, but not very hard; many people are struck with pangas and spears; if Njombo's enemy had not used bad medicine, perhaps Kimani would have recovered. As it is, there will be heavy fines to pay; Njombo is poor, and so Kupanya will have to help him to find many goats."

"But Kupanya has promised to send the murderer to the D.C.," I said, feeling rather at sea.

"Kupanya will find someone to send, and perhaps pay him some goats; there will not be any trouble," Sammy said.

It all seemed very much involved, and I was sorry Njombo had gone; I liked him, he was always cheerful and smiling, he had a merry eye, and he wore a neat little bead-edged leather cap, made from a sheep's stomach, with a rakish air.

"Njombo is buying a wife," Sammy added, "and now all his goats will have to go to Kimani's father, so he will not be able to pay for her."

"I hope he will come back," I said.

"Yes, he will come back, for he will need rupees to buy goats to pay Kimani's father. Kimani was a worthless man, but now he has died he will bring wealth to his father." That seemed to be Kimani's only epitaph.

I could not mourn Kimani, as I had not known him; but next morning the dove with the broken leg lay in its moss-lined box stiff and cold, its half-closed eyes not red at all, but dull brown.

There had been so much life in its palpitating, downy chest, it had put its head on one side and pecked so keenly at its food, that I could not believe it would never fly again. I had felt certain it would recover, and the blow was bitter. Tilly found me in tears and suggested an honourable funeral, so I dug a grave and interred it underneath a young fig tree, and made a small cross.

The little duiker was a comfort, and let me stroke her warm body while she waggled a stumpy tail. But she would not allow me to touch her black velvet muzzle, which was soft as shammy-leather. She had thick, stiff hair with a faint tinge of blue about it, and a line down the middle of her back. Sometimes she twitched her ears and lifted her muzzle and I knew that she was testing the air for the least suspicion of a whiff of other duikers, for news from home, as it were, and that if such news came, she would feel restless and perhaps disappear. We called her Twinkle. When she came, her legs had been like long, thin twigs and her eyes enormous; gradually the rest of her body grew to match their scale, and she attained a great deal of self-possession. She walked about freely, and came into the house, and nibbled titbits from my hand.

The houseboys grew used to her; although the Kikuyu killed duikers and other buck whenever they could, because of damage done to their shambas, they did not eat the flesh of wild animals, so Twinkle was safe with them. But Juma warned me against the Kavirondos. "They will eat her if they see her," he said. "They will eat anything, even hyenas." This was untrue, but they would certainly have eaten Twinkle. Although we had no Kavirondos on the place, the Palmers' cannibals were not far away.

A few days later a *toto* arrived with a wicker basket and a chit for Tilly. Inside the basket, on a bed of leaves, sat two green chameleons, a present to me from Lettice. "I hope they are a he and a she, but no one seems able to tell," she wrote. "At any rate they appear to be friends." Tilly and Robin thought of various fancy names for them but in the end we called them George and Mary, because Robin thought their crests looked like crowns, and they had the dignified, deliberate movements proper to royalty.

If I put them on a tartan rug, Robin told me, they would explode. I believed him, and refused to try the experiment. Their repertoire of colour was not very wide, but they could change from green-all-over to a patchy greenish-brown with touches of yellow (suitable for bark) in about twenty minutes. It was fascinating to watch the lightning dart of their long, forked tongues—as long as their whole bodies—which would nick a fly off a leaf too swiftly for the eye to follow. They were just like miniature dragons. When they had gulped a fly whole, their expression of complacent self-satisfaction seemed to intensify and they sat completely motionless. Robin said they looked like aldermen at a city banquet who had eaten themselves into a stupor. But their expression was not stupefied: it was watchful, calm and impassive.

We built a large cage of wire netting around a shrub, where they could lead a natural life. To begin with I caught flies for them, but they ignored my offerings. They were independent creatures, and waved their legs as if they were cycling when I picked them up, wriggling desperately; yet they were not frightened of me and never tried to run away. One day I proffered a chameleon to Njombo who shrank back with an expression of extreme distaste.

"They are bad things," he said, and refused to tell me why. His aversion was odd, since chameleons did nothing but good, and had no bite or sting. But Alec Wilson came across an explanation in one of his instructive manuals or periodicals that contained some native legends. The chameleon, apparently, had been entrusted by God with an important message for the first man, who was living somewhere near Mount Kenya. "You must take this message and not linger by the wayside," it was told. "You must deliver it before the moon wanes."

The chameleon started off in fine fettle but soon forgot the purpose of its journey. Various adventures befell it which I forget, and which in any case probably changed with the teller; it visited the underworld, and met some unpleasant ogres. At any rate by the time it recollected its mission, resumed its journey and eventually arrived, the time limit had expired.

"Now look what you have done," God thundered. "The message you carried was to reprieve the moon from its monthly extinction, and man from death. Now it is too late. Henceforth the moon must disappear each month and every man and woman must die, and all because you did not obey my instructions." So ever since the poor chameleon, who could have saved mankind, had been shunned. In a sense that protected it, for shunned things were not molested. No one, for instance, would have dreamt of harming a hyena, or even a vulture.

I discovered gradually that a legend existed to fit every bird and beast, but the Kikuyu very seldom told them to Europeans; they were for women and old men to repeat to children in the smoky, firelit evenings. When my dove died, and Sammy found me mourning by its grave, he told me a story I often recalled when I heard these birds cooing on three notes which the Kikuyu imitated in their name for dove: Da-toooo-ra, the second syllable soft, liquid and very drawn-out.

There was a girl, Sammy said, called Wanjiru, who lived by a river, and her mother beat her so severely as to break her back. When her bones were scattered on the grass, the doves picked them up in their beaks and decided to put Wanjiru together again. So they joined her bones with links of the fine chains made by Kikuyu smiths and worn by Kikuyu people, and hid her in a cave.

Along came some girls to draw water. Each helped the other to lift a full gourd on to her friend's back: but no one would help the smallest girl, who was Wanjiru's sister, because she was disgraced by her mother's cruel behaviour. So she sat down by the stream and cried. Wanjiru heard, and emerged from her cave to lift the gourd into position on her sister's back; but she warned the girl to keep the secret of her hiding-place.

After a while, the secret leaked out. Wanjiru's parents hid in the grass and, when she emerged from her cave to help her sister, they sprang out, captured her and took her home. But the doves were having none of this. They flew into the hut and demanded from Wanjiru's mother all the chains she wore as ornaments. When she refused, they pulled out all the links that held Wanjiru's bones together. So she fell apart, and her mother put the bones back in the cave. But the story ended happily. For a second time the clever doves re-assembled Wanjiru and she lived in the cave, obedient now to their instructions never again to help her family.

Chapter Nine

WHEN the New Year came round, most of the farmers went to Nairobi to the races. Tilly and Robin stayed at home their first year, but next time the Palmers persuaded them to go, and I was sent to Mrs. Nimmo's.

Mrs. Nimmo was kind, but too motherly. Tilly was so taken up with the daily business of living that she had little time, and perhaps even less inclination, for a broody hen approach to parenthood. Life was there for me to take part in, and always offered plenty to do, but things were not invented for me, I was not labelled as a child to be handled with care and given special treatment. Mrs. Nimmo, being so far childless—the prolonged absences of Mr. Nimmo perhaps did not give her much encouragement—was inclined to lavish her maternal love on me. This I found embarrassing, though not without its compensations, for I was given things to eat that I enjoyed and made to feel important. On the other hand she disapproved of the amount of time I spent pottering about on my own or talking to the Kikuyu, and tried to curtail my liberty.

Mrs. Nimmo was a large, strong, often flurried woman who gave the impression that she was about to overflow. She was not exactly fat, but generous in build, and compounded of a strange mixture of indolence and energy. Sometimes she would wear her hair in curling-pins half the morning and slop about in bedroom slippers, yet she was extremely fussy about the neatness of her living-room, the way meals were served and such matters (often overlooked in our household) as cleaning one's boots before entering the room.

In some ways she was in advance of her time. Kitchens, for instance, were generally regarded rather like a witch's lair, to be left strictly alone. They were small, smoke-blackened places filled by a wood-burning range (generally bought second-hand) and a great many people who always clustered there, relatives of the cook's perhaps, or just passers-by. The cooking was performed in large black pots that were never scoured, like French stock-pots. Everything was encrusted with a black deposit of wood-smoke, the window was blocked up by old sacks to prevent the least whiff of fresh air, it was much too dark to see and the intrepid white explorer stumbled over *totos* crouching in corners, took alarm at peculiar smells, and emerged with smarting eyes and choking lungs into welcome daylight. From this black and overcrowded hole emerged food which was always hot, apparently nourishing and, if the cook was given half a chance, often appetizing as well. No good came of hankering after hygiene, and no cook would stay for long if his employer nagged him about it. This arrangement suited Tilly, who had not been taught to cook and preferred the work of farm and garden. So she put the matter out of her mind, and left the kitchen to Juma.

Mrs. Nimmo, on the other hand, was a conscientious woman who liked to keep a grip on things. A state of war therefore existed between her and the cook; sacks were always being torn down, *totos* evicted and cooking-pots scoured. But after she had blown through the kitchen like a tornado things returned to normal in a few days and the recipes she had laboriously taught the cook vanished from the bill of fare. Her cook went about, on these occasions, with the air of a most long-suffering man, as indeed he was, and Tilly sometimes wondered why he did not leave. The reason came to light some time later. He had engaged a Kikuyu smith to copy her store-room key, and used her house as a sort of cornucopia flowing with sugar, fat and paraffin.

When white people discovered such goings-on they naturally regarded them as thefts and inveighed against the morals of the natives. But I do not think the natives regarded them as thefts at all. The Kikuyu were perfectly honest with each other; crops grew unplundered, homesteads were fortified only against evil spirits, if a woman left a load of millet by the path-side, or a man a snuff-horn or spear, it would be found intact on its owner's return. But Europeans were outside the ordinary stream of living and their property, therefore, exempt from ordinary laws; it sprang up like grass after rain, and for a Kikuyu to help himself was no more robbery than to take the honey from wild bees.

"You must eat up your milk pudding," Mrs. Nimmo was always saying to me—I can hear her now, her flat yet singsong lowland voice, and see her kind yet curiously impersonal smile, her round snub-nosed face whose separate features, in themselves pleasing enough, did not seem quite to coalesce into a personality. I can hear her saying: "You must eat up your milk pudding, it's good for the complexion": or, "You must eat up your porridge, it's good for the brain."

"I thought that was fish," I protested.

"Well, it's fish too, dear; porridge is good for everything, it will make you grow into a big, fine girl."

"But I don't want to be a big, fine girl. I want to be a jockey."

Mrs. Nimmo clucked like a hen and looked disapproving. My home life shocked her deeply, and I heard her remarking to Alec Wilson, who rode over a day or two after I came:

"It's no business of mine, I'm sure, but whenever are they going to send that child to school? It's not right, letting a child grow up like a native."

"They mean to send her to a boarding school at home when the coffee bears," Alec explained.

"When the coffee bears! I mean to have a castle in Spain when my ship comes home."

Alec tried not to smile; it was generally believed that Mr. Nimmo was making enormous sums from his ivory poaching, and Robin thought that he was burying rupees under the floor of his hut, like the Kikuyu, or investing them in herds of cattle in Uganda. Meanwhile, Mrs. Nimmo was kept so short of cash that she could scarcely afford to buy fifty eggs for one rupee or a hen for sixpence, the current prices, and owed her labour force several months' wages.

"Mr. Nimmo is most disappointed that he cannot get here for the New Year," she added in her most formal tones. "He writes that he is detained by business in the Belgian Congo. But I expect him home next month."

This was a formula she used constantly; so far as anyone knew, Mr. Nimmo never wrote, but simply turned up between safaris at infrequent intervals, drank a great deal of whisky, sacked half the labour force, complained of Mrs. Nimmo's extravagance and went away again.

Alec was not going to the races, he did not want to spend the money. Nor was our neighbour Victor Patterson, who was expecting visitors. So Alec had come to ask Mrs. Nimmo to a party to see the New Year in. She had to refuse because of me, but Alec took pity on her disappointment and accepted her eager offer to give the party herself.

"But what will I do for the dinner," she cried in deep distress, "when there's no prime beef to be had in the country, and no decent turkeys either, and the fowls the size of starlings, and the mutton tough as old boots?"

"The food will be secondary, at least with Victor," Alec said. "And he'll bring his own whisky, I expect."

Mrs. Nimmo clucked, and hoped that everything would be kept respectable: Mr. Nimmo would not countenance any doubtful goings-on under his roof.

"You mightn't believe it, my husband is very particular when he's at home. But then, he's used to the best. His father was one of the most respected men in Dundee, and twice made Provost of the city. And I haven't always lived like a tinker as I do here. My grandfather was a Writer to the Signet, and my great-uncle Andrew became the Lyon Knight at Arms."

Alec made a respectful departure, leaving Mrs. Nimmo to bustle about in a frenzy of food-gathering and preparation, of tidying-up and of chivvying her cook, who looked aloof and indifferent; to him there seemed no reason for this sudden galvanizing activity, the day was a day like any other and no wedding feast, circumcision or betrothal had occurred.

"Oh for a good, juicy undercut of prime Scots beef, or a fine Midlothian turkey!" Mrs. Nimmo lamented. "Or even black-face lamb or a salmon straight from the burn! This is a heathen country and there's nothing worth the eating in it. The flour's so coarse and crusty I cannot even make a scone my mother wouldn't have thrown out of the window. I like young Mr. Wilson, he's a nicely-spoken young fellow, but that Mr. Patterson. . . . Well, I suppose he can't help being an Australian, and one must take the rough with the smooth out here; but I hope his friends are not more of the same sort or I don't know what Mr. Nimmo would say. He is very particular whom he entertains."

I did not see much of Victor Patterson's friends, for I was sent to bed soon after they arrived, but I often heard Mrs. Walsh spoken of, and saw her once or twice afterwards, and she was the kind of person who burns a little mark into the memory, like a flame. Indeed she was a flame-like person, small, thin, red-haired and vibrating with energy. Her eyes were blue and very bright, her colour high and she spoke with a strong Irish brogue. She was not an Australian at all, but had lived there for many years with a husband now dead, with whom she had gone at seventeen to make a fortune on the goldfields of Western Australia. She made no fortune but lost all she had—that is to say, her husband, and her two small children, of whom one was drowned, the other bitten by a poisonous snake; and so she left Australia alone and friendless, at less than thirty years of age, to find a living in South Africa.

She moved up to the east coast, just after the railway had been built, with a second husband, a quiet Englishman called John Walsh, and they remained together until the end of their days. Everyone called her Pioneer Mary. By the time she came to Thika for the New Year of which I am speaking, the start of 1914, she was a well-known character, for she travelled all over the Protectorate, and in German territory, to trade with the natives, sometimes in an ox-cart and sometimes on a mule, sometimes with her husband and sometimes alone. She had no fear, and went among tribes as yet untouched by European influence, and more or less outside European law, with a rifle slung over her shoulder, but she never had to use it except to provide herself with meat. She cared little where she went, or what she did, or whom she talked to. Sometimes she would drive her ox-cart on to the platform of a railway station—which was not really a platform, just a flat place hardened by murram—and offer goods for sale to the native passengers: oranges, bananas, eggs, cooked chickens, or things they loved to buy like coloured cotton handkerchiefs and combs and ornaments and mirrors, or anything else she had been able to pick up cheap in the bazaar.

The natives she employed feared and respected her, and perhaps thought her a little more than human, for, although womanly enough in looks, she displayed, in their opinion, nothing of a woman's character; she was forthright, hard and sometimes fierce, and none of them ever molested her. Whenever I saw her she was cheerful and friendly, although it was easy to believe in the temper for which she was famed. There was something about her that put you a little on your guard, as if in the presence of a lioness that was tame and purring, but had claws tucked under her pads.

At Mrs. Nimmo's she was all purr and no claws. She looked admiringly round the grass-walled living-room, which Mrs. Nimmo had decorated with green branches, coloured candles and paper streamers.

"Well, now, look at that!" she cried. "Isn't this the homeliest sight in all the world? Mightn't we be back now in the old country with the snow outside and the church bells pealing and the waits ready for their glass of port wine? Well, now, for the mercy of heaven isn't everything as neat and tidy as a fusilier's coat on his wedding day!"

She went on in this strain for some time, with Mrs. Nimmo drinking it in. The grass hut's basic furnishings were meagre, but Mrs. Nimmo had brightened them with bits and pieces (as she called them) of her own, such as brass warming-pans and charcoal-holders hanging on the reed-screened walls, brasses worn by cart-horses over the big open fireplace, and a spinning-wheel that gathered cobwebs in a corner. There was a big log fire. On a packing-case covered with a red chenille table-cloth stood a potted spruce, conveyed with considerable difficulty from Nairobi. Tinsel streamers, glittering balls and other baubles hung from its branches. She had made the tree bloom with candles, red and blue and yellow; if you half-shut your eyes it looked like a dark, crouching animal with golden fur and silver harness, and was something very wonderful to me.

Pioneer Mary pulled from the enormous pocket of her bush-shirt an untidy parcel, saying that she would have bought me something fine and entertaining, a toy or a book, if she had known there was to be a child, but this was all she could find. It turned out to be a very small crocodile, about eight inches long, stuffed with grass and clumsily skinned, but engaging because it was a complete reptile in miniature, down to its tiny claws and little bumps along the backbone and prickly teeth jutting from ferocious jaws. It was extraordinary to learn that crocodiles were born like this, complete: little, snapping, predatory creatures from their moment of introduction on to this earth. I cherished my baby crocodile, and kept it for several years until it was eaten by a puppy.

"I'm glad you like it," Pioneer Mary said, "though it's not much of a present to be bringing to a child, and I wouldn't say a crocodile was overflowing with the Christmas spirit, even when it's newly born. But you'd not be caring for the trinkets I have with me for the niggers, and where would I be finding a shop for toys and pretty things? Now we must rest the bones of the old year as well as wishing strength for the new. Let's have the bottle, Jack, and wish Mrs. Nimmo the best of health and happiness, and her good man also, and God bless all our friends and damnation to our enemies."

Mrs. Nimmo looked displeased; she did not drink herself, and regarded with misgiving the three lean, inelegant colonials who had invaded her home.

"I'm sorry, I have no soda water," she said in rather chilly tones.

"No need to gas my booze," Victor Patterson answered. "I leave the gassing to the politicians." When he laughed his teeth behaved as if they led a separate life and were saying something on their own. His long, thin jaws had been champing quietly like a horse; now he walked to the door and spat loudly and suddenly. "Dry as a ship's biscuit," he added, looking at the night. "It's a fair cow."

Robin had once remarked that he thought Victor too Australian to be true; he suspected him to be a bishop incognito who had learnt the language at the Berlitz School, or a disguised absconding financier. In fact he had been at different times a prospector, a sheep-station hand, a dock worker and various other manly, open-air things. His leathery, sallow face reminded me of an old pigskin wallet of Robin's, but his eyes were blue and childlike, only bloodshot round the rims.

I rather liked Mr. Patterson, if only for his wayward teeth; but these had failed to conquer Mrs. Nimmo.

"I hope those two gentlemen won't get rowdy," she remarked to Alec, who came with her to the door when she led me off to bed.

"I hope so too, but I shouldn't like to guarantee it."

"A woman needs her husband at a time like this. Mr. Nimmo won't put up with any horseplay in his home. If there should be trouble, Mr. Wilson, I shall look to you."

Alec glanced at his fellow-guests. Both Victor and John

Walsh were powerful, slow-moving, determined men, as hard as rocks, and just as immovable.

"In that case you had better lock up the breakables and have the mules saddled for a quick getaway," Alec advised.

"Well, really! What a thing to say! You're not very gallant, Mr. Wilson."

"I know my limitations. If there should be trouble, you'll find me hiding under your bed."

Surprisingly, Mrs. Nimmo giggled, and quite a different look came into her face. She no longer appeared to disapprove of the party, but rather to expect something of it.

"The things you say!" she exclaimed. "Please look after the guests while I settle the bairn for the night."

I resented very much being settled and wanted to join the party, but there was no getting round Mrs. Nimmo. If only I had been left to Pioneer Mary, I felt, how different it would have been! Cleaning teeth, folding clothes, saying prayers would scarcely have bothered her. The drums were thrumming somewhere in the distance for an African counterpart to Mrs. Nimmo's party where there would be dancing in the firelight, singing and stamping, with beer for the elders and love for the young. A hyena howled from the next ridge, going with relish about its grisly but hygienic business. The darkness was pricked by the squeak of a bat, pierced by an owl's call and shattered by a sudden outburst of barking. I could not get to sleep, and some time later slipped out of bed and crept from my rondavel into a grey starlit night that smelt of jasmine and coffee. There was bustle in the kitchen and laughter in the lighted living-room. It was easy to see in through a window; they had finished eating and were sitting near the fireside round a pool of flickering blue flames that darted to and fro like butterflies. Then one of them would seize a blue leaping flame in his fingers and put it into his mouth.

I nearly cried out, it looked like magic, and the people weird and unfamiliar in the dancing light. Could this be some secret rite of adults, one of the queer, remorseless matters that they sometimes hinted at but never openly related? Then they paused and roared with laughter, and filled their glasses and began to sing. The blue flames died and I could see they had a dish before them; they had been dipping for raisins set alight with brandy and making their wishes for the New Year. They sang loudly; Pioneer Mary was herself seemingly alight, her red hair streaming, her shirt half-buttoned, her boots kicked off, and a glass never out of her hand. To my surprise, Mrs. Nimmo was joining in the songs and waving her arms and tapping the ground in tune.

"If we could have a reel now, wouldn't that be fine?" she cried, and soon they had one, she and Alec and the Walshes, while Victor Patterson summoned queer sounds from a comb and a piece of toilet paper. Mary danced like a fiend all over the room, uttering at intervals wild beast-like shrieks, kicking her legs up and clapping her hands, much to the distress of Mrs. Nimmo, who pranced with agility but wanted desperately to keep to the steps, the order and the time. Mr. Walsh danced steadily and Alec did not know the steps at all. The two women pushed him about, laughing at him, and he played the fool, and when the reel broke up Mrs. Nimmo sank into a chair with Alec on her knee, to everyone's great entertainment. This was not at all the Mrs. Nimmo that I knew, nor Alec either. It all seemed rather silly, so I went back to bed.

I was awakened later by shots. Through my window I could see the moonlight, and a jingling of bridles and a shuffling of hooves came to my ears. Voices in the house were shouting, then two more shots clapped through the darkness and were followed by a terrific crash, a cry of pain and then a woman's screams. I burrowed under the blankets, where it was warm and comforting and, I believed, bullet-proof. When I cautiously protruded my head the screams had stopped and been replaced, surprisingly, by laughter, perhaps of an hysterical kind, mingled with a stamping and snorting of mules.

I reached the window just in time to see a figure leap on to a mule and gallop off with a rifle in its hand held up like a banner, pursued by two more mounted cavaliers. The rifle went off again as the cavalcade vanished into the moonlit bush, sending back mournful echoes from the ridges; one of the men raised his voice in a wild halloa and sent more echoes chasing after. The halloas grew fainter, the echoes died and silence majestically resumed possession of the night.

A wail came from the house and a figure staggered on to the veranda crying: "Never again! Never, never again! They came to me from my grandfather who was Writer to the Signet; when I was a little girl, mother carried them up the stairs before her as carefully as a hen with chickens and now that woman . . . that miserable wretch . . ."

"I warned you to lock up the silver," said Alec, who was standing beside her looking after the departed revellers, "but I never thought of the warming-pans."

"I'll take her to law! There's a hole right through the centre of the largest of them. . . ."

"Nice shooting." Alec spoke admiringly.

"Ach, that's all you think about, no one cares a mite for my poor warming-pans!"

"You hardly need them here, Mississimmo," Alec said in a voice that sounded as if his mouth was full of feathers.

"Maggy to you, Mr. Wilson, now we're old friends." An unexpected and perhaps unintended giggle escaped from Mrs. Nimmo. "You did look funny, dodging down behind that chair when the gun went off."

"Not cut out for cannon-fodder," Alec replied with dignity.

"If Mr. Nimmo had been here he'd never have allowed it."

"I think I'd better go home."

"What, and leave me unprotected with that band of tipsy brigands galloping about? Is *that* the act of a gentleman?"

"Perhaps not . . ."

"Your place is to protect me, Mr. Wilson."

"Alec to you, Mississimmo—Maggy."

"Alec, then."

"My place is by your side?"

"I am a lone woman . . ."

"Not tonight, Maggy."

"Of course, I don't mean . . ."

"Ah, but I do," Alec said with unexpected loudness. He seemed to have swallowed the feathers and to find his mouth dry and hollow.

"Oh, how can you!" Mrs. Nimmo cried, but she did not sound really distressed. Alec stepped up to her in order, apparently, to whisper his reply, and as the conversation appeared to have ended I returned to bed, and dreamt of hooves thundering up deep black valleys towards firelit caves, and cannonades from battlements, and shouts of victory; but I was riding Margaret the mule whose pace grew slower and slower, and carrying George and Mary who had become the size of crocodiles and were weighing me down. Blue flames came out of their nostrils, they turned their faces towards me and opened their enormous jaws and there was Pioneer Mary dancing a jig among their teeth, each of which was the size of a large native drum.

It was not a restful dream, but this did not prevent my waking refreshed to a morning new-washed in dew. Doves were cooing, weaver-birds twittering and shrikes calling; sunshine threw a square of gold on to the earth floor and from outside came that familiar overture to the African morning: the swish-swish, swish-swish of a twig broom sweeping the path gently and rhythmically, swish-swish, swish-swish, like the whisper of waves on a beach, broken by pauses and the padding of feet and the melody of high voices calling to each other in hope and laughter, for night was done with and the sun climbing up the sky. Even the sun was newly washed, according to Kikuyu legend, which held that it sank into the sources of the rivers and at night was carried down to the sea for a cleansing dip, to emerge clean and bright every morning.

The houseboy and a *toto* were clearing up the living-room, which looked as if a bull had been loose in it all night. Warming-pans and charcoal-carriers lay on the floor, the spinning-wheel was prostrate and the furniture all awry. When Alec appeared he looked bleary-eyed and ruffled, and walked like someone who would rather not be seen. However, he nodded to me, winced a little at the motion and said:

"If there's one piece of advice I would offer to a child at the outset of life, it is, don't see the New Year in with a mixed party of Scots, Irish and Australians; it's an explosive mixture, like T.N.T. In fact don't see the New Year in at all, but if you must, find a maiden aunt to do it with and be sure she's a tee-totaller."

"Did they shoot anything?"

"Only Maggy's warming-pans, I think."

Breakfast was a silent meal: at least, Alec was silent and ate very little. We had poached eggs. I always played a game with poached eggs, which was to cut the white away bit by bit until only the round yolk was left, and to postpone as long as possible the moment when I pricked the yolk to release a yellow flood:

just as, in the oval tin tubs we bathed in, I used to lower each bent leg as slowly as I could until a small white island of flesh on top of each knee-cap remained in an expanse of water, and then very, very gradually reduce the margins of the twin islands until at last the waters closed over them.

Mrs. Nimmo, unfamiliar with this practice, asked sharply: "What are you doing, child, with your egg?"

At this moment I pricked the yolk with my fork and remarked with satisfaction: "Look, it's bleeding!" To my surprise, Alec rose with a groan and rushed from the room.

"Is something the matter?" I inquired.

"He's not quite himself, poor fellow," Mrs. Nimmo said. She was more concerned about the damage to her property, especially to a sampler bearing the text: "Many waters cannot quench love, neither shall the floods devour it," done in cross-stitch in purple on a mustard-yellow background. There was a tear through the middle of the "quench".

"To think it came down to me from my aunt Kate, who worked it before she ever married and went to India! It has a great sentimental value to me, a *great* value. Treating my house like some low saloon! What Mr. Nimmo will say when he comes home, I cannot for the life of me imagine."

"I'll buy you something better," I promised, for I had plans to get a pony and win a great many races. Each race, I knew, resulted in a silver cup, which must surely be worth a lot of money.

"That's a kind thought," Mrs. Nimmo said, patting my hand. "And so you shall, when your ship comes home."

"I haven't got a ship," I objected.

"We all have one, in a manner of speaking, but sometimes they take a long time to come home."

This was a new idea—everyone with ships sailing about on some distant ocean, apparently quite out of control. I wondered what had happened to Tilly's and Robin's.

"Do they ever sink?" I inquired.

"Unfortunately they do."

That explained matters. The Palmers' ship I knew to be approaching with a grand piano and some stuffed heads inside.

Alec Wilson reappeared, looking pale but rather better, and took Mrs. Nimmo's hand.

"Thank you for your hospitality, and everything." He spoke rather awkwardly, his eyes on her face.

She withdrew her hand, pursed her lips and answered with formality:

"It was kind of you to stay, Mr. Wilson; I must admit I shouldn't have liked to have stopped here alone with the bairn, with those wild, godless creatures about."

"Any time you need protection, Maggy, send for me."

"Thank you, Mr. Wilson, I'll remember that, but I don't expect it to be necessary. Mr. Nimmo will be home any day."

I wondered why Mrs. Nimmo was treating Alec less as a friend than as a slight acquaintance; but Alec did not seem to mind, and rode off quite cheerfully, although complaining that his mouth felt like the inside of a parrot's cage. The next day I, too, rode home on Margaret, escorted by Njombo who (as Sammy had predicted) had reappeared, as jaunty as ever so far as I could see. His head had been shaved, and shone like a sovereign. Now that he had become a murderer I vaguely expected some change in his appearance, but that was the only one.

"There has been a holiday at memsabu *Ngwari's*," he remarked. (*Ngwari* was the word for francolin, and they called Mrs. Nimmo that because she chattered such a lot, on a continuous and monotonous note.) Most of the Kikuyu took little interest in our customs and behaviour, but Njombo had an inquiring mind and sometimes tried to find out what we were up to. "Perhaps it is to ask God for rain. Everything is parched in the shambas."

"It was not because of rain," I explained. "A new year has started."

This made Njombo thoughtful. The Kikuyu did not reckon time in years, new or old, or in any way cut it up into sections. It flowed on like a stream. They had rainy seasons and dry intervals: millet rains which were short, and just over, and bean rains which were longer. As a rule, after every millet harvest they held a circumcision ceremony, and the youths and maidens who were initiated received a general name, such as "locusts" if there had just been an invasion, or "much millet", "smallpox", "burning forest", "hungry birds", "ear-rings", "maize mill", according to some event of note, or interesting incident. Of course the age of circumcision was not the same for everyone, but this system did provide a rough guide; people of the small-pox age-grade, for instance, were circumcised in 1894 and therefore now in their early thirties. Njombo's grade was called "sheets of iron", presumably to mark the introduction, in his district, of corrugated iron roofs.

"There cannot be a new year," he remarked, after some reflection, "when no one can plant seeds because it is dry, nor harvest crops because they are finished. No, that is just a story; the memsabu with the rifle and the red hair is a powerful magician and she has come to help us with this business of rain."

I asked Njombo how she had helped us, or would do so in future.

"She eats fire," he said.

"Yes, I saw that. The others ate it too."

"There will be rain, we shall see. Perhaps your father will give her a cow, then she will make a sacrifice to cause his coffee trees to grow, and to make his wife fertile. The spirit of the red memsabu is very strong."

That Pioneer Mary had a vital power above the ordinary was as plain to me as to Njombo. While I was wondering whether I could ask her to use it to get me a pony, a reed-buck bounded across the path and skimmed away into the long grass and bushes with splendid leaps, almost like a bird flying. Njombo hurled a light spear he was carrying after the buck, but the blade missed and embedded itself in the bark of a fig-tree. Njombo loped after it, retrieved the spear and returned looking very downcast. He stood for several moments gazing at the tree and then bent down and scooped a little hole from the red earth by the path-side. Margaret, growing impatient, jiggled and tossed her head.

"Wait," Njombo commanded. He gathered several leaves from a shrub with a big mauve flower, crushed them in his hand, mixed them with some powder from a horn dangling from his neck, stuffed them into the hole and then pushed the earth over them with his foot.

"It is bad to strike that tree," he said sombrely, and we continued on our way, Njombo quite subdued. Some trees were sacred and some were not, and we had no way of telling which was which; but the Kikuyu always knew, and on several occasions had refused to touch one that Robin told them to fell.

Evidently Njombo had been unlucky with this particular fig. He wore many charms on his shiny body: two goat-horns, including the one from which he had taken the powder, a bracelet with small wooden rattles on his right arm, a leather purse on a chain and, on his right leg, a little wooden cylinder containing dust and powdered leaves taken from seven different paths and mixed with good-luck medicine, to protect him against the evils to be found on all the roads and paths of the world.

In spite of these, the ill luck to be expected from the striking of a sacred tree had slipped through his defences. Even the path that crossed a small stream, fringed with banana trees, dividing our land from the Nimmos' (I began to see) was full of dangers more subtle and sinister than any to be apprehended from the lions and rhinos that once had sheltered there, and had now retreated to the plains before the savage onslaught of mankind.

Chapter Ten

TILLY was trying to educate me in such time as she could spare from the farm and garden. Luckily I liked reading and she left me alone a good deal with the book of the moment, but we were not well placed to get hold of the right kind of literature, and sometimes I had to fall back on old copies of *The Field*, manuals of instruction on everything from lace-making to the erection of simple stills (Robin was putting one up to distil essential oils) and the volumes of a pocket encyclopedia in minute type.

These I found rather beyond my capacity, and when Tilly was safely occupied I would abandon them in favour of trying to catch George or Mary in the act of eating a fly, or of looking for birds' nests, talking to Njombo and Sammy, playing with Twinkle, or of other non-educational pursuits. We had an atlas, and Tilly put me on to tracing maps. The strong, oily smell of the tracing-paper enthralled me, and I loved its crackle and its springiness, but found it hard to control. After tracing them, I transferred the countries on to drawing-paper, put in rivers, towns, railways and mountains and painted everything in gay if blotchy colours, which was very satisfactory.

After a while, both Tilly and I grew tired of this and I took to inventing countries. All of them were islands which contained a lot of swamps, because I enjoyed making the neat little symbols used by map-makers to indicate marshy land. They were also mountainous, because a lot of contour lines made them look dramatic and important. When this palled, Tilly read aloud an essay on gardens by Francis Bacon, and told me to design one on the lines he recommended.

The garden's main outline, all in squares, was clear enough, but I found it difficult to represent a hedge with arches and, over every arch, a little turret with belly enough to receive a cage of birds; and then, between each arch, a figure made of broad plates of round coloured glass for the sun to play upon. However, I had no doubt that all this would look very gay, not to mention the alleys, coverts, mounts, fountains, pools and arbours with which his thirty acres were liberally sprinkled.

From the garden, we proceeded to the house, and the table allocated to my studies became strewn with rough designs of banqueting houses, towers, turrets, chapels, cellars and butteries. The house, as I remember, was divided into two, one side for dwelling and the other for feasts and triumphs, which I hoped would be numerous; and I wondered who would occupy the infirmary set aside for sick princes, as we did not seem to have any of those. When completed, I counted over fifty rooms, and asked Tilly who would fill them, but she told me not to be so unimaginative.

I was sitting one day designing a cloistered court with statues when Lettice Palmer walked in, smelling faintly of heliotrope and looking, as she always did, fresh and elegant, although she had ridden over in the heat of the day. She carried in her bag a little book with sheets of thin paper in it and she would tear one off and rub it over her face when she grew hot or dusty, and this would miraculously restore her cool, unshiny appearance.

She looked at the papers strewn around and observed:

"Your father seems to be going from one extreme to the other, in the matter of houses; is he trying to out-do the Sackvilles, and build a rather larger Knole?"

I explained about Bacon, and Lettice took up the book and glanced through it. She had taken off her heavy hat and her red-brown hair was as glossy and smooth as a newly-opened horse-chestnut. Her skin was like one of the waxy, heavy-scented frangipani blossoms that drenched the night air, and one could see tiny little blue veins on her temples, like rivers on one of my maps, and two faint lines at the corners of her wide mouth. She wore a thin silk blouse and riding skirt, and her waist was slender as a wasp's; you could see the motion of her bosom when she breathed, like a bird's when you hold it palpitating in your hand.

" 'There was never a proud man,' " she read, " 'thought so absurdly well of himself as the lover doth of the person loved: and therefore it was well said, that it is impossible to love and to be wise.' Pompous old prig! Now come, I've a surprise waiting for you outside."

A syce stood on the lawn, or what was destined to become a lawn, holding two ponies, her own alert South African and one

I had not seen before: a small, white, dumpy animal with short legs, a short neck, and a suspicious expression.

"You've got your wish," she said. "Make the most of it, because when you're older that will very seldom happen to you, and when it does, you will often find you wished wrong."

As I did not understand her meaning, I did not reply.

"Well, have you been struck dumb?"

This was even more embarrassing, and I was still tongue-tied.

"This pony is a present for you," Lettice patiently explained. "That's what you wanted, isn't it? Or have you changed your mind, and would prefer a party frock or a talking doll?"

I shook my head, now much too overcome for speech, and gazed at the pony, which gradually changed before my eyes. From a stumpy, rough-coated Somali it became a splendid milk-white charger, fleet of foot and proud of eye, and yet not too proud to acknowledge me as its friend and master. It looked at me, I perceived at once, with a meaning withheld from other people, a look of recognition and mutual conspiracy.

An ability to match my thanks to the gift was quite beyond me; I muttered a few disjointed words and patted the pony. His nostrils were soft and springy, like woodland moss, and his breath sweet. He cocked an ear as if to say that he accepted my advances, and understood that he had come to stay.

"You'll have to find a name for him," Lettice said. "Something very fine and grand like Charlemagne or Galahad. He came from a place called Moyale."

That was the name that stuck to him, Moyale. I thought of several others but Njombo paid them no attention. Moyale did not mean anything, but he could pronounce it.

Tilly and Robin were nearly as surprised and overcome as I was. Tilly grew pink with embarrassment and was almost grumpy, she did not like receiving presents on a scale much too lavish to reciprocate, yet of course Moyale could not be returned.

"Ian Crawfurd got him for me," Lettice said. This was a name I had not heard before, but one that was to crop up often in my elders' conversation.

"It came down with a batch from the Abyssinian frontier," she added. "They drove the ponies through the desert where only camels live as a rule, but there had been rain. One night they were attacked by raiders and had a pitched battle, and another time lions broke in and stampeded the ponies, and they lost three or four."

More than ever did Moyale become an object of romance and enchantment. Caparisoned in gold and crimson, with a silver bridle and a flowing mane, he had carried princes on the tented battlefield, and galloped through the night to bring news of victory to maidens with hibiscus flowers in their dark hair, imprisoned in a moated fortress.

"I hope that he is salted," Tilly said.

"You aren't going to eat him, surely?" Lettice inquired. But this was a term, Tilly explained, to indicate that a pony had recovered from horse-sickness and was thenceforth immune.

Njombo, who was used to mules, professed himself delighted with Moyale. "What a pony!" he cried. "He will gallop like a zebra, he is strong and healthy and yet not fierce; now you have a pony fit for King George."

We found a brush, and groomed him every day. His hide had many scars and gashes, and a brand on the flank. To me these scars were relics of spear-thrusts and sabre-strokes delivered in battle. Certainly Moyale had not led a sheltered life, and he was at first suspicious of Njombo and myself, but he soon grew tame and learnt to enjoy sugar and carrots. We had no lump sugar, and fed him on dark brown *jagoree* made by Indians from local cane, that had a heavy, burnt, rather sickly flavour.

For a prince's charger full of battle-scars, he was surprisingly placid. I think he had a lazy nature which he was at long last able to indulge. He would amble peacefully along with one ear cocked forward and the other off-duty, as it were, in a resting position, but life had imposed a wary sense upon him, and sometimes I could feel a current of alertness running through his body. Once he shied violently and threw me off sideways into a prickly bush, but waited politely for me to remount. His main fault was a hard mouth, an inevitable result of the long, brutal bits used by Somali and Boran horsemen. Our mild little English bit must have seemed feather-light to him and, had he wanted to, he could have ignored it; but he was not ambitious, and perhaps knew when he was well off, freed from the spurs and whips and curbs and thirst and hunger of the Abyssinian deserts.

Soon after this Ian Crawfurd arrived, to stay with the Palmers, who asked Tilly and Robin over for the evening. I had to go too, as I could not be left, and they arranged for me to sleep there, rather than ride back late at night. I was given a tent, much to my satisfaction, for there was nothing I liked better than tents. By day their hot, jungly smell, as thick as treacle, was delightful, and the dark-green gloom inside reminded me of Turkish delight. At night they had the atavistic charm of caves: a warm, protecting, secret cave, a refuge and a private kingdom. Lying on the camp-bed, you could make shadows on the canvas by holding your hand near the lantern; on the ground, each sentry-stiff blade of grass threw its pencil of shade. You could imagine yourself looking down upon a great forest in which an ant, staggering along with a tiny crumb in its mandibles, was like a monstrous pachyderm carrying off a rock to drop upon the heads of its enemies.

Tilly wanted to tie the flap back to admit plenty of air, but I implored her to shut it.

"There's nothing to be afraid of," she said.

"There are the cannibals."

"Cannibals! You must control your imagination."

I reminded her about the Kavirondo who had perhaps—though no one seemed to know—eaten the man Njombo had killed.

"Nonsense," Tilly said. "That was just an invention of Sammy's. In any case, they only eat people who are dead."

All the same, she did close the flap and leave the lantern burning. The tent was close enough to the living-room for me to hear bursts of laughter now and then—in fact, most of the time. Ian Crawfurd was a young man who left a wake of laughter as he skimmed along. Hereward Palmer was the best-looking man I knew, but Ian Crawfurd was much more attractive. He was even fairer—his hair looked almost silver in the lamplight—and his face drew your eyes because its expression was always changing, like cloud-shadows on mountains, and because the bones were so beautifully formed. They seemed to have been very carefully moulded out of some malleable material like plasticine, whereas Hereward's were rigid, as if cast in iron. The hollows of his cheeks and temples were soft and delicate, like curves in Chinese porcelain. I do not mean that there was anything effeminate about his looks; on the contrary, he was strong and lean, but he did not walk heavily, like Hereward, he walked with precision and spring, like a tracker. When he spoke he often tipped his head to one side a little, and his eyes, blue-grey in colour, were candid and clear.

Ian Crawfurd was a friendly person who found life entertaining and agreeable, as indeed it could be for the young, healthy and adventurous. He had arrived on horseback attended by a tall, thin, proud Somali who wore a shawl of bright tomato-red wound loosely round his head, and who appeared to disdain all that he saw. To him, no doubt, we were fat, effete, root-bound heathen southerners who consorted with dogs and ate pork; only loyalty, the virtue next to courage, obliged him to come amongst us, like an eagle in a parrot cage.

When I awoke, a blade of sunlight had thrust under the flap of my tent, and outside the doves gurgled like cool water tumbling from a narrow-necked jar. Also came the three notes in a falling cadence, half a whistle, half a call, of a nondescript but vociferous bird the Kikuyu called the "thrower of firewood"—why, goodness knows. I got up to pay my morning visit to Moyale and found Ian Crawfurd at the stable preparing for an early ride. His hair shone like kingcups in the morning light. He wore a leather strap, for some reason, on his right wrist, and looked as slender-waisted as a whippet in his shirt and breeches.

"I'm glad you liked the pony," he said. "I picked him out from a batch of twenty or so; I thought he was the nicest, if not perhaps the most beautiful."

"Did he belong to a prince?"

Ian Crawfurd looked thoughtful, and replied that, in a sense, he had. "He belonged to a Ras, and a Ras is a kind of prince, if frequently a villain also: I daresay the two go together more often than not. The Ras didn't want him to leave Abyssinia, even though he accepted a red cloak and a Winchester rifle and gave me his word; so he had to be smuggled out, with his nineteen companions."

I had heard of watches being smuggled, and scent; but ponies . . . ?

"That's a long story," Ian Crawfurd said. "Too long to tell before breakfast; let's ride up the ridge and you shall tell me who lives where, and what sort of animals you'd turn them into if you had been apprenticed to a witch who knew how."

Everyone (he went on to explain) had some affinity with a bird or beast or reptile—and not always the one that you would think. Doves, for instance, were unpleasant characters who squabbled, scolded and were greedy and cross, whereas eagles were very shy, and cobras liked nothing better than to curl up in someone's bed and go peacefully to sleep in the warmth, and only spat when they were terrified.

I thought Mrs. Nimmo might become an ostrich because she had a large behind which waggled when she hurried, and he assigned to Captain Palmer the giraffe because he was long and thin and had large feet and a thick hide. A bat-eared fox for Alec Wilson for his large ears and big brown eyes; for Victor Patterson a greater bustard with whom he shared a long stride, long neck and toughness—"and both need to be hung," Ian Crawfurd said.

When I mentioned Lettice Palmer, he laughed and shook his head.

"We must leave her out of it," he said.

"But why?"

He pointed with his whip at the sun, which was climbing quickly above the tawny ridge towards some fluffy clouds as light as meringues. "Suppose the sun entered the sign of Virgo, the tide turned and an eagle perched upon the Sphinx all at the same moment, it might really happen; and we should look fools if we got back to breakfast and found our hostess had become a wallaby."

I felt disappointed in Ian; like nearly all grown-ups, he had started something sensible and let it tail off into stupidity. But when I looked at him it was impossible to be annoyed, he was so gay and spirited, and smiled with such goodwill; he had in him the brightness of the morning, you could not imagine him ill-tempered and morose, and whatever he did, you accepted.

"Perhaps she'd be a sort of bird," I suggested, determined to persist with the game. "With lovely feathers. A kind sort, of course."

"I'm not sure there are any," said Ian, who did not seem to have a high opinion of birds. "Rather, I think, 'the milk-white hind, immortal and unchanged', if that isn't blasphemous."

We turned our ponies, who became immediately transformed from sluggish, heavy-livered creatures into prancing steeds, tossing their heads and stroking the ground with their forefeet. On the outward journey Moyale had treated his surroundings with a lordly indifference, but now every bush became an object of the deepest suspicion, to be approached with pricked ears, wide nostrils and stiff legs. I rode Moyale in a state of bliss shot through by stabs of anxiety. He could have done just what he liked.

We took a short cut through the bush and Ian, leading the way, suddenly pulled up his pony and signalled to me with his riding-crop. Our ponies, responding instantly to a current of warning, stopped their jiggling and stood stock-still. I caught a glimpse of some moving object in the long grass. It was part of the excitement of any ride that you never knew what you might encounter; apart from reed-buck, duiker and other small game there were plenty of leopards about, and lions came now and then on visits from the plains.

Then I saw Ian relax and urge his pony forward. The grass reached above the ponies' knees. We halted on a low hump and saw below us nothing more ferocious than a circle of beaten-down grass, like a miniature race-course, about two feet across—a perfect little circle; and round the ring a single black and shiny-feathered bird, with a ruff like a Tudor courtier's, only black too, with head thrown back and wings outstretched, was prancing and hopping, like a demented ballet-dancer, first on one leg and then on the other, and springing into the air. In the middle of the circle, on a tuft of grass, a small, drab bird sat and brooded, rather hunched, thrusting a neck forward and backward as if something had stuck in its throat.

"Whydah-birds," Ian said softly. "Watch them, you don't often catch them at the game."

We watched in silence while the birds performed their antics ten or twelve paces away. The dancing cock seemed about to stumble and fall, then recovered and leapt in the air as if to take off, only to land again. But after a while the central hen evidently grew bored and started to peck at some seed-heads in the tuft of grass. Whether because of her indifference, or for some other reason, the cock's attention also wandered, his ruff subsided, his wings drooped, his tail sagged and suddenly he took off and flew away. We waited to see whether the hen would follow him. But no, she had other plans; and presently a second black and shiny cock landed in the ring, ruffed up his neck feathers, arched the long plumes of his tail so that they curved back almost to his head, and began to prance for all the world like a jet of black water leaping from a fountain in the grass.

I do not know how long we should have watched them if Moyale, growing bored, had not snorted and sneezed. There was a chattering of alarm, a flapping of wings and both birds took off and vanished over the crest of the ridge.

It was their mating dance, Ian Crawfurd explained. One after the other, cocks came to parade in their finery before the female, who squatted in the centre with a bright appraising eye; after a while, she would choose one for her mate.

"What happens to the others?" I inquired.

"They fly away, and look for another hen to fascinate with their splendid plumage and their strong, masterful hops."

"Then there must be some over," I suggested, "who don't get a mate."

"Yes, there are the doomed, perpetual bachelors; no nest to go home to, no little chicks to find insects for, no one to puff out chests and sing about when other cocks go by."

"It sounds very sad."

"Yes, it is. There was once a cock who loved the fairest of all the whydah-birds—the darkest, perhaps I should say, the darkest and the kindest; but another cock, a cock with blacker wings and longer tail-feathers, had made her his own. So she shared the nest of another, and sat by his side, and when her chosen mate danced before her, she nodded her head at him to say bravo, bravo. The first cock knew that she could not be his, because he came too late, and hadn't got such black wings, or such a long tail. So he flew far away into the mountains and looked for worms and beetles and things like that. Sometimes he found them, but they did not taste very good, and he knew that they never would, so long as he had to eat them all by himself, with his lady-love so far away."

Ian Crawfurd paused, I thought to collect words for the ending; but that seemed to be all. I did not like inconclusive stories.

"What happened then?"

"Nothing happened—and that's the way to tell a true story from a made-up one. A made-up story always has a neat and tidy end. But true stories don't end, at least until their heroes and heroines die, and not then really, because the things they did, and didn't do, sometimes live on."

"Does every story," I wondered, "have to have a hero and a heroine?"

"Every story, since Adam and Eve."

That story, I reflected, if you came to think of it, scarcely had an ending either; it started well, but tailed off into Cain and Abel, and I could not remember what had happened to Eve. Ian Crawfurd, I supposed, was right, but it was unsatisfactory, for everything ought to have a beginning, a middle and an end.

Chapter Eleven

AHMED the Somali was waiting to welcome Ian back, clad in a white tussore silk robe, a green sash and his loosely-wrapped tomato-red turban. He bowed and brought a cupped hand to the centre of his forehead with a wide sweep of the arm. There should have been an embroidered cloak and a sword for him to receive from his master; as it was, Ian threw his binoculars to this haughty noble, and expressed the hope that, in the absence of camels' milk, he had found suitable nourishment.

Ahmed wore the mettled air of a highly-bred race-horse. His long, thin, grey fingers seemed curved to grasp a dagger's handle, his eye was proud and lonely as a kestrel's. With the air of one conferring a dukedom on a retainer he inclined his head and replied:

"I have eaten, bwana."

At breakfast, Lettice Palmer remarked: "Ahmed makes me uneasy; I can never quite get over the feeling that I ought to be on my knees like a Circassian slave offering him a bowl of rose-water. He's the only *regal* character I've ever encountered."

"I had the same sort of fear myself at first," Ian admitted, "but his manners are so perfect he's managed to make me feel like a Caliph born to command the services of princes; so we are both satisfied."

"I had a jemadar very like him once on the Frontier," Hereward announced. "A splendid fellow; he once killed four Pathans single-handed and recaptured a Maxim gun after he'd been hit in both legs."

"And ate them all for breakfast," Lettice said sharply. She immediately looked contrite, and asked Hereward how the farm work was getting on. Hereward replied meekly; he was her slave. He had the farm labour organized in gangs called after colours: the blue squad, the red squad and so on. In his office, a cubicle divided off from the store, he kept on the wall a large map of his farm studded with pins bearing little coloured flags, so that he could see at once where each squad was, or ought to be. It was his intention to create a healthy spirit of inter-squad rivalry, but in this the African response was disappointing; if rivalry existed, it was not expressed in terms of work.

He was, moreover, plagued by a distressing tendency on the part of his men to wander from one squad to another as the spirit moved them. If he put the blue squad on to clearing tree-stumps, a hot, strenuous activity, and the red squad on to thatching shelters for coffee seedlings, which took place by the river in the shade, by ten o'clock he would find the red squad twice its proper size and the blue squad sadly diminished. The respective headmen, tackled on the subject, would merely look hurt, shrug their shoulders and make some excuse bearing no possible relation to the truth, but applied as an emollient to irritated feelings. This, among Africans, was an expression of politeness, a desire to please; but of course it only angered white men, and especially Hereward.

"Every one of these fellows lies like a trooper, and not one has an inkling of the meaning of discipline!" he would cry. Then he would add, with an air of martyrdom: "I suppose I must just go on trying to knock it into them, that's all."

He did try, very hard, and it was unjust that Lettice found his efforts ludicrous. As a rule she concealed her feelings, but Ian's presence made this more difficult. That day at breakfast, while Hereward was holding forth, I saw their eyes meet across the table and then drop to their plates. Their mouths twitched just a little, and simultaneously they both picked up their knives and forks and resumed their eating.

I was always sorry when the time came for me to leave the Palmers'. Their living-room was quite different from ours, although the shape was much the same, and the reed lining, and the lizards in the roof. Their furniture had many curves and curlicues and decorations, and no doubt looked even more out of place than ours, but it was entertaining. There were cushions made of dark-green velvet, and others of a striped golden satin which shone like the insides of buttercups. Zena and Chang had a special cushion each. Flowers stood about in cut-glass vases and porcelain bowls. Lettice had a china-cupboard full of shepherds, musicians, pedlars and the like posturing in arbours of leaves and flowers of every colour one could think of, all intertwined, and modelled with astonishing delicacy. I daresay these were not very valuable, but they enthralled me, each leaf and flower, each foot and finger, were so enchanting and exact. Hereward said it was absurd to have such things in a grass hut in Africa, they would only get broken, but Lettice dusted them herself.

They had several pictures, too. The one everybody admired was a portrait of Lettice looking splendid, but aloof and rather impersonal, not as I knew her at all. It was beautifully painted, but one could not feel the life in her face. It was by a fashionable portrait-painter and had been in the Academy. Hereward admired it very much. I preferred two other paintings in the room. One had been done by Lettice herself, so it had no value, but I always looked at it when I came in. It was a picture of a ravine in Scandinavia with tall, snow-weighted pines and dark, mossy rocks and a waterfall, and it had an air of silence and mystery and long nights; one could imagine black bears prowling under the pines, and a cold, resinous atmosphere, and unseen creatures lying in wait. The other was entirely different: some sailing boats rocking on a very blue river, and people fishing from a bridge, all broken up, like the sunlight on the water, into flashing surfaces of brilliant paint. It was the gayest thing you ever saw, but Hereward said it was a hideous daub; it even made him angry, I could not think why. It was true that you could see the brush-strokes and the gobs of paint, so perhaps it was unfinished and raw, but all the same the boats danced before your eyes on the water, you knew it was a warm, sunny spring day and that the fishermen were enjoying it all.

Apart from these interesting things, and many others, and quantities of books in fresh, exciting jackets, the Palmers' room always smelt delicious. Dried rose-leaves and lavender mixed with patchouli in Chinese bowls were no doubt responsible. Even the garden-house—the privy—had a few touches other people's lacked. Instead of an ordinary roll of toilet paper, Lettice arranged sheets of Bromo in a spiral like a pack of cards, in a flat, open basket, and put a lavender bag on top. A copy of the *Meditations of Marcus Aurelius* bound in green leather lay beside a pile of copies of the *Revue des Deux Mondes*, but personally I found the *Sporting and Dramatic Life*, which was also present, to be more congenial. A maximum-and-minimum thermometer hung on the back of the door and Lettice was training honeysuckle up the walls.

Our own house was less exciting, and rather cramped. We lived and ate in a single, square room full of furniture, ranging from the commode I have mentioned, and a good mahogany writing-table (always piled high with account books, letters, bills and catalogues) to a roughly carpentered deal table, home-made chairs with seats of cowhide thongs, a couple of old arm-chairs upholstered in leather, whose stuffing protruded from several rents. a pouffe or two, and various other necessary things. One side was occupied mainly by an open fireplace which, with its chimney, was the only object made of stone. A Victorian fire-screen worked by Tilly's mother stood incongruously before it, quite dwarfed by the aperture, like a mouse guarding a cave.

You could not secure pictures to the reed-matting walls, or not for long—several had fallen down; there was no ceiling, only a forest of poles above us lashed together with creeper-twine, and insect-rustling thatch; the floor, until it was cemented, undulated so much that all the furniture wobbled, and bits of wood or wads of paper were constantly being stuffed under legs to achieve an equilibrium that never lasted. We always had a lot of flowers, jostling for position among books and paint-boxes, magazines and veterinary medicines, Tilly's embroidery, Robin's sketches of machinery, my birds' eggs and everybody's oddments; sometimes they found themselves in tall silver vases or a Chinese porcelain bowl, sometimes in a jam-jar, whichever came first to Tilly's hand.

The living-room was flanked on one side by Tilly's and Robin's bedroom, which they shared with several dogs, and on the other side by mine, which was divided into two, half for me and half for the tin bath. My half held little beyond a chest-of-drawers made by a local *fundi* and a camp-bed, with a colobus monkey skin on the floor beside it. The camp bed was always on the point of being replaced by something better, but I was glad that it never was, for I could snuggle into it, as into a burrow, in a manner impossible on proper mattresses, and knew its creaks as one knows the voice of an old friend. A collection of wooden or china animals stood on the chest-of-drawers, but no looking-glass; indeed for some time no such thing existed in the house, except for a little pocket glass from Tilly's handbag which was propped up on a packing-case in the bathroom for Robin's use when he shaved.

Now and again, the bathroom was transformed into an emergency ward. There was an old man called Rohio who lived in the reserve and used to come and see us sometimes; his son Karioki drove the ox-cart that fetched our water from the river, and in between whiles prodded at the garden weeds with a hoe. (This he had held, to start with, by the business end, and used the handle for dislodging weeds, possibly because a digging-stick was the traditional Kikuyu tool, but possibly also as a protest against Robin's insistence that a journey to the river completed by eight o'clock in the morning did not constitute a full day's work.) Rohio was a friendly soul who liked nothing better than a long, leisurely chat about the weather, the crops, people and affairs. Once or twice he brought me small presents, such as a stick of delicious, cool sugar-cane to suck, or a bagful of groundnuts.

He appeared one day looking hunched and ill, and with a nasty cough. Tilly gave him a dose of strong medicine and advised him to go home at once and stay in bed. He gave the long Kikuyu "ee-ee-ee-eee", which meant almost anything, rubbed his woolly head with a skinny hand and walked off unsteadily, as if drunk, although this was not the case. That was in the afternoon. Just before sundown, Karioki appeared on the veranda and said: "Rohio has been taken ill."

"What kind of illness?"

"Of the chest. He cannot breathe, he needs medicine. . . ."

"Oh, dear," Tilly said in English, "we've promised to dine tonight with Alec, he is making an event of it, we can't let him down. . . . Take me to your father," she added in Swahili, and they went off to the huts.

The upshot was that Rohio, who was by then unconscious, was carried in and submerged under a heap of blankets in the bathroom. Tilly dared not dose him for fear that he would choke; he had a high temperature, and she diagnosed pneumonia.

"All we can do now is to hope he'll sweat it out," she said. "We had better go to Alec's, as there's nothing more I can do for him, and in any case there's no food in the house."

Robin and Tilly seldom left me alone, but they had such

faith in Sammy that occasionally, if they went no farther than our nearest neighbours, they would place me in his charge. On such occasions Sammy came and sat on the veranda, and as I dropped off to sleep I could hear him through the open door talking in low tones to various companions. On this occasion I could hear also a sound like a kettle with a loose lid boiling hard, and coming from old Rohio next door. Robin had said that to be unconscious was like sleeping deeply, so I knew that he was not in pain, and the sound did not keep me awake.

When I awoke, the morning sun had laid a bar of gold across the red earth-floor of my room. I dressed quickly, and looked in through the bathroom's open door. (We never shut our doors at night.) A form lay huddled on a pile of blankets, ominously still, and there were no sounds of a boiling kettle. I felt chilled all over; Rohio must be dead.

I found Tilly out with Sammy, setting tasks for the day. It had been, she said, an eventful evening. At Alec's the mules had been unharnessed and put in the stable, and the buggy had been left under a tree. When Robin came out with a lantern after dinner he had seen a number of shapes vanish into the night, and heard weird and blood-chilling noises.

"I thought I'd got 'em again," he reported, "especially when I saw the grass had turned white, and seemed to be frothing like beer." This was stuffing from the cushions of the buggy strewn all over the ground; the upholstery was torn and hung in shreds over the wheels. About the scene there lingered a faint, foetid smell of decay.

"Hyenas," Alec said immediately. "They've been very uppish lately; the other night I woke to see one at the foot of my bed, trying to gaze into my eyes."

When Robin and Tilly reached home in the sadly-ravaged buggy, Sammy met them with the words: "Rohio is almost dead. He cannot recover. The time has come to carry him outside. . . ."

"That is not our custom," Tilly snapped, thinking of the ravenous hyenas, and their long, sharp fangs. The crisis had come upon the sick man; he was fighting desperately for every painful breath and it seemed impossible that the struggle could continue.

"His heart can't stand it," she said sadly. "All I can think of is a drop of brandy; it couldn't hurt him, and anyway I'm afraid. . . ."

Robin fetched a bottle kept for emergencies and opened it, and Tilly managed to get a little down his throat.

"It can't do harm, and it may do good," Robin advised. "Try a little more."

While Sammy held the lamp above them, they went on pouring brandy in spoonfuls down his throat, until the whole bottle was finished.

"Well, that's kill or cure," Tilly remarked. They piled the blankets over him and went to bed, telling Karioki to wake them if there was any change. They had the hungry hyenas very much in mind. Tilly had a theory that the dogs would howl if Rohio died.

The dogs did not howl, and next morning Rohio had turned the corner and was sleeping naturally. He stayed for several days in the bathroom, fed on beef tea and gruel, and in a surprisingly short time was able to walk without help. Karioki shaved his head as bare as an egg, which was a sign of recovery. Rohio's delight at seeing again the sunshine and trees, and life going on all round him, was touching.

"God has helped me, and you have helped me," he said to Tilly, "and now I shall become as strong as a buffalo, and walk over the hills, and beget children—even I, an old man whose sons have been circumcised. Your medicine is powerful, and my heart is strong."

No words for thanking people existed in the Kikuyu's language, and Europeans often accused them of ingratitude. It was true that they took help for granted, and very seldom, if ever, felt that it imposed upon them any obligation to help their benefactor in return. Europeans had many true stories of retainers who had turned and bitten hands that had fed them generously, and this trait had caused much disillusionment. Perhaps gratitude was simply a habit Africans had never acquired towards each other, and therefore could not display towards Europeans; or perhaps Europeans were looked upon as beings of another order to whom the ordinary rules did not apply; if they wished to help you, they would do so for reasons of their own, and were no more to be thanked than rivers for providing water, or trees for shade.

Old Rohio proved an exception to all these rules. Although he never thanked us in words, he did so by his actions, and after his recovery, whenever he came to visit Karioki, he always brought Tilly a present: perhaps some eggs in a little woven basket, or a load of sweet potatoes on the back of one of his wives. He would squat down in the shade of the veranda, take snuff, and doze or simply sit until she appeared, and then he would rise and proffer his present with a little nod that set his long ear-ornaments (strips of leather encrusted with beads) swinging like a pendulum; and he would clasp her hand between his own and shake it gently, as one does a branch with fruit on it, and tell her the news of his family.

Although Njombo had returned from the reserve, Hereward still did not know that he had killed the headman, and kept on pressing chief Kupanya to produce the guilty man. Kupanya kept on putting him off with long, vague messages, so Hereward resolved to go and see the chief, and to combine his visit with a guinea-fowl shoot. The guinea-fowl were regarded as a pest by the Kikuyu because they came into the shambas and scratched up seed, and boys hunted them with sticks and hit them down from trees at night when they had gone to roost. The Kikuyu therefore welcomed the idea of a shoot, and so did we, because we grew tired of eating tough native sheep or oxen with very little flavour, or small skinny fowls, and looked forward to a meal of plump, succulent birds. So off we set one morning on mules and ponies with a picnic luncheon packed in saddle-bags: the Palmers with Ian Crawfurd, Alec Wilson and our three selves.

At first we rode through the khaki grass, the scattered erythrinas and fig-trees, the clumps of dark-green aromatic bush that we were used to, seeing very little sign of life beyond a flock of glossy-coated goats with their attendant, a small naked boy. But quite soon we entered the reserve and, although no boundary was marked, the nature of the country quickly changed. Circles of round huts appeared, each fenced with split poles, and the hillsides were patchworked with small, irregular plots of cultivation. Each young maize plant showed up against the rich red of the turned earth like a halma peg on a chocolate-coloured board.

The women in the shambas straightened up to watch us and

some ran for shelter like bolting hares, their babies bobbing on their backs, for they had never seen mules or ponies before and thought that they were evil spirits or monstrous objects like centaurs; the whole concept of a man sitting on a beast was wild and strange. The shrill call of women ahead and still invisible came to us from beyond the bush and forest patches; sound carried easily from ridge to ridge.

After a steep climb up a slippery hillside we paused to rest our mounts and gaze about us at the chequered ridges, the forest darkening the scene ahead, the thatch of huts poking like mushrooms through bush and floppy-leaved banana trees which partially concealed them. The Kikuyu liked privacy; each homestead was bush- or forest-sheltered, each had its own twisting path that could be guarded by spells. The country was greener here than on our farms, and more fertile; the rainfall, you could see, was higher, the air more crisp, and the bush full of wild flowers, bright flowering creepers and big flowering shrubs, especially one, a kind of cassia, that bore spikes of golden florets as vivid and as bold as gorse.

"We have seen nothing but women and children," Lettice remarked. "Surely there must be men about somewhere."

"Lying under trees asleep, or swilling beer," Hereward announced, "while their wives do all the work. Lazy scoundrels."

"Lucky dogs," Robin said wistfully.

Hereward's moustache bristled. "Young dogs should be made to work, if they won't do it voluntarily. No discipline, that's what's the trouble. This Government——"

"I suppose we were all like that once," Lettice interrupted hastily, "going about in woad and making human sacrifices, until the Romans came. It seems odd to think that we were civilized by Italians."

"You can hardly call the Romans Italians," Hereward objected.

"I don't know what else you can call them."

"This Italian Mission farther up the ridge," Alec remarked. "I suppose it's civilizing the Kikuyu, though so far the results are pretty ghastly."

"If you find anything missing, that's the place to look for it," Hereward added. "They say all these mission-boys are thieves."

"Perhaps we ought to look there for my scent-spray and that copy of *Eugène Grandet,*" Lettice suggested.

Hereward mounted his pony in a huff, wearing an expression like a camel's, and Lettice went rather pink. Before she could think of some emollient observation, Ian had come to the rescue with a remark about Muslims which gave Hereward an opportunity to praise their virtues. Although himself a stout Christian, Hereward had no wish to attract members of the subject races into the fold, but rather resigned them to the Prophet, whose views on discipline, strong drink and women he considered very sound.

Kupanya was waiting for us under a large fig-tree outside his fenced enclosure, which had almost the dimensions of a village, because he had so many wives and children.

"Do people become chiefs because they are rich, or rich because they are chiefs?" Lettice inquired.

"The two advance side by side," Ian answered.

Kupanya had dressed up in a cloak of grey monkey-skin and wore a kind of shako made of some other fur, together with a great many ornaments and charms. This was a compliment to us; normally he wore a blanket like everyone else, and merely carried a staff with a brass knob on it to indicate his chiefly status. Round him sat a circle of old men with wizened faces and scrawny limbs, apart from one or two who had run to fat. They displayed wise, lined, authoritative faces, and the dignity of those whose word is always obeyed.

"Those are the real rulers of the tribe," Ian said. "Kupanya is more or less a figure-head."

Njombo had told me that Kupanya had been a noted warrior in his time and had killed several Masai, and even wounded a European. His prowess with the spear had won him a generous share of booty, and so, by the time his age-grade had taken over the control of local affairs, he had become a man of substance; and his character had made him a man of authority. When the District Commissioner had looked about for a suitable chief, Kupanya had seemed an obvious choice.

"His wealth has grown like a gourd," Njombo commented; and now indeed he looked a little like one himself, large and full and ripe.

He gave us native beer, which Hereward spat out with a

grimace, and Ian sipped with interest, remarking that it tasted of sour yeast. Alec said that it would give you a bad headache if you drank more than a mouthful. Remarks about crops and weather would have continued for the rest of the day if Hereward had not grown impatient.

"I have been waiting for you to send in the man who killed my headman," he said. "Now I am tired of waiting. If you do not send him immediately to Fort Hall I shall summon the police askaris and they will come and find him."

"And this man," Kupanya asked, "if we can find him, he must go to Fort Hall?"

"Certainly."

"And then?"

"There will be a case, with a judge, and if he is guilty, he will go to prison."

"And if he is not?"

"He will be set free, but then the askaris will come and look for the real culprit, and they will go on looking till they find him. So you need not think you can satisfy us with an innocent man, and that will be the end of it."

"Why should I do such a thing?" Kupanya asked in shocked tones. "Am I not a chief, and is my first wish not to help the Government?"

"In that case your task is easy. You must find the murderer, and send him to the D.C."

"Have I the eyes of a spirit, not of a man? Can I see into the hearts of people and tell their business?"

"Very well," Hereward replied in his no-nonsense tone, "I will send for the askaris."

No one liked having the askaris in, they were as bad as locusts, and in some ways worse, for locusts did not eat rupees or menace daughters. Kupanya tapped the ground with his brass-tipped staff and looked thoughtful and sulky. After a conversation in Kikuyu among his fellow-elders he rose with dignity from his three-legged council-stool and said:

"Wait, bwana. If God will help me, I will find the man." Then he stalked off, followed by several elders. The others remained squatting in a circle and passed round a horn filled with beer. Their eyes were rheumy and some of them grew sleepy as the day grew hot.

All sorts of people had by now crowded round the fig-tree to look at us. Tilly and Lettice had been provided with cushions on which they sat gracefully, their riding-skirts spread round them, in the shade. Many of the young Kikuyu men, who smelt powerfully and richly, though not unpleasantly, of rancid fat and red earth, wore short leather cloaks which failed to hide their genitals; when they pressed too close, Hereward shooed them off, looking embarrassed.

"Perhaps we should not have brought the ladies on this expedition," he murmured to Alec; but Tilly overheard.

"Perhaps we should not have brought the gentlemen," she suggested, indicating a number of well-greased, shaven-headed girls who had nothing on but very small triangles of leather and strings of beads, and whose breasts were still half-formed and therefore firm and in the right position.

"Nakedness doesn't seem to matter when people are black or brown," Lettice remarked. "White bodies look like clay waiting to go into a kiln. Natives look as if they've been fired and finished; perhaps that's why they don't strike one as indecent."

"Lettice, please!" Hereward remonstrated. "And in front of a child!" He sounded deeply distressed. But then Kupanya returned, bringing in tow a slim, drooping lad who looked as if he might evaporate at any minute, or disintegrate into a puff of wind. His lips were large and loose and he wore a glazed, helpless expression.

"This is the man!" Kupanya announced in tones of doom, as if he had emerged from single-handed combat with Goliath in chains at his heels.

"He doesn't *look* like a murderer," Lettice remarked.

"Nor do I expect he is one," said Ian.

"Ask him," Kupanya said, gesturing grandly towards the subject of the conversation.

"Did you kill my headman in the fight?" demanded Hereward.

"Yes, bwana."

"Why?" The man looked up for the first time, quite startled, as if this were a new idea.

"Why?"

"Yes, why, idiot; one doesn't kill people for no reason."

There was a rapid exchange of Kikuyu remarks.

"I killed him because he hit me first. I hit back, and he fell down and died."

"Well, that'll be for the D.C. to decide. This man must come back with us today," Hereward ordered. The young man, as he turned to go, smiled and said in halting English:

"Good night, sir. Save all sinners."

"Good heavens! Where did you learn that?"

"Good morning, sir. God save the King."

"A mission-boy!" cried Hereward.

"Yes, bwana," the young man said, relapsing now into Swahili. "I can read a book, I can write a letter."

"It is a pity he did not stick to that," Alec remarked.

"You see?" said Hereward. "What did I say? First thieves, and now murderers."

"He still scarcely looks up to it," Lettice objected.

"Just shows you, what these missions teach them. You'd better send two strong men with him, Kupanya, to see he doesn't escape."

"He will not escape," Kupanya replied.

Chapter Twelve

THE guinea-fowl could not be shot until the sun was more than half-way down the sky and so we found a shady tree some way from Kupanya's village for the picnic. In our circle of cool shade, as if under a rustling green parasol, we inhabited a different world from the sun-soaked Kikuyu ridges that stretched to meet a far, enormous sky, blue as a wild delphinium and decorated with vigorous clouds that threw shadows as large as islands on to the hillsides and valleys. It was as if we sat in a small, darkened auditorium gazing out at a stage which took in most of the world.

"If one followed those little rivers to their birthplace," Lettice inquired, "where would one be?"

"On top of the Aberdare mountains, where it's bleak and cold and marshy, and the lions are said to have spots," Ian replied.

"And down there?" Lettice gestured with a sandwich towards the far distance where a brown smudge on the horizon showed us the beginning of the great plains.

"The valley of the Tana, where there's perhaps the finest concentration of game in all the world."

"I must go there one day," Lettice said.

"You would find it unhealthy and hot."

"That is part of its attraction."

Alec Wilson, with an air of plucking up his courage, observed: "That's not the sort of thing you're cut out for, Mrs. Palmer. That's to say, marching and camping and that sort of thing isn't the life for a lady of your—for someone who—well, I mean . . ." He grew not pink, but positively red, in his confusion.

"For someone as incompetent as I?"

"No, no, of course, I didn't mean to imply . . ."

"I'm sorry: I know you didn't." She smiled at Alec with unusual warmth to make up for her remark.

"You mean that Mrs. Palmer is too good for Africa," Ian suggested. "You are probably right."

"That is rather a large claim," Lettice said.

"Surely it isn't a question of which is superior, Lettice or the continent of Africa," Tilly suggested. "It's a question of adapting ourselves to the conditions."

"It might be dangerous to carry that too far," Lettice replied. "That is perhaps what the natives have done. I doubt if Hereward would like me to carry firewood about on my back with nothing on but some beads and a bit of greasy leather, and to share a hut with goats and hens."

"I have no wish for my wife to be a savage," Hereward agreed. Somehow one always got the impression that he was in uniform.

"This is a savage country, so perhaps it might be better. An ability to sketch in water-colour and sing German *Lieder* is not very useful if there is an outbreak of plague or a puff-adder has got into the kitchen."

"There is no need for the womenfolk to concern themselves with such things," Hereward replied.

"That is a very gallant attitude, but they do not always have men to do it for them. Whenever I look at a Kikuyu woman toiling up a hill with a baby and a load of produce on her back weighing about a hundred pounds, I feel guilty."

"How ridiculous!" Hereward exclaimed. "They are only natives. Do you expect to lower yourself to their level?"

"I sincerely hope I shall never have to try."

"Surely," Tilly put in, "the idea is that they should rise to ours."

"Do you suppose," Lettice mused, "that one day they will become adept at water-colour sketches and German *Lieder*?"

"It seems unlikely," Robin reflected, watching a procession of three women, bent under their loads, plodding past us, their copper coils flashing back the sunlight, turning their shaven heads, gripped by leather bands, a little sideways to look at us with patient, bovine eyes.

"Surely that's the whole point of our being here," Tilly remarked. "We may have a sticky passage ourselves, but when we've knocked a bit of civilization into them, all this dirt and disease and superstition will go and they'll live like decent people for the first time in their history." Tilly looked quite flushed and excited when she said this, as if it was something dear to her heart.

"That is not the whole point of *my* being here," Alec Wilson put in, during a pause that followed. "I didn't come to civilize anyone. I came to escape from the slavery one has at home if one doesn't inherit anything. I mean to make a fortune if I can. Then I shall go home and spend it. If that helps to civilize anyone I shall be delighted, but surprised."

"Of course it will help indirectly," Tilly said.

"They must have an example," Hereward agreed.

"Do you think that we set an example?" Lettice inquired.

"I should have thought it was obvious, my dear. Even if it's only a matter of soap and water, and clean houses, and rudimentary hygiene, and proper clothing and—well—decency."

"And the way the women get treated," Tilly added.

"Mr. Crawfurd hasn't given an opinion," said Lettice.

"Well, as to that, I don't think Ahmed (for example) is at all likely to follow our lead where women are concerned. In fact, if there's one thing that really shocks him, it's the way our women behave."

"It hardly seems his place to be shocked," Hereward said.

"He's horrified (if that's a better word) first of all at the way they answer back, and secondly at their idleness. To see a man working while a woman lolls about offends his sense of decency. And as for the way in which wives mix with other men, he thinks it quite shameless."

Hereward went rather red and looked as if he was going to splutter like a firework, but so many things occurred to him to say at once that he said nothing. Alec remarked soothingly:

"Captain Palmer hasn't told us yet why he came here—to set an example, or to make money."

"I came to play a small part in building a new Colony under the Crown. That seems to me a good enough reason for anyone. As for the natives, they are very fortunate to come under British rule."

This declaration put a full-stop to the conversation, as Hereward's remarks were apt to do, whereas with Lettice and Ian, or Robin and Tilly, talk would volley gently to and fro until halted by some external event. We lay under the tree in silence, watching the sky wink at us through gently-moving leaves and hearing the rustle of heavy-seeded grasses, the far tinkle of goat-bells, the never-ceasing chirruping of crickets that seemed to concentrate the essence of heat and brightness into sound. In this high afternoon, human noises were suspended and you could almost hear the earth drinking in the hard sunlight, and the frail, dry pattering of insects' feet.

Ian lay on his back creating for himself, it almost seemed, with his bright hair, a little tarn of sunlight. It had become a fashion among the younger men (set I think by the Cole brothers, Berkeley and Galbraith) to wear round their shoulders one of the light, fine woollen shawls affected by the Somalis, and Ian had one, on which he was reclining, that exactly matched the sky. Lettice was propped on one elbow, scratching patterns in the soil with a twig. On Tilly's dressing-table stood a little pin-tray made of mother-of-pearl whose cool, smooth, iridescent lustre, haunted by the ghosts of colour, was the nearest match that I had seen to Lettice's complexion.

Ian was watching her with a look of concentration, almost of puzzlement. She raised her eyes and they gazed at one another in silence. Not long ago, Robin had blasted some rock out of the quarry. After he had lit the fuse, we had waited several hundred yards away for the bang. Now I had the same sort of feeling, as if we all waited for something big and dramatic; but of course there was nothing like that to come in this peaceful, drowsy afternoon lull under a tree.

An ant carrying a speck of food hurried across the dusty plain under Lettice's eye. With a twig, she gently pushed it aside to change its direction, but each time it turned back to resume the course on which it was set.

"Such a little thing," she remarked. "And yet its resolution is stronger than mine. I shall tire of this battle of wills before the ant."

"You are playing the part of fortune, who is rightly called a woman," Ian said.

"The part is too big for me." Lettice threw aside her twig. "Let the ant carry his prize to his family."

They were silent for a little, Lettice tracing a pattern in the dust with a forefinger, while the probing sunlight, piercing the canopy of leaves, threw on her reclining form a dappled pattern of light and shade. I could not see whether Ian was watching her, or the world of sunshine outside. The others were busy with a conversation; when they paused, the crickets' chirping, the goat-bells, the rustle of leaves wove themselves into a backdrop of sound. Ian spoke very quietly, so that I could hardly hear.

"Lettice, you have me at your mercy like that wretched insect. I think that you have paralysed my will."

"I have done nothing," Lettice said gently, digging her forefinger into the ground.

"You have existed. You exist now. And that is enough."

"Hush," Lettice murmured. "You are indiscreet."

"So is a volcano, so is a typhoon, so are the flames of a blast furnace. It is too late for discretion."

"Too late. . . ." Lettice echoed, in a voice that sounded stiff and strange. She was breathing quickly, as if she had walked uphill. There was a pause while she seemed intent on controlling her breathing; then she looked across at him and smiled.

"You must not try to hypnotize me, Ian; you are like the Ancient Mariner. You must think of the ant. I only caused it inconvenience; then it hurried on."

"It knew where it was going to; that is the difference between ants and men. But now you have set me on my course."

"What are you two talking about?" Hereward inquired, breaking off from his discussion.

"Ian is describing the habits of ants." Lettice pronounced the word like aunts, and the others looked interested.

"It's true that some of them have queer habits," Robin remarked. "My aunt Constance keeps a collection of toads on Clapham Common, and breakfasts off stout and oysters; and my aunt Veronica, who is over eighty, lives alone with six unmarried daughters and will speak to none of them, but plays the harp all day, and is surrounded by pugs."

"Ian was speaking of the kind of ant with six legs and jaws longer than its body."

"I have no aunts quite like that," Robin said reflectively. "At least so far as I know; but what with the beast of Glamis, one never can tell what might be found on the top floor of any Scots castle."

"Surely we've filled in enough time talking nonsense," Hereward said, springing to his feet. "Where have the beaters got to? Fast asleep, I suppose!"

The shoot got under way. I stayed with Lettice and the mules and ponies; the men were to beat homeward down the valleys, and Tilly, who was learning the sport, went with them. She was frightened of the gun at first but soon learnt to control it, and Hereward remarked admiringly that she would make a splendid little shot.

"It is much less alarming when you fire it off yourself than when other people do," Tilly explained.

"Like sins," said Lettice.

"What sorts of sin?"

"Any sort. When other people commit them, you are startled, but when you commit them yourself, they seem absolutely natural."

"I hope you don't speak from experience, my dear," said Hereward.

"Oh, no. I am quite well read."

I rode with Lettice along the winding paths while shadows began to advance up the red and green hillsides, turning the intervening valleys into pools of darkness. The round thatched huts on the ridges glowed like fresh honey and, on the hillsides, a feathery grass with pink and silver seed-heads bent before the breeze in a manner that, for no reason, always made me feel sad.

The beaters made a great deal of noise walking through the shambas below us, waving sticks. Guinea-fowl are great runners; the difficulty is always to get them off their feet. We heard a number of bangs and a good deal of shouting, Small buck were also about, and this worried me, for any duiker in the district might well be a relation of Twinkle's, or might leave an orphan behind it, if it were killed, who might never be found, and die in the bush.

"Why don't they shoot goats, instead of duikers?" I wondered. "There are far more."

"For one thing, the goats belong to people," Lettice explained. "And for another, they would not provide sport for the guns."

I inquired why.

"Because they stand still, and don't run away."

Obviously this was sensible of the goats, and I felt a new respect for them. It was the same, I noticed later, with birds; if a guinea-fowl sat in a tree Hereward would not shoot it, but waited until someone made it fly away. This increased the likelihood that he would merely wound the bird, but once when I remarked as much he grew angry, and said that I did not know the meaning of the word sport.

I was quite right about the duiker, however. We heard cries, and saw one bounding away among the crops below us and disappear into a patch of bush, which the beaters quickly surrounded. Hereward and Tilly advanced side by side into the duiker's refuge. The little buck broke out and tried to escape up the hill, but a Kikuyu threw a stick and turned it. A few moments later it reappeared on the far side of the bush, once more to be turned back by stick-hurlers. Finally it tried to break back between Hereward and Tilly. I do not know which of them shot it, but it went down with a dreadful squeal which made Lettice put her hands to her ears. I think it was shot in the spine and its back legs were paralysed. Hereward ran towards it and, after another shot, it lay still.

I ran down the hill to where it lay. It was a female, with a whitish belly and no horns, and soft grey-brown fur. Its feet were clean and sharp and delicate as those of a dancer.

"I hope it hasn't got a child," I said.

"It has a child in its belly," one of the Kikuyu remarked. He took out a knife and slashed it up the middle. The flesh parted like an envelope slit by a paper-knife and all its red and blue intestines tumbled out and lay in a quivering pile. The man thrust his hand in and pulled out a perfect little baby duiker, its fur already on it, waiting to be born. Even its tiny feet, no larger than a finger-nail, were perfectly formed; even its eye-lashes were ready. It lay there half-entangled in a slimy sac of tissue that the beater had torn aside, and looked so tragic that I burst into tears.

"A pity," Hereward conceded. "No way we could tell it was in that condition."

"Poor little thing," Tilly said, trying to comfort me. "But perhaps the baby would have grown up to be eaten by a leopard, or caught in a trap."

This only seemed to make matters worse. The Kikuyu quickly stripped the duiker of its guts and threw them into the bush with the unborn baby, and slung it on a stick to carry home. Its head hung down pathetically, and blood dripped from its mouth.

"I want to go home," I said, suddenly terrified lest Twinkle had escaped and been chased and killed.

"We will go home together," said Lettice, who had now arrived, "and leave the rest of you to slay more guinea-fowl."

Several of the beaters came with us, among them the young man Kupanya had picked out as the murderer, who had evidently not yet gone to Fort Hall. He seemed to have forgotten all about his troubles, and had been beating with enthusiasm and energy. To mark his status as a mission-boy he wore a pair of khaki shorts, whereas everyone else had a blanket. After a while our escort broke into snatches of song. These songs, always in a minor key, were plaintive and, to my ears, melancholy, but they were not songs of sorrow. As a rule they celebrated some triumph of battle or of love. Perhaps this song celebrated the death of the duiker and its unborn baby, and was its sole brief memorial. The singer no doubt made its death into a triumph for his skill in running, and for the marvels of the white man's rifle. But the triumph seemed to me a very mean one, and it was a long time before I could forget the duiker that had been so peacefully browsing on the hillside, a nest perhaps prepared for its child, and was overtaken so roughly by the pain and terror of death.

At the last stream to cross before reaching home, Ian was waiting for us, sitting on a boulder with his blue Somali shawl flung over his shoulder. When he mounted his pony his movements had the same sort of grace as those of an antelope, lithe and economical. Hereward stumped about like an intruder, but Ian moved as if, like the antelopes and the Kikuyu, he had grown from the soil.

"I have shot enough guinea-fowl," he said. "The others have gone to beat the last lot of shambas. Hereward is happy, he is teaching Tilly, and thinks that she is hanging on his words."

"You mustn't be unkind about Hereward," Lettice objected.

"Perhaps not; but he is such a fine specimen, he ought to be stuffed."

We had to ride in single file in order to keep to the narrow paths, but when we reached a stretch of open grazing, Ian again drew up beside Lettice.

"You will be going away soon," she said, looking ahead of her, and not at him.

"Yes: we have planned another Abyssinian safari. But I hope it will be my last."

"Have you made a fortune, and mean to retire?" Lettice asked lightly.

"Neither: but after a while I think the pursuit of freedom only turns one into a slave."

They rode in silence and I followed behind them, not at all interested in the conversation, and anxious to get back to Twinkle. Yet I could feel again a tension in the air that made their words memorable.

"There was a scandal when I ran away with Hereward," Lettice said. "You know that I was married before."

"I am afraid all that makes no difference," Ian said, rubbing the backs of his pony's ears with his whip. "But of course it is very interesting."

"Well, it is the plot of many hackneyed plays and novels. I was married at eighteen to a man much older than myself. I believe there was a rumour that my father lost me at cards, but I should doubt if that was the case. It's true this man was pushed down my throat, so to speak, by my parents, but I think that I imagined myself in love."

"There's an Eastern flavour to this story," Ian commented. He had tied the blue shawl round his waist, and rode close to her side. "Ahmed would think that it was all a great fuss about nothing. The only point of interest for him would be the sum your father lost at cards."

"Perhaps his is a better point of view, but I was not acquainted with it at eighteen. And I was most unhappy, which was inconsiderate of me, since the arrangement suited everyone else so well. Hereward was sympathetic, handsome and kind. He was also impulsive, and we eloped. Of course he had to send in his papers, and it was some time before I realized quite what that meant to him. Hereward is a born soldier. So now here we are. He gave up a lot for me and I hope that he will find this life a compensation. I think he will: I think he is discovering a new purpose. So now you understand, Ian, why you must keep your freedom, or find someone else to surrender it to."

Ian was silent for so long I thought he had forgotten where he was, and when he did remember he spoke so quietly I could scarcely hear.

"You have warned me off, but I am not the type to go in search of tigers in Bengal, or the highest peaks of the Himalayas. Nor to feel my heart bleed for Hereward. We are both young, and time is on my side."

"It is when one is young that time is too precious to waste."

Ian pulled up his pony and laid a hand on the reins of hers. "Look at that sunset: time can never be wasted when there are such sights to look at, and such things to enjoy."

The sunset was, indeed, spectacular. The whole western sky was aflame with the crimson of the heart of a rose. Deep-violet clouds were stained and streaked with red, and arcs of lime-green and saffron-yellow swept across the heavens. It was all on such a scale that the whole world might have been burning.

"Wonderful, but extravagant," Lettice said. "There is no restraint in it."

"Yes, it is the sort of sky that angry Valkyries might ride across," Ian agreed.

"There is more beauty in a butterfly's wing or a seashell than in that sunset; but it has a barbaric splendour in it, and an element of terror."

They went on talking about the sunset and ideas it suggested to them, which were many; each mind fertilized the other. I did not listen, for the crimson sky, the golden light streaming down the valley, and then its obliteration by the dusk, as if some great lamp had been turned down in the heavens, filled me with the terrible melancholy that sometimes wrings the hearts of children, and can never be communicated or explained. It was as if the day, which was unique, and could never come again, had been struck down like the duiker and lay there bleeding, and then was swallowed into oblivion; as if something in each one of us had died with it, and could never be recalled. I felt it desperately important that the moment should be halted, the life of the day preserved, its death indefinitely postponed, and that the memory of every instant, of every fleck of colour in that tremendous sky, should be branded on my mind so as to become as much a part of my existence as an eye or hand.

The Kikuyu, however, paid no attention to this great tragedy of the death of the day. They talked of unknown things in liquid, musical voices, and spat, and sang, and hitched their blankets on their shoulders. I felt like a missionary tormented by the sight of thousands of innocent souls perishing merely because they lacked the words that would have saved them. When I pointed to the sky in which the red had all but faded and said: "Look, it is good," which was the only word available, they glanced up politely, nodded, and one said: "Yes, it is good," and went on with his conversation.

Perhaps he had words for his feelings, and his feelings were like mine, but I could never know, and this, too, was disquieting. The sunset vanished, the night came swiftly and it grew cold. We made our ponies trot, and soon a light came into view that had been put on the Palmers' veranda to guide us in.

Chapter Thirteen

ONE day Sammy said he was going to get married, and would like a few days' leave.

"You have two wives already," Robin said. "You are becoming very rich." He spoke a little resentfully, as Sammy's pay could not in itself have brought about this state of affairs and many things upon the farm often disappeared, especially maize-meal locked in the store. Robin kept the key, but Sammy was always having to borrow it, and in any case a Kikuyu blacksmith who could make fine chains for snuff-horns, and keen-bladed swords, would think nothing of copying a key.

"My father has great wealth in Masailand," Sammy said, as if guessing Robin's thoughts. "He has many daughters, and their bride-price makes him rich."

"Very well," Robin agreed. He added to Tilly, with a touch of regret: "If each of Aunt Veronica's daughters had realized a large sum, she would have been a rich woman, and might have left it all to me."

"If Sammy goes to his reserve, it may be six months before he comes back to work," Tilly pointed out.

"Luckily the bride is here. She's a Kikuyu—so far as I can make out, a relation either of Kupanya's, or of Njombo's, or of both. So he won't have to go away, and the ceremony will no doubt take place on the farm. I wonder what we ought to give him for a present?"

When he inquired, there was no hesitation about the reply: a fat ram, or, better still, a bullock.

Robin's experience had taught him already that the present of a bullock had to be carefully handled. It was remarkable how, whenever Christmas approached, or some big event like circumcision, the very best ox would break its leg and have to be shot. What angered Robin and Tilly was not so much the deception as the suffering caused to the ox, which probably had its leg cracked by a pick-axe or an iron bar. Perhaps the Kikuyu were not deliberately cruel to animals, but they were horribly callous. If they did not actively enjoy watching an animal suffer, they certainly did not mind, and it never occurred to any of them to put a beast out of pain. In their eyes, I suppose, pain was simply a thing that had to be suffered, whether you were a beast or a man; and as for beasts, they did not seem to give them credit for having any feelings.

A small and skinny bullock was marked for the feast and tethered near the house to be fattened on maize and sweet-potato tops, and Robin announced that if any other beast were to be injured, everyone would be fined two rupees and the carcass sold to Indians at Thika. The ox-teams remained intact.

No special ceremony seemed to be involved in Sammy's marriage, merely the making, transport and consumption of large quantities of beer, The liquor, made from sugar-cane, fermented in large gourds which sat like squat, plump-bellied elders round the fire in the middle of a hut bubbling quietly away, with driblets of froth, like the old man's saliva, trickling down their narrow necks.

Once the beer was ready, various women attached to Sammy's household stoppered the big pots with leaves, strapped them on their backs and set off for the homestead of the bride's father, who was one of Kupanya's fellow-elders and friends.

About this time, Njombo reappeared from a further visit to the reserve. The sparkle had gone out of him, he was listless and almost sulky, in spite of the stone stables, now completed, and two new ponies, a handsome bay called Lucifer (a name he did not quite live up to, in spite of Arab blood) and Dorcas, a chestnut mare. Whenever Sammy appeared near the stables, Njombo looked the other way or walked off, his face blank and stony. The gay little cap he had worn, made from a sheep's stomach, had been abandoned; his ears lacked ornament, his blanket was of the plainest, he had given up laughing and joking with his friends. When I asked Sammy what was wrong he replied with contempt: "Njombo is a fool. If a man cuts down a banana tree in his shamba, can he see bananas in his cooking-pot?" This did not seem to clear up the matter.

I cannot remember how I discovered the truth, that Sammy was marrying Njombo's intended wife. Poor Njombo could not pay the bride-price, everything he owned or could borrow had to go towards the blood-fine owing to the family of the

Palmers' murdered headman. So Sammy had stepped smartly into the breach, and carried off the girl.

No one disputed the justice of this, not even Njombo, but he had, for a Kikuyu, an undisciplined spirit and he could not help resenting his fate.

"Perhaps it would have been better to have gone to prison," I suggested.

"How could I go to prison? If I had done so, who would have paid the debt?"

Meanwhile the mission-boy produced for Hereward, whose name was Kamau, had gone to Fort Hall and been arrested, and would soon be tried for something he knew nothing about.

"That is unfair," I suggested.

But Njombo was unsympathetic. "*Huyu*," he said—that man, that creature—"he is like a bustard who stalks about in the long grass and looks with envy at the ostrich. His father owes a debt to Kupanya, so he must help to pay it."

It was about this time that the District Commissioner came from Fort Hall to make inquiries about the murder. He wore a khaki uniform with shining buttons and a large topee with a badge in front, and was attended by a retinue that impressed us with its smartness and size. When he went on a walking safari, he was preceded by thirty or forty porters carrying loads, but this time he rode up on a mule without his camping outfit, and stayed the night. At first he was rather stiff and distant in his manner. He was an official, and it was incorrect to be too friendly with riff-raff on the farms. Tilly had laid out a small steeplechase course, and after tea he was made to join in a race with several of the neighbours. These steeplechases led as a rule to several falls and much hilarity, and by the end of this one the District Commissioner, Mr. Spicer, was laughing and joking like everyone else. He apologized for not having come before, but said he had about a quarter of a million Kikuyu to deal with and only one assistant who was down with fever, and he himself had been collecting hut-tax; and in any case chief Kupanya had sent in a prisoner.

Next morning he held an inquiry. He sat on a camp chair under a tree while everyone squatted round him. One after the other, witnesses recalled the fight which had led to the death of the Palmers' headman. The accused youth, they said, had seized a *rungu* (one of the heavy-headed clubs that warriors carried) and bashed the headman in self-defence.

"If it was in self-defence," Mr. Spicer asked, "why did the accused receive no injuries?"

The headman, they said, had gone for him with a knife, and Kamau's agility had saved him from injury.

"Who is paying blood-money to the dead man's family?"

This question provoked such a mesh of explanations involving relationships and goats, that Mr. Spicer was soon wrapped round in argument like Gulliver pinioned by Lilliputians, quite unable to break out. He selected three or four witnesses, instructed them to report at Fort Hall in so many days' time, and came in to breakfast.

"I hope that boy will not get a very long sentence," Lettice said. "He looked so under-sized to be a murderer, and not at all fierce."

"Mission-boys," Hereward exclaimed with distaste. "The ruin of perfectly good natives. Just what you'd expect."

"I always suspect mission-boys," Mr. Spicer agreed. "Not of the crime, but of being picked out to be accused of it; no one likes them very much. But if all the witnesses agree on oath, and the accused man says he's guilty, then it's difficult not to convict. However, in this case there's the plea of self-defence. . . ."

"Let us hope it succeeds," Lettice remarked. "Even so, it's sad to think of him languishing in prison."

"They very seldom languish," Mr. Spicer said. "I have to count the prisoners quite often, and there are nearly always too many. The first time I did this, I found the prison population almost twice as large as it should have been. Food was short in the reserve and the warders had found places for a great many of their relatives, who treated the jail more or less as a club, and gave part of their rations to their wives. It is a very easy jail to escape from, but all our trouble lies the other way, in keeping people out."

"All the same," Lettice persisted, as he prepared to mount his mule, "I hope you won't be too hard on that poor little creature."

Mr. Spicer put on his topee, and seemed at once to change from an ordinary person into someone altogether more grave, resplendent and aloof. Even his expression altered, and his tone of voice. He adjusted his topee with its glittering badge, said distinctly: "I think you may trust in British Justice," and rode off.

"That hat has a kind of magic in it, like Samson's curls," Lettice reflected. "His self-assurance roosts in it, and can be taken on and off."

"Well, it is the Uniform," Hereward said with understanding.

For a month or two we heard no more of the case, and then one day Kamau the mission-boy reappeared, looking much fatter, and pleased with himself, and wearing a new shirt.

"I am not guilty," he said, using the English words, though stiffly, as if they were a bad fit.

"Well, it is no affair of mine," Robin replied. The foundations of our stone house were being laid slowly, with the aid of Hereward's Indian *fundi*, and his mind was full of the complications of building. Kamau said he would like to work for us, and that he was a clerk, who could look after stores and tickets. Robin doubted this, but signed him on for a very small wage in this capacity. Sammy shook his head afterwards, and said that nothing but harm would come of it.

"Why did the D.C. return him?" Sammy demanded rather crossly. "He said that he had killed the headman. And all the witnesses agreed."

"Perhaps the D.C. thought that they were all lying," Robin suggested. "As indeed they probably were."

"It is not a good thing," Sammy said firmly, without explaining why. He had, of course, become an ally of Kupanya's, which was a great help to us, as we never went short of labour. I sometimes saw his young wife, Kupanya's daughter, about her tasks near Sammy's homestead, or on his shamba, which occupied the choicest part of our farm. She was called Wanjui, and was jaunty and attractive, with supple limbs as soft as new-moulded clay, and was scarcely more than fifteen years old. Now that she was married her head was shaven and she wore a beaded leather apron and a great many coils of wire, for Sammy was a rich man and could afford to keep her well. She went with his second wife (the senior was in Masailand) to hoe the shamba, or plant maize, or harvest millet, according to the season. So far as we could see she was gay and happy and, if she regretted Njombo, she showed no sign. Njombo was a younger and more dashing sort of man, but not nearly so rich.

Some months later, after the rains, Sammy reported to Tilly in a gloomy manner that Wanjui was sick, and asked her to provide medicine. After Tilly had visited Wanjui in the cavern of her hut, she sent for Maggy Nimmo. Mrs. Nimmo always came under protest, saying that she was a nurse no longer, and had no equipment, and was always expected to do doctors' work, but as a rule she did come, jogging over on a mule in a very long divided skirt.

"It's the usual story," she said to Tilly when she had looked at Wanjui. "A miss, and all sorts of dirty messes applied to make matters worse. How these women live at all is beyond me, mutilated as they are for a start. What can one do for the girl in that filthy dark hut with every sort of infection? There's only one chance, to get her into hospital."

By now a branch line had reached Thika, and a train ran each way three times a week. This made us all feel very civilized. The train was not well equipped for sick people, and the five miles to Thika in an ox-cart or mule-buggy were still an obstacle, especially in the rains, when the two streams we had to cross engulfed their home-made bridges and turned into impassable torrents. Still, for eight or nine months of the year a sick person, if not too sick, could be got to Nairobi in six or seven hours with luck, provided that he fell ill on a Monday, Wednesday or Friday.

Tilly fixed up some blankets in the mule-buggy to make a bed. When everything was ready, Sammy appeared in the doorway looking sheepish and said that Wanjui had refused to go.

"Then she must be taken," Tilly said.

Sammy shook his head. "Some relatives have come . . . there are two old women . . . they have their own medicines. . . ."

Tilly was furious, but it was no good. Sammy himself would have sent her, but in this emergency the word of a husband carried little weight. The matter had been taken over by Kupanya's family. Mrs. Nimmo reported that two old crones were in possession of the hut and that a witchdoctor with a gourd full of spells was squatting outside, and a goat tethered near him ready for sacrifice.

"That girl will die," she said, "if she doesn't have proper treatment. If I had my way I'd take her in by force."

This was impossible. Sammy now supported the old women, and Wanjui remained in her hut. They had managed things in this way for centuries, and in any case the journey would very likely have finished her off. Kamau came up and said that he wished to pray for Wanjui, but this could only be done in his hut, so he wanted leave for the rest of the day. Robin replied that he could pray just as well in the office, but Kamau said that God would not listen to him there, and they had a theological argument.

My own interest was centred on the goat marked down for sacrifice. It was all so unfair on the innocent goat that I resolved to see if I could rescue the animal. This had to be a single-handed, secret business, for I knew that Tilly would forbid the exploit as firmly as the Kikuyu would resist it. In fact I was not supposed to know what was going on at all, but as I was doing my lessons in the sitting-room where most of the discussion took place, the gist of the matter did not escape me.

After lunch, instead of resting on my bed as I was supposed to, I slipped out to Sammy's compound, where I expected everything to be in a state of drama and activity. But it seemed to sleep as usual in the sun; a few small children played around in the dust, a woman sat in the shade of a hut making a basket out of creeper-twine, there was no sign of Sammy or the old crones. And where was the doomed goat? A little corkscrew path took off from the compound and vanished into a plantation of tall maize. I followed this through a green, rustling forest, and came to an uncultivated patch round a tree. In the shade of the tree several men were squatting, doing something that I could not see on the ground. I watched for some time without daring to move, lest they should be angry, lest I had stumbled on some secret rite. But there did not seem to be anything secret about it and the men did not look round, so I walked up to see what was going on.

I was too late to save the goat. Its inside had been slit open, some of its organs lay on the ground and it had been partially flayed—all sights to which I was well used, and did not find remarkable. The point was that the goat was still alive. A man held its jaws to stop it bleating, but for a moment I saw its eyes, and the feeble twitchings of its raw and broken legs. I then turned and ran all the way back. Tilly found me on the lawn scratching Twinkle's back, a treatment of which she was very fond. She started to scold me for neglecting my rest, but noticed something wrong, and inquired whether I had been out without a hat, an error that was thought by everyone to result in instant death.

"Nothing must ever happen to Twinkle," I said.

"That would be a dull life," Tilly pointed out. "She's getting big enough to look for a husband."

"Then we must get one for her."

"One duiker is quite enough," Tilly said firmly. She had been obliged to have all the flower-beds surrounded by wire netting, but Twinkle leapt over these and the beds had now become more like prisons than features of a garden, with barbed wire entanglements all over the place. Now and then Twinkle would butt people in the backside and then walk off unconcerned, as if contemptuous of the fuss they made. Tilly lived in the hope that the call of the wild would operate, but I was convinced that Twinkle was too fond of me to leave us for the bush.

"Sooner or later," Tilly added, "Twinkle really will have to go."

"No, no, whatever happens, nothing must hurt Twinkle."

Tilly looked at me, and also at Twinkle, and said that she wished we had never kept her in the first place, but as it was, we would look after her. I was obsessed with the fear that Twinkle would be used for a sacrifice. She had become very bold, and walked in and out of the house with an imperious, self-confident air, picking her way like a queen. The Kikuyu said that she was very fat, and we ought to eat her. I knew that she was safe from being eaten by the Kikuyu, but not from being tortured and killed.

When I had cut my hand on a broken bottle, Tilly had sealed over the gash with some stuff that glistened like transparent silk called Newskin. That evening, the world looked to me like a smooth coat of Newskin painted over a deep, throbbing wound. The surface shone like healthy flesh, but just below it everything was anguished and horrible. There was the innocent goat, its life agonizingly torn from its tissues, and there was Wanjui, who could have been saved and comforted, helpless in the hands of the old crones, dying in the darkness of the hut; our lives went on as usual, and we could do nothing to alleviate all this pain. Next morning Sammy, who had grown sullen and almost rude, said that Wanjui was dead. Later in the day I noticed smoke coming from his compound. She had died in the hut, which had therefore to be burnt down, while her body was taken out into the bush for the hyenas.

Chapter Fourteen

TROUBLES did not come singly to Sammy. Not long after this, a dreadful thing happened to his eldest son, a boy of circumcision age. Materials for blasting were kept under lock and key, and only Robin and Sammy were supposed to handle them. One day Robin noticed that some of the detonators had gone. Things were always being stolen, but not detonators, and he could only hope that some had been lost, and no one had liked to admit it. Sammy denied all knowledge of the missing articles, and after a while the interest died down.

One afternoon when everyone was dozing (even Tilly was indoors) we heard an explosion from the direction of Sammy's huts and, after a pause, women's cries and people shouting. Tilly hurried out, telling me to stay indoors, but I followed out of curiosity and saw a man and a woman bringing towards us, as it seemed, a pillar of glistening red, like raw meat. I darted back into the house and resumed the painting of flowers in a seedsman's catalogue. Tilly was away a long time and looked dishevelled and exhausted when she came back, and her blouse had blood-stains on it. She wrote a note to Mrs. Nimmo and sent a boy to fetch Robin, and then sat down and took up a neglected piece of embroidery, and cut short abruptly anything I said.

Sammy's son had tried to beat out a detonator between two rocks, to make an ornament. One arm (as I learnt later) was hanging by a shred and his face was a red sponge of pulp. Somehow Tilly had managed to stem the bleeding until Mrs. Nimmo arrived to make a more professional job, but of course it was a matter for a surgeon. This time there was no argument. The mangled boy was wrapped up and put in the buggy and driven to the Blue Posts, and Major Breeches, who owned a motor-car, took him to Nairobi, a journey of between two and three hours.

Sammy went to Nairobi about a week later and returned to report that the boy was alive but had lost an eye and an arm. An atmosphere that was not exactly sullen, but was not cheerful either, prevailed on the farm. Robin complained that people skimped their work even more than usual and no longer sang when they cleared bush or weeded. Several of the regular and, up till now, reliable Kikuyu disappeared. Sammy said vaguely that they were ill, or had sick relations. It was curious how pervasive such an atmosphere could be. The air was bright and sunny, rain came when it was needed, flowers bloomed, work progressed, and yet there was something oppressive and uneasy. Hereward said that it was all imagination and we needed a change. Fortunately, one was in sight; Ian Crawfurd had written to suggest that, when his latest journey in the north was over, he should take the Palmers, Tilly and Robin on a game-shooting safari.

"Get away from all this pettifogging detail for a bit," Hereward approved. "Good for Lettice, especially. Stop her moping."

"Is Lettice moping?" Tilly asked. "I hadn't noticed it."

"Difficult country for women," Hereward said vaguely. "The vertical rays of the sun." He had taken to riding over quite often to ask Tilly's advice. Perhaps he found her cheerfulness and energy inspiriting. Tilly never moped, and disregarded the vertical rays of the sun.

Njombo had now been back at work for some time and he, too, shared the general malaise. Now that we had three ponies, his job was an important one, for they needed more attention than mules. He had a real talent for looking after them, and was intelligent, so he was one of the few individuals, apart from Sammy and Juma, whom we looked upon as a prop and stay.

It was therefore very disappointing when one day he disappeared without a word to anyone. When Robin made inquiries, he was told: "Perhaps Njombo is sick," but no one seemed to know, and Sammy simply shrugged his shoulders and said that Njombo was as foolish as a chicken, and that others could be found to do his work just as well.

This was untrue, and Sammy knew it. Although desertion, as it was called, among the labour was quite common, and could be dealt with through the District Commissioner, farmers did not as a rule pay much attention unless it was on a big scale, or connected with theft or some other crime. But on this occasion Robin was annoyed. Njombo had a position of trust, and had gone off without even leaving a message. Robin sent an urgent summons into the reserve, but nothing happened, so he rode up in a temper to see Kupanya. The chief received Robin with his usual bland courtesy and presented him with a chicken, which ruffled Robin further still, because he had forgotten to bring anything to give Kupanya in return.

"I will send for this man," Kupanya said, when he had heard the complaint, "but it may be that he is sick."

"If he is sick then he should have treatment," Robin replied.

"There are doctors for white men and doctors for black men. It may be that he has come to consult a black man's doctor."

"Then he is a fool," Robin retorted, unable through the limitations of the language to denounce superstition and quackery, as he would have wished. "Tell him to come back at once or I will bring a case against him before the D.C."

Njombo did return about a week later, and received in silence the dressing-down from Robin which he no doubt expected, and did not assimilate. He had lost weight, and looked a sick man. His return only seemed to accelerate matters. Quite suddenly he shrank, his bones stuck out, his cheeks grew hollow and his skin dry, as if something had literally been drained out of him. Robin said he looked as if he had been attacked by vampires, and Tilly dosed him in vain with Epsom salts, cough mixture, cooking port and quinine.

Once a month, Robin drove into Nairobi in the mule-buggy to fetch the wages, which came out in little sacks of rupees lying at his feet. Such a visit was now approaching, and it was decided to take Njombo to the hospital. As he would never give his consent, he was merely told to come with us in order to look after the mules. When we reached the native hospital Robin marched him in and he was virtually captured by the orderlies. His listlessness was now such that he showed little fight, although he rolled his eyes in his distress. Robin explained matters to a European doctor, who said that he would do his best.

"But don't think we're sure to cure him," he added. "There are dozens of tropical diseases we haven't even names for, let alone treatments."

I missed Njombo, whose fondness for the ponies almost matched my own, but noticed that Kamau was trying to insinuate himself into an escort's position. He discovered that I was collecting wild flowers and would appear with one in his hand and offer it to me hesitantly, perhaps thinking I was looking for a special kind. He was always delighted when I took it and thanked him, and pressed it in an old catalogue from the Army and Navy Stores. I was rather sorry for Kamau, no one seemed to like him, and Robin said he was a very bad clerk and almost certainly dishonest, and had sacked him several times. Kamau paid no attention and always turned up smiling in what he evidently hoped was an ingratiating manner, so he stayed on.

I told Kamau that Njombo had been taken to the hospital. He shook his head.

"Njombo cannot get well."

"Yes, he can. The doctors will give him medicine."

"The medicine of doctors is not strong for Njombo."

"Njombo is like everyone else."

"But there are bad men, wizards. . . ." Kamau looked cold and hunched, as if against a wind. "Njombo was foolish to bring harm to Sammy's son."

"Sammy's son was foolish, to hit that thing like a cartridge with a rock."

"It hurt no one else. People saw Njombo digging up the stone. . . . But these are bad things. When the bwana goes to Nairobi, I would like him to bring me a watch."

Kamau was more interested than the other Kikuyu in what we did, wore and possessed, and wished to copy us; Robin thought him a thief. He refused to say any more about Njombo, and no one else mentioned the name. It was as if Njombo was dead already, dead and forgotten. It was noticeable about the Kikuyu that when anyone was dead, the gap had to be closed immediately, no one spoke the name—like a rent that is quickly mended, to make the garment look as whole and serviceable as before.

And then one day Njombo reappeared, his legs like sticks, very frail and hunched like a sick chicken. It was a wonder that he had managed to walk from Thika. His skin looked grey. He carried a note which said:" I cannot do anything for this man. There is nothing wrong with him except that he has made up his mind to die."

This was a blow, not merely to the hopes Tilly and Robin had entertained of Njombo's recovery, but to their faith in European medicine, which they had believed fully a match for heathen superstition or toxicology. Tilly put him in her sick-bay and ordered Juma to feed him on beef tea. He had no will or life of his own, and refused the beef tea, and no member of his family came to nurse him. It was sad to see him, who had been so bold and smiling, reduced to this pitiable condition, like a blighted plant whose roots have rotted; and to be helpless to apply a remedy.

"I don't see how it can be poison," Tilly said, "because he eats nothing; the sickness must be in his mind. We must convince him that the spell, or curse, or whatever it is, is all imagination, and hasn't really any power to hurt him."

"That is rather difficult," Robin pointed out, "when it so obviously has."

"Only because he thinks so. It's a question of faith."

"Perhaps the Church could help," Robin suggested. "It's their business, in a sense."

Tilly caught at this, and we all rode up to the Italian Mission which lay a few miles inside the reserve. Everything there was of the simplest—a plain mud-and-wattle church, an open-sided shelter for a school, a cluster of huts. The Fathers were small, bearded, dark and always welcoming, but they knew scarcely any English, so conversation had to be conducted in pidgin Swahili. Although devoted, pious and hard-working men, they did not escape criticism both from Europeans, who accused them of living at a level little, if any, higher than the natives', of destroying African standards and of teaching a creed almost as full of superstition and magic as the one they hoped to demolish, and from some, at least, of the Africans, who not only mistrusted alien teaching at variance with Kikuyu custom, but objected to the Fathers' need for land. In order to support their mission, which was very short of funds, the Fathers had planted coffee, and perhaps it was not easy for the inhabitants to understand that these were men of God, and therefore entitled to plant their trees in an area that the Government had promised to reserve for the Kikuyu, and not to give to Europeans.

The Fathers led us into their living-room, furnished with little more than a roughly-built home-made table, a few camp chairs and several holy pictures and statuettes, and offered us wine. When Tilly attempted to present our problem in her limited Swahili they listened sympathetically, nodded and smiled.

"We hope that you will come and drive out this bad spirit, like the pigs of Gadarene," Tilly concluded.

"Has the sick man had the water of God?" inquired the spokesman for the Fathers. Tilly was puzzled for a moment, but then realized that he referred to baptism, for which Swahili had no word—just as there was no word for Holy Ghost, which became simply the Bird, or for the Virgin Mary. She said that Njombo had not been baptized.

"Then we cannot drive away the bad spirit."

Tilly was indignant. "But do you not preach that the Word of God is stronger than Kikuyu magic?"

"If God has not yet caught a man, he does not belong to God, he still belongs to Kikuyu custom. If the water of God had been placed upon his head . . ."

"Surely you cannot say because he has not yet had this water on his head, you cannot help him?"

The priests sadly shook their heads. They were sorry, but firm; Njombo was outside their province. Only the sheep within the flock could be saved.

"Very well, then: you must quickly give him the water."

The priests exclaimed and gestured. "He must first wish for water, learn, understand. Perhaps in one month . . ."

"He will be dead in a few days."

They shrugged their shoulders regretfully, and smiled. One of them reflectively picked his teeth. A peculiar kind of white topee, quite round and with a flattish crown, was clamped down on their heads, and the toes of their black, cracked boots pointed towards the Heaven they served.

"This is ridiculous," Tilly complained in English. "They won't save Njombo's life because he hasn't been baptized, and they won't baptize him because he's dying. If *that's* their idea of Christianity . . ."

"I see their point," Robin said. "Unless Njombo really believes in their form of magic, it can't save him. And he's too far gone now to take it all in."

Tilly was upset and thwarted, and had little use for the poor priests after that. All the resources of our civilization were unavailing against the word of some obscure, ignorant and heathen wizard with his beans, bones and powders. She felt the humiliation personally, especially as Njombo was, so to speak, ours. He was under our protection and we had failed to carry out our part of the implied bargain; this was what stuck in her throat.

On our return we found Alec waiting, and consulted him. He got on well with the Kikuyu and, probably because he was a bachelor and had no one else to talk to, generally knew more than our other neighbours of what was going on. Besides his native name of Bado Kwisha, he had a second one that he was not supposed to know: this was bwana Dungbeetle, which did not sound complimentary but was not meant to be unkind. Alec claimed it as a tribute to his persistence, for nothing is more patient and resolute than a dungbeetle, which will push its little kneaded ball of muck along a rough, uphill path with infinite care and resolution; but Njombo told me that this was not the reason at all, but that when Alec sat on a pony—he was a clumsy horseman—he looked as if he was trying to push it along, and kicked his legs like the insect they had named him after. I tried hard to see the likeness, and never could, because the dungbeetle was so thickly armoured and spindly-legged, although I did see that Alec tried in an ungainly way to shove his pony forward.

"There is only one man who can save Njombo," Alec said, "and that is Sammy; it was he who put on the spell, because he thinks it was Njombo's magic that blew up his son; and he must take it off again."

"You make it sound like a mackintosh," Robin protested. "Sammy simply ignores what I say."

"Well, we must look for his Achilles heel. And that is easy, with a Masai."

"You mean his cattle."

"Of course. If you round them up and tell him that you'll cut their throats unless Njombo recovers, or hand them over to Njombo's father, I think your Sammy will very soon come to heel."

Robin tried this, but it was not a success. His trouble was that he was never really convinced of his own authority. A little worm gnawed away at the back of his mind: what shall I do if they refuse? How shall I make them obey me? To squash the worm, he assumed a very stern demeanour and spoke abruptly, like a sergeant on parade. This was most unlike his ordinary manner, which was dreamy and benign. It was extraordinary to watch the change; like a coin tossed in the air, he could show two absolutely different sides of his nature, and yet both were the same.

He summoned Sammy to his office in a corner of the store, smacked the table with his palm and said:

"Sammy, you are the headman and you have had a quarrel with Njombo which is very wicked. You are behaving not like a man who can read, but like a savage. Do you not understand that these Kikuyu customs are bad and old-fashioned? If Njombo dies, you will be a murderer."

"I do not understand what you are saying," Sammy stubbornly replied.

"You will understand very quickly when I seize your cattle and shoot every one of them myself. Every one. I shall do this, Sammy. If by tomorrow evening you have not undone this thing, if Njombo does not begin to recover, that is what will happen. Every one of your beasts will die."

Sammy glowered like a black mountain and his eyes rebelled, but he said nothing. While he was enraged, Robin's threat did not convince him.

"Very well: finish Njombo's illness or your cattle die," Robin barked. "Go at once and arrange it. At once. That is all."

Robin knew that, if he had the chance, Sammy would spirit his cattle away to a friend in the reserve, so he had them driven into the thorn-protected *boma* where our own oxen spent the night.

"What shall I do if Sammy *doesn't* de-witch Njombo?" Robin wondered. "I can't really kill sixteen head of cattle, and have the D.C. after me. I suppose all this is highly illegal."

"So is bewitching people; you could have Sammy run in."

"Oh, yes, run in! One has as good a chance of getting a conviction in a witchcraft case, as a mule has of winning the Derby."

Tilly would not let me see Njombo who lay, she said, immobile in his dark hut, fading away like an old photograph. His ribs stuck out, his pulse was very feeble and he scarcely seemed to breathe. "He's committing suicide by sheer will-power," she said. The hut in which he lay took on a mysterious and sinister character, as if set apart and charged with threatening powers. I kept approaching it nervously, expecting to detect a black presence hovering by the door, or ghostly shapes flitting in and out of the roof. It looked dead itself, lacking the faint blue film of smoke that always hung about the thatch of a hut full of life and people.

Chapter Fifteen

AS the day developed, everyone realized that nothing was being done to de-witch Njombo and that our bluff had failed. Robin got out his rifle and left it about in obvious places as a hint.

"A lot of dead cattle won't save Njombo," Tilly remarked. "I think that one of us ought to see Kupanya. Njombo is his relation, and surely he must have some authority."

"Sammy married his daughter," Robin pointed out. "That was what started all this trouble, I suppose."

"If Njombo dies, we can report the case and make things awkward for him with the Government. At any rate we can try."

Robin did not like to leave the farm with so much tension in the air, so Hereward offered to escort Tilly, and I was allowed to go with them. We set off in the heat of the afternoon up the red path to Kupanya's, Hereward spruce and upright in a perfectly cut pair of breeches and shining boots on a well-bred, lively polo-pony, and myself jogging behind on Moyale, who had by now grown fat and wilful, and put his ears back and shook his head when I pummelled his ribs with my heels to urge him on.

Hereward took a forthright view of our troubles. "If you don't mind my saying so, Robin's too lenient with these fellows. As for Sammy, I'd put him down and give him twenty-five and that would be an end of the trouble."

"It would also be an end of Njombo," Tilly pointed out.

"That's a lot of stuff and nonsense, if you ask me. He's been poisoned, that's the long and short of it. You aren't on guard over the fellow day and night, you don't know who's creeping in there filling him up with some revolting brew. By George, the trouble you go to over your boys! It isn't every woman who's willing to take on the jobs that you do. Robin's a lucky man."

Tilly reddened, muttered something about Robin having a lot to put up with and urged her pony into a trot, so that Hereward had to drop behind in single file. It was the time of day when heat presses down upon the earth and squeezes out the energy, when men idle in the shade like trout lying nose-to-current on the bed of a stream, when even doves can barely muster the desire to coo. Women sat straight-legged under bushes, their pangas beside them, suckling their infants, even flies were drowsy and settled again and again on the ponies' faces and on our hands and arms, ignoring our flaps and twitches. Rains were brewing; the air was stifling and heavy, distant ridges looked as sharp and hard as if they had been cut out of cardboard.

Kupanya's group of huts was deserted, except by one or two naked children and an old crone, her face as crinkled as a walnut, plaiting a corn-bag with crabbed fingers. One had a sense of watching eyes, yet Hereward's calls received no answer.

"Should have brought a hunting horn," he remarked. "That would have fetched 'em out."

A child scurried from hut to hut, a woman put her head out of a door and withdrew it, a sense arose of slowly awakening activity. At last, after an even longer pause, Kupanya emerged from a hut as reluctantly as a very tight cork drawn from the neck of a bottle; he looked bleary-eyed and was clad only in a blanket he was still adjusting over one shoulder. When he expected us, he dressed up in his monkey-skin *kaross* and looked imposing. In dishabillé he looked imposing in a different way: strong, well-muscled, agile, his healthy skin shining like the barrel of a well-kept rifle. It was easy to believe that not so long ago he had slain Masai, raided cattle and danced with his body garishly painted, with rattles on his ankles and feathers in his pig-tailed hair.

Hereward explained our mission in his barking voice and poor Swahili, as if giving orders on parade. The chief listened with a heavy afternoon face and briefly answered:

"Njombo—I do not know this man."

"Do not give me lies! He is one of your own relations."

"If he has left my land to work for Europeans he is not mine, but theirs."

"Whether he is yours or ours does not matter," Tilly said. "Listen carefully. Someone is trying to kill Njombo with medicine. If this does not stop at once, today, or at any rate by tomorrow morning, we shall tell the D.C. that you have allowed it. And then the D.C. will send askaris to arrest you. He will put you in jail and fine you hundreds of goats, and take away the staff of the chief. And he will give that staff to another. That is the plain truth. And here is our warning. If the magic has not been taken off Njombo by noon tomorrow, the D.C. will know about it before the sun sets."

Kupanya stood for a while in silence with his eyes on the ground, and a look as heavy as the thunderstorm we could feel mounting up just beyond the horizon. The air was motionless, the flies clung, and when a goat picked its way across the compound, the little puffs of red dust that its feet created hung there and drifted back on to the ground as slowly as thistledown.

"I do not understand these words," Kupanya said at last. "All this has nothing to do with me. If the D.C. wishes to come, I am ready for him."

"The D.C. will not come," Tilly retorted. "He will send askaris to take you away with bracelets on your wrists. Have you not heard that the Governor has said there must be no more bad magic? So now you must put a stop to this affair. You have till noon tomorrow; and if Njombo dies first, the D.C. will know that you have murdered him."

With this parting shot, Tilly sprang on to her mount and we rode off without waiting for protests or denials.

"You handled that splendidly," Hereward said with enthusiasm. "By George, I wouldn't like to come up against the rough edge of your tongue!"

"I only hope he doesn't call our bluff," Tilly replied quickly, for she disliked compliments, and might not have been sure whether this was one or not. "If we do send to the D.C. he'd probably do nothing at all, at any rate for several weeks."

"You've got the chief rattled, my dear."

"There's going to be a thunderstorm."

It was extraordinary how quickly a huge black cloud had appeared from nowhere and filled the sky. The air grew blacker and more sinister and the ridges crouched beneath a lurid, leaden light as if waiting for the crack of doom when the earth would spew up its dead. A cold wind shook the trees like a vicious cavalcade of ghostly horsemen riding the air, and then a fork of lightning lit the whole scene with an unreal whiteness, as if a crack in the surface of reality had for an instant revealed an underworld full of hidden devils and advancing doom. Trees bent before the onslaught and perhaps dug their roots into the ground.

The crash that followed brought our ponies to a halt, quivering all over. We slid off them and held tightly to their bridles. The whole air was electrified, explosive and black. Huge raindrops came down as cold as ice and with a personal malignance. It felt as if they wanted to tear the clothes off our bodies; the drops splashed over our feet and the next flash of lightning blinded us, and for several moments everything was invisible and yet full of painful light.

"The bananas," Hereward shouted, and started to run with his pony plunging beside him. We were near a stream between two ridges, and banana trees with their arching fronds grew beside it, dropping over the water. The storm burst fully as we reached the banana clump. The air was filled with fury, as if a wild, colossal monster was setting on the earth with tooth and claw to tear it to shreds. The banana fronds were quite unable to offer shelter, they were whipped about like shreds of rag. We huddled together with the quivering ponies and in a few moments were drenched to the skin. It was terrifying, yet there was something splendid and invigorating about the raging wall of icy water assailing us, a grey wall that blotted out all vision, and the roaring of the wind, and the crashing and cracking and reverberating of the thunder, and the violence of lightning flashes that split the sky. It was all so purposeful, the fury did not seem wanton, but directed—at whom? Not at ourselves, huddling by the stream, we were too small and insignificant, but it was hard not to believe, as the Kikuyu did, that God himself was in a fury and was raging through the storm, and that the lightning was the flashing of his sword as he lunged at the devils who had offended him.

The storm rolled down the valley, leaving us cold and soaking wet, but exhilarated and thankful. The thunder was still loud, but the wind slackened and the water-wall thinned out into heavy drops. The ponies began to toss their heads and dance about in thick, chocolate-brown mud.

"That was a near thing," Hereward said in a stiff voice. "I

don't want to see lightning as close as that again. Are you all right, Tilly?"

"You can see I am," Tilly replied crossly, thereby showing that she, too, had been badly frightened.

"I'd never have forgiven myself if anything had happened to you."

"It would hardly have been your fault, Hereward. And it would have happened to us all."

"Well, there are many worse ends. I sometimes think it would be the best way out for me."

"What nonsense!" Tilly cried, trying to tighten one of Lucifer's girths. "Why should you wish to get out of anything? You have everything you want."

"I am glad I have given that impression." Hereward sounded anything but glad, in fact rather offended, yet determined to forgive the offender. "I think most men would include his wife's affection among the things he wants."

"Are you trying to say that Lettice . . ."

"I may be a fool of a soldier, but I'm not blind as a bat."

"Oh, come off it, Hereward. . . . I wish you'd help me with this girth."

Hereward, his moustache at the bristle, responded with agility, slipping a hand over Tilly's as he reached for the wet leather and obliging her to wriggle it free.

" 'Nuff said, my dear. I think we understand each other. You're a very plucky woman, you know."

"I'm a very wet one. And I want my tea."

It was not a pleasant ride back. The cold and slippery saddle rubbed my bottom, everything clung to the skin and poor Moyale slid and slithered up and down slopes now traversed by miniature red rivers. The tempest had left a sky full of storm-wrack through which a red and savage sun reappeared to suck a white miasmic mist out of sodden pastures.

The storm had deluged the farm, and lightning had blasted a fig-tree half-way up the river slope. Robin said that he had felt the flash strike the earth, and it was like the entry of the demon king in a very expensive pantomime.

Hereward hurried back to Lettice, who, he said, hated thunder and hid in a cupboard, or under bedclothes, with her Pekinese.

"Poor Hereward," Tilly said. "He's absurd, but one can't help feeling sorry for him."

"Pompous ass," Robin commented. He was not often unkind about other people but his enthusiasm for Hereward had waned, because of a manner he thought patronizing. "I can't think why Lettice ran off with him."

"In his way he's quite attractive, but not nearly so attractive as . . ." Tilly noticed me, and added: "Go and take off your wet things at once and have a good hot bath."

If you were a Kikuyu, I thought, you never had a hot bath and so it must be hard to get warm and dodge chills; on the other hand, your skin was oily and the water flowed off, as from a bird, or from Twinkle, whose thick pelt kept her skin as warm and dry as if no rain at all had fallen.

The rain brought out the *siafu.* Those fearful black rivers of implacable insects poured between their low mud banks over the garden, across the veranda, through the kitchen quarters. The Kikuyu put hot ashes round the house and their own huts to deflect the vicious armies, and stood the legs of our beds in sardine-tins full of water. These were the only things that would turn *siafu* aside—ashes and water. Tilly put the dogs on leads when she took them out, for if one of them should step among them it would rush about in a frenzy, very likely straight into another *siafu* trail; dogs had been killed in this manner.

Of all things in the world, I feared *siafu* most. Silent, determined, innumerable, they would overwhelm you in an instant, swarm into your nose and hair and eyes and kill with a remorseless cruelty. Not that I had ever heard of a man or woman being killed by them, but it always seemed possible. They had destroyed cattle and horses. And where were they going, these creatures with armour-plated bodies, pincer-jaws and baneful juices, always in a hurry, never pausing, surging forward in those countless, terrifying millions, a never-ending stream of close-packed bodies that might flow on for several days? Where had they come from, what force was driving them on? Had each individual ant a brain, a heart, a will? If this were so, how did it come about that all these individual creatures, million upon million of them, acted together as if they were one, as if that long black coil of separate insects was a single creature with a single heart and brain and will? These were mysteries as deep as the universe that no one could solve.

And what about Njombo, alone in his dark hut, unconscious, but still breathing? If the *siafu* passed over his body they would strip it to the bone, as they stripped hens and chicks and puppies, all helpless things. The same thought occurred to Tilly and she told Juma to spread ashes round his hut, but when she went out later she found that nothing had been done.

"The ashes are finished," Juma said sulkily.

"Very well; then you must lift Njombo out and carry him here to this veranda, where he will be safe."

Juma recoiled, muttered something and vanished into the kitchen. When Tilly went to investigate in half an hour, ashes had been spread round the dark and silent hut.

Although protected by the sardine-tins of water, I went nervously to bed, afraid that somehow the biting armies would find a way round our defences and imagining that every rustle from the papyrus-lined walls, which rustled constantly, signified an invasion, and that the ants would trek along the ceiling and drop down on to the bed. Tilly allowed me to keep the safari lamp burning low, and on the whole this made matters worse, as in the dim shadows which it threw I seemed to see the moving masses of the enemy. In the night heavy rain fell, without thunder, which I hoped would drown the armies, or at least discomfit them.

Apart from the rain, the night was very silent, but once I awoke to hear the bone-chilling howl of a hyena, close to the house. Hyenas were said to be cowards, but in their midnight howlings there was something intimate, knowing and sly, as if they were saying: it will be your turn one day, your flesh will rot as other people's, you too will join the great legion of the faceless and dissolved. The hyenas were no doubt waiting for Njombo, and perhaps while I lay in bed their jaws were pulling at his limbs, so that there would be no more Njombo, nothing to show that he had lived, laughed and existed, and everything that was a man had ended in a few moments of satisfaction for these heavy-shouldered shadows of the night.

I was awakened, as always, by the high, metallic ring of iron on iron (a bar struck by a rod) that was our daily summons to work. In such a soft and golden morning, alert with the praise of birds, night fears were silly; the *siafu* had gone, the doves were cooing, Twinkle sparkled like a queen, her fur dew-beaded, and picked fastidiously at shrubs that shot miniature cascades of cold water over her black, quivering nose. The Kikuyu greeted us and each other with smiles, one could not imagine the existence of terror and pain. Yet Njombo lay as before in the dark hut—alive still, Tilly reported, but only just; his limbs were so light and fragile it was a wonder there was any blood in them. She had propped him up and tried to make him drink but he seemed too weak to swallow.

"It's today or never," she said. She told the syce who had replaced him to saddle a mule and be ready to start at noon with a note for the D.C., hoping that news of this would convince Kupanya's spies that we meant business.

"What will happen," Robin asked, "if Sammy and Kupanya pay no attention?"

"Then we must put Njombo into the mule-buggy and take him to Fort Hall, dead or alive. That will force a case, anyway, and get someone into trouble, even if it doesn't save his life."

The strangest part of it all was that none of Njombo's relations had turned up to look after him. A Kikuyu is normally embedded in his family like ore in the rock, or a tooth in the jaw: organically a part of it, unable to conduct a separate existence. Yet here was Njombo cast aside like a bad tooth, alone and abandoned to the care not just of strangers, but of aliens from another world. When I saw Kamau, later in the morning, I asked him what had kept Njombo's family away.

"They are afraid," he answered.

"Afraid of what?"

Kamau gave me a sideways look. "Afraid . . . of his sickness."

"My mother is not afraid."

"It is not a sickness that attacks Europeans. . . . There is a man who has some baby porcupines. Would you like to buy them?"

"Will Njombo die?"

Kamau looked upset. "Tch, tch, this is not my affair, nor an affair for children. . . . There are two porcupines, as big as that." He held out his hands.

"Where has Sammy gone?"

"Kupanya has sent for him."

"Then perhaps he will bring back medicine for Njombo."

"Sammy cannot give the medicine. There is a man . . ."

"A sort of doctor?"

"It is bad to speak of such things. Is it true that in England there are cattle as large as elephants, and men who are neither red nor black, but blue?"

Kamau was very interested in England, and sometimes we gave him old illustrated magazines. He had the King and Queen on the wall of the office and several other pictures from the *Illustrated London News*, including part of a naval review upside-down. As he had never set eyes on the sea, or heard of it until the other day, we found difficulties in explaining a battleship, or indeed any kind of ship at all. "Like a cart on top of water," was the best we could do.

After breakfast Robin went out as usual to the shamba, Tilly attended to business in the office and store, and I was employed drawing pictures of a sabre-toothed tiger being stalked by a prehistoric man, since, for the moment, our history lessons had switched from the Civil War back to the Pleistocene, owing to the arrival of a book on Early Man.

Tilly returned to the house at noon and called on Juma to prepare beef tea. She looked angry and stern; and, glancing at the book on Early Man, remarked: "All those centuries, and nothing much has changed—except of course the hairiness, but that's only on the surface, it seems. When the coffee comes into bearing I think we must get a piano. Lettice would teach you; would you like to learn?"

"Very much," I said, imagining my hand sweeping up and down the keys to create rivers of splendid melody, and the plaudits of a large audience.

"There's not much music in my family," Tilly reflected, "but Highlanders must have some in them, if they could only be kept away from pipes. . . . Well, I suppose I mustn't put this off any longer."

Juma appeared in the door without the beef tea, and said:

"It would be best to leave this thing alone a little longer, memsabu."

"I told them that at noon . . ."

"Kupanya's is a long way off, and if you wait a little perhaps something will be arranged . . ."

"I will wait until two o'clock," Tilly agreed. She looked at once much more cheerful, and began to think the bluff was going to work after all. "It is like walking on ice," she remarked. In reality, it was like living in one world while another co-existed, but the two scarcely ever meshed. Sometimes, when Tilly made a cake, she let me use the beater, which had a red handle that you turned. The two arms of the beater whirled round independently and never touched, so that perhaps one arm never knew the other was there; yet they were together, turned by the same handle, and the cake was mixed by both. I did not think of it at the time, but afterwards it struck me that this was rather how our two worlds revolved side by side.

Robin came back from the shamba much enraged by Sammy, who had left many things undone, and vanished in a most irresponsible way. But at lunch-time we heard that Sammy had returned, and Robin sent for him. No Sammy came, only a message to say that he would report later.

"I think that's a good sign," Tilly said, when Robin showed symptoms of explosiveness. "Sammy may have brought a wizard with him to work the magic, and perhaps there is something going on now."

"I think we've both gone off our heads," Robin grumbled. "We know it's all a lot of tomfoolery, the whole thing is illegal, and here we are playing their game, instead of bundling the whole lot of them in to the D.C. and letting him knock some sense into their heads."

The afternoon slipped by without any striking event, and silently. I had expected something dramatic, perhaps a sound of drumming and song, or the mewing of spirits, or at least a goat's bleat: for all the time I was wondering whether some broken-legged, half-flayed animal was paying with its agony for the restoration of Njombo's hope of life.

At about four o'clock Sammy came to the door. He did not smile, as usual, but looked sulky and subdued, gazed at his feet and said gruffly:

"Come to see Njombo."

At any other time his almost hectoring tone would have angered Tilly, but now she was too relieved and hopeful to mind. She returned in about half an hour with news of victory. Njombo had opened his eyes and allowed a little beef tea and brandy to trickle down his throat. Like the inaugural sap of spring, life had begun to stir hesitantly in his blood.

"When I propped him up, it was like holding up a feather, his very bones seemed weightless," Tilly said. "There was chalk on his face and arms, and a queer smell. Heaven knows what had been going on in there, but whatever it was, I think that it has saved Njombo. And now you must read the riot act to Sammy, and tell him that if it ever happens again he'll be imprisoned."

"We have no proof it was Sammy," Robin pointed out.

"We have no proof of anything. In fact proof itself seems to be an exotic, like those poor little oak trees we planted. Thank Heaven it's over, unless he relapses. And now I want my tea."

How much does one imagine, how much observe? One can no more separate those functions than divide light from air, or wetness from water. It seemed to me that, after tea, everything was different; songs came from the Kikuyu huts, the women laughed like gurgling water as they carried firewood home, the previous day's storm had vanished. Some years later, we had a parrot in a cage fitted with a green baize cover to snuff out the light at bed-time. How odd it must have been for the parrot, I thought, to see day turned to night in a single second; and now it seemed as if a cover had suddenly been lifted from the farm, and daylight had burst upon us all again.

Alec Wilson came over next day full of gossip. It was Kupanya, he said, who had saved Njombo, and Kupanya had intervened only because the storm, coming immediately after our visit, had convinced him that God was angry, and did not wish Njombo to die. "Kupanya didn't give two hoots for the D.C.," Alec said, "but he was a bit reluctant to take on the Almighty."

"It's always a good thing to have friends in high quarters," Tilly remarked.

The chief had sent for a wizard, who had broken the spell, and so cheated Sammy of his revenge. Sammy was furious, for he believed that Njombo, out of jealousy and spite, had killed his young wife by witchcraft and caused the detonator to injure his son. There was no doubt at all that if Kupanya had not changed his mind, Njombo would have run down like an unwound watch, and died.

"I should never have believed it," Tilly said, "unless I'd seen it with my own eyes."

"I suppose we believed in it ourselves until not so very long ago," Alec said.

"Many of us believe in it now," Robin amended. "One of my cousins near Argyll made a wax image of her neighbour, a grumpy old man who won a lawsuit against her about the salmon-fishing, and stuck pins into it, and he got such bad rheumatics that he had to go abroad to take a cure, and ate some bad fish and died of food poisoning."

"He might have got rheumatics anyway, especially in a damp Scotch castle," Alec pointed out.

"It was quite a dry castle," Robin replied, rather huffed. "And the point was he died of poisoning."

"He was over seventy," Tilly said.

"Well, cousin Margaret *thought* she'd killed him, anyway, and was so much encouraged she started on his factor, but the man went to Canada and she never heard whether it worked."

It was remarkable how quickly Njombo recovered, considering that he had been, as Tilly said, as near a goner as made no difference, and looked as bony as a barbel when he first emerged from the hut. He never spoke of his experience to any of us, and we never questioned him, but I always looked upon him as a man who had been raised from the dead.

Chapter Sixteen

ONE day Hereward rode over to ask for Robin's help. The piano had arrived at the station in a crate, and required the united efforts of both farms to convey it to its destination.

"We shall need two span of oxen," Hereward said. "I think we shall have to cut some trees down first to widen the road."

The actual operation took on a military character, with men stationed at strategic points to direct the drivers, others held in reserve at steep places to add manpower to ox-power, and various people warned to keep the track clear on the morning of the move. The worst danger-point was a river crossing with a steep bank on either side. The stream had been roughly bridged with logs, but these were submerged in rainy periods and sometimes washed away, and the banks put a severe strain on our teams. Wagons sometimes ran backwards and Hereward was afraid the grand piano might end up on its back in the stream. His stuffed heads had come too, in several crates, but he scarcely mentioned these, having perhaps concluded that to bring horns to Africa was like conveying cloves to Zanzibar.

We all rode down to Thika to see the crate loaded into a wagon. A gang of lifters had been assembled, a much larger group of onlookers had assembled itself, the Indian station-master bustled round and Hereward, looking as usual perfectly turned-out in jodhpurs, barked brisk orders that no one obeyed and deployed forces who merely ignored his plan of attack.

"I wonder what the boys think is inside," Tilly observed. "A house, perhaps; it's almost as big as one of theirs."

When Njombo, who had by now recovered, and accompanied us on a mule, did in fact inquire, the limitations of our Swahili forced her to reply:

"It is a thing with which you make a noise."

Njombo, startled out of his calm, let out a long exclamation and remarked: "It must be a very big noise indeed."

"Not big, but good. You make it with your hands."

"But who will be able to?"

"Memsabu *Mrefu.*" Hereward's official native name was *mrefu,* meaning tall; but he had another meaning praying mantis, never used to Europeans, I suppose because they might have considered it an insult to be compared with an insect that could be crushed even by a child.

"How can memsabu's hands use such a thing?" Njombo asked sceptically. "It would be a giant's affair."

Tilly gave up trying to explain the piano and stood in the shade of the station-master's tin office to watch Hereward and Robin marshalling their wagon and teams into a suitable position. The piano was eventually loaded upside down, and this made Hereward angry, but he was powerless to reverse it. Lashed to the wagon, it swayed off along the rutted track, a far cry from the concert halls and drawing-rooms for which its makers had doubtless intended it.

"Stupid notion, really," Hereward commented. "Lettice would have it, but what use is a piano out here?"

"I suppose Lettice will enjoy playing it."

"Oh, well, if it makes her any happier, I shall feel it's been well worth while. You're her best friend out here, Tilly, so I can say this to you. I'm worried about Lettice. I sometimes doubt if this is the right life for her. She gets queer notions into her head."

"I haven't noticed it," Tilly said cautiously.

"At one moment she wants a special room built for the piano, a rose-garden with a fountain in it and Italian statues; next day she talks of selling up and going to live in Yorkshire of all places, and pulling strings to get me back into the regiment—which is out of the question, of course. Now she's got it into her head that the natives are trying to poison Chang and Zena; she chops up their food herself and insists on sleeping in the dressing-room with the little beggars and locking the doors. All fads and fancies, one extreme to the other. I wish you'd speak to her, Tilly."

"I shouldn't worry, Hereward; I expect it's the altitude, or the vertical rays of the sun."

Hereward gave a sharp bark like a jackal.

"Just what I told her, but now she wants to go off on this safari of Crawfurd's. Stupid idea—for her, I mean. All right for a fine, strong woman like you."

Tilly looked displeased at the compliment. "It might be good for Lettice. And they say Ian Crawfurd is a splendid shot and knows the country inside out."

"A young puppy, if you ask me. But of course I don't expect my opinions to carry any weight."

We had reached the river, and a crisis was developing upon the farther bank. Egged on by a tremendous shouting, cracking of whips and general furore, the oxen had taken a run at the steep part of the bank and would have crested the rise had not the crate unfortunately caught on the branches of a tree. The oxen heaved in vain, the wagon started to slide backwards, dragging the little beasts after it, and Robin, who was riding by the team, bellowed, "Stone, stone, stone," at the top of his voice. Everyone took up the cry; it echoed round the hillside like a battle-cry while the sliding wagon gathered pace, the frantic oxen scrabbled with their little hoofs and several people tried to hang on to the spokes. A couple of Kikuyu at length rushed up with boulders to put under the wheels, a simple expedient which arrested the runaway in the nick of time. The crate, dislodged by the tree, was now hanging dangerously over to one side, and a few more yards would have seen it topple over and smash itself against the rocks.

A considerable audience had by now sprung out of an apparently deserted countryside to proffer advice, while the drivers and their mates re-told the more dramatic parts of the episode with a great many gestures and pieces of mime, so that one could see again the oxen heaving, the wagon creeping forward, the impact of the tree, the wagon slipping, the oxen giving way, the threatened disaster, the yawning abyss, the heroic struggle of the driver to arrest the wagon and finally the brilliant last-minute triumph of the two men with boulders who flung themselves into a position of danger and saved the day. It was all much more exciting than the actual incident, and I thought Robin and Hereward unkind to cut it short and insist upon the unroping, rearranging and securing of the crate, while the oxen panted, and the audience watched with fascinated eyes.

"Silly idiots," Robin said. "They forgot the wheel-chocks. And I told them about three times."

"What can you expect?" Hereward agreed. "I suppose God gave them brains, but they'll do anything to avoid using 'em."

One could see, then, that the drivers had not been very bright; but what a story they would have to tell when they got home!

The wagon reached the Palmers' without further adventures, and a week or two later we were asked over for a piano-warming. By now they had moved into their stone bungalow, which seemed to everyone the height of luxury; it had three spare rooms, teak floors, bow windows, a bathroom and gables in the Dutch style, with curlecues. Lettice had hoped for a tiled roof, but this was too expensive even for Hereward, and they had fallen back on the usual corrugated iron, painted green.

"You've done your hair in a new way," Tilly remarked. Lettice wore it piled on top of her head in soft, gleaming swathes and she had a fillet of small bronze leaves somehow woven into it.

"I thought I had better dress up like a concert pianist, even if I can't play like one," Lettice explained. "My fingers feel like sausages and make sounds like the wild asses that stamped on Jamsheed's grave, but never mind, I thought we might all sing choruses. Ian has come back, did you know? And wants us all to go off soon with him on the safari."

It was good news about Ian, and I went off hopefully to find him. I had been reading about Prester John, so Abyssinia had become a place of riches and mystery, where princes wore crowns that flashed with rubies, and dwelt in castles set on the cloud-enfolded crests of lowering mountains.

Ian said he had met a prince, but without a crown, though he did have jewels set in the handle of his sword, which he used to cut off chunks of raw meat at a banquet; and a cup-bearer, a boy of twelve or so, had poured the wine from a golden goblet, and knelt on one knee before his prince, after the taster had taken the first sip. And although Ian had seen no castles, he had visited a monastery on top of a hill so steep that no pony could clamber up, inhabited by holy men with long beards, and by five princes, relations of the Emperor, whose eyes had been burnt out in their youth, so that they could never lay claim to the throne nor lead armed revolts against the Lion of Judah.

Hereward was moved to exclaim: "Revolting cruelty! What barbaric devils they are."

"Yes, they are barbarous," Ian agreed, "but they did it to preserve unity and avoid civil wars."

"I see no need to make excuses for them."

"Their point, I suppose, is that it's better to blind four or five young men than to plunge the country into dynastic struggles later on, at the cost of thousands of lives."

"I don't believe they thought of that at all," Hereward said. "You'll be defending next their habit of mutilating prisoners, like the wretched Italians taken at the battle of Adowa."

To change the subject, Ian told us about another and more fortunate prisoner he had met in Addis Ababa. This was a Scot left over from Lord Napier's campaign, now an oldish man of considerable substance and influence with the Emperor. Ian and his friends had wanted to buy more ponies, but Menelik had forbidden their export; the British Minister said he could do nothing and they might as well go home. The Scots ex-prisoner, however, had fixed the whole thing in three days, at a cost to Ian of a hundred pounds in Maria Theresa dollars.

Hereward looked disgusted and said in his stiffest tones: "If you'll forgive me for saying so, I think that an Englishman who resorts to bribery in a nigger country betrays our name to the world."

His words fell like lead into a pool; there was a plop and then silence, while everyone searched for something to say. Lettice observed:

"If the Abyssinians are used to bribery they will go on doing it, and Ian can't reform them single-handed. Besides, when in Rome . . ."

"I have never been able to understand the difference between a bribe and a tip," Robin said. "Yet you are a blackguard if you do give the one, or if you fail to give the other. It is very difficult."

"I suppose it's a question of timing," Ian suggested. "One comes before service, the other after. Would it make you think any better of us, Hereward, to know that we gave him his *pourboire* after he had smoothed our path with Menelik, and not before?"

"You can split hairs if you like," Hereward replied gruffly. "Right's right and wrong's wrong to me."

"You are lucky to see things so clearly," Lettice said.

"There's no luck about it. Right and wrong are there for everyone to see. They are often inconvenient, and therefore people pretend they're obscure as an excuse for dodging them. That's all."

"It is quite enough," Lettice observed. "I can see that I must deputize for Orpheus, without any of his genius. You must please be charitable to me, if not to the Abyssianians or to Ian's morals."

Our ears had grown accustomed to rhythm and dissonance, to cadence and chant, but not to melody. Although Lettice may not have been a player of the first quality, the skill of her hands, darting like butterflies above the keys, in summoning from the instrument a torrent of harmony seemed to me a kind of miracle. A hissing lamp threw a circle of light over her gleaming chestnut hair with the bronze leaves in it, over her pale skin and her dancing hands, and over the piano's shining surface, still and deep as a lake among mountains; this was a moment of magic revealing to us all, for a few moments, a hidden world of grace and wonder beyond the one of which our eyes told us, a world that no words could delineate, as insubstantial as a cloud, as iridescent as a dragon-fly and as innocent as the heart of a rose.

When she had finished her piece there was a silence no one cared to break, it seemed to have a tangible existence of its own. Lettice herself dissolved it by arranging some music and starting to sing. Probably her voice was not the equal of her playing, but it was true and gentle, and she sang lively little songs in French. Ian jumped up and stood beside her, looking over her shoulder, as natural and easy as one of the Somali horsemen whose lives he often shared. I suppose the music had tautened our perceptions and made me see them, together in the lamplight, as something other than they were, more handsome and accomplished, more of the spirit and less of flesh and blood, more of the ideal and less of the matter-of-fact—or had woven for reality a richer garment than it usually wears.

At any rate, they looked very fine, and full of laughter as they sang together songs as light as bubbles, and as gay. Ian's voice was clear and simple and made me think of sherry poured into a crystal glass the Palmers had—the look of it, not the taste, which I did not know. I cannot remember any of the songs that evening except one in which we all joined, the French-Canadian jingle *Alouette*; and afterwards, whenever I heard this little tune, it reminded me of that evening, and Lettice at the piano with Ian by her, the others joining in with more enthusiasm than accuracy, the sense of gaiety and friendship, and the room with a spicy scent peculiar to everything that Lettice owned.

Chapter Seventeen

MOST of the cannibals went home when the Palmers' house was finished, but two or three settled down with wives and families, a little group of aliens stuck like a splinter into the flesh of the Kikuyu. The women wore nothing but a triangle of leather, no larger than my hand, dangling from a string round their waists, but made up for it with a great deal of thick, heavy wire coiled round their arms and legs so tightly that the flesh bulged out like inner tubes on each side of the coil. They walked with a free, upright gait, carried things on their heads instead of on their backs and smoked clay pipes with long stems. The Kikuyu, whose own women wore leather aprons to their knees, thought them indecent, bold hussies and had as little to do with them as possible.

They soon acquired goats which, like all livestock, spent the night in thorn-fenced *bomas* intended to keep out marauding beasts. In this objective, the Kavirondo's *boma* failed. They lost several goats, and accused the Kikuyu of stealing them. The Kikuyu denied this hotly, and blamed a leopard, whose spoor they pointed out nearby. The Kavirondo retorted that the spoor belonged to a harmless hyena and stuck to their charge, and so a *shauri* developed which came to Hereward for settlement.

This word *shauri* was one we used a great deal. It could mean a quarrel, a lawsuit, an arrangement, an agreement, a discussion, a concern—almost anything. Here it meant a contest in rhetoric between Kikuyu and Kavirondo spokesmen. After several hours of this, Hereward gave a judgement of which he was proud. If the Kikuyu are so sure there *is* a leopard, he said, let them catch it, and their case will be proved. If they fail, and if no better evidence can be furnished, they must restore to the Kavirondo a number of goats equal to those which disappeared.

"Unsporting, in a way," Hereward commented. "Traps, I mean. Much rather walk him up and bag him in the open, but there doesn't seem to be much chance of that."

Tilly warned Hereward to take special care of the dogs. They were a favourite food of leopards, who would risk almost anything to catch one. But Hereward had taken the side of the Kavirondo, and was not unduly disturbed.

He paid for this—or, rather, poor Chang did. The Palmers were at dinner, the double doors giving on to their veranda were open and Chang was curled up in a wicker chair outside. Chang and Zena went everywhere with Lettice and it was unusual for Chang not to be at her feet, but he was less than six or seven paces away, and no one imagined any danger. Even just after it had happened, they did not realize anything was wrong. Lettice heard a sort of thump, and something like a tear or gasp, and a faint noise that might have been the chair scraping on the tiles. Hereward got up to look, and saw nothing.

It was dark outside, no moon. Lettice called Chang and when he did not respond Hereward felt in the chair, which he noticed had been slewed round to one side.

Of course there was a great hue and cry. Everyone called and walked about with lamps held high, but saw nothing. At last one of the Kikuyu shouted: he had found the spoor. It was not very clear to Hereward, but everyone else agreed that it was a leopard, unmistakably. No sign of Chang was ever found. I wondered if his hair, poor Chang, would give the leopard indigestion, but Juma said their stomachs were like mincing machines. Once I was shown some leopard droppings that had in them bits of undigested fur from the pelts of mice, of which leopards are fond, though you would think mice too small. By such standards, Chang was quite a large meal.

Lettice drove herself almost into a frenzy with remorse and self-blame. "If I had only called him. . . . If I had only for one single second imagined . . . If only . . ." It was too late. Zena was seldom out of her arms, and she refused to be comforted.

"You've still got Zena," Tilly said.

"They were inseparable. It's like Pyramus losing Thisbe, or Juliet, Romeo; how can Zena live without him? How can I? I expect it's a punishment, only why should it be wreaked on Chang?"

"The best thing is to get another quickly, even when you feel (one always does) that you can never, never bear to have another in his place. Like a tooth."

"No, I shall never get another; I ought to live in a solitary fortress somewhere, fed through a hole in the wall; I bring disaster on everyone I love."

"I don't think you should blame yourself *quite* so much," Tilly suggested cautiously. "Leopards are one of the country's natural hazards, I suppose."

"Hugh has had appendicitis, did I tell you?" Lettice seldom spoke about her son. "He very nearly died, poor little boy, and what good am I to him as a mother?"

"Perhaps you should bring him out."

"That is the one thing I've been hoping for; but Hereward . . . I daresay he's right, in a year's time Hugh will have to go to school, and here there's nothing; but even a year, that seems an eternity; a year would mean everything to me. Now I feel that if he came, I should let him get bitten by a snake, or eaten by a lion, or he would get dysentery or typhoid or malaria. . . ."

When Tilly got home she told Robin that she was going to get another Peke for Lettice, to take her mind off Chang.

"They are very expensive," Robin pointed out.

"Surely the price of a single Peke won't make or break us."

"No, but the bank . . ."

"Well, then, we must blue a bit of capital." That was Tilly's sovereign remedy, but Robin said regretfully:

"I'm afraid it is too late for that."

"I daresay there's something we can sell," Tilly concluded hopefully. She had some turkeys, reared with much care for the Christmas market, and every morning she emerged from what she called her muddle-room, next to the store, with streaming eyes and a red face, having been chopping up the onions they so much appreciated. Now she decided that a pair sold for breeding ought to fetch the price of a small Pekinese.

Meanwhile, a leopard hunt was under way. Hereward went out at dawn with an enormous rifle and an array of amateur trackers, gun-bearers and beaters, but the spoor was soon lost in the bush and long grass. There was no knowing which way the beast had gone. It could follow our little stream to its junction with the Thika and proceed right down to the Athi Plains without encountering much in the way of human habitation. Most of this country had been a no-man's-land between the Kikuyu of the forested uplands and the Masai and Kamba of the plains, so it was neither one thing nor the other, forest nor veld, mountain nor plain. Upstream, the leopard would come to the reserve, which was much more populated, but on the other hand it could also reach forest, and eventually the whole wild mountain range of the Aberdares. Even Hereward had to admit that the choice was too wide to permit of his putting his mind, as a hunter should, into that of the quarry, and locating it by a sort of telepathy, so he reluctantly agreed to fall back on low cunning, rather than to rely on the manlier virtues of skill, endurance and courage.

When it came to low cunning, the Kikuyu were in their element, and it soon appeared that everyone was an expert leopard-trapper, but that many different kinds of trap could be made. You could arrange a contraption by which a poisoned spear fell on top of the quarry, you could dig a pit with poisoned stakes into which it would tumble, you could set a noose for its neck, you could conceal an iron gin that seized it by the foot, you could build a small stockade whose gate closed behind it to capture it alive—there seemed no end to the different techniques. The only thing in common to nearly all methods was the use of goats as bait. Poor goats, they were destined to suffer every kind of torture for the convenience, pleasure or superstition of man.

I forget which kind of trap was first constructed, but I do remember that instead of the leopard it caught a hyena, which none of the Kikuyu would drag away. Hyenas were unclean because they ate corpses, but more than that they were a favourite haunt of dead men's spirits; the creature whose baleful eyes you saw glinting in the darkness just beyond the halo of firelight might, for all you knew, be your grandfather or your uncle, come perhaps to embody retribution for some insult or injury inflicted on him while he was alive.

The fur of this dead hyena was a dingy sort of grey with dirty white spots. Its powerful shoulders tailed away towards long, sloping hind-quarters, a structure that gave it a curious loping motion. Njombo looked at the beast with distaste and said that all hyenas were lame. When I asked why, he pointed at some piebald crows hopping about at a safe distance beyond the vultures, and told me one of his children's tales. Long ago, it appeared, the father of all the piebald crows possessed a gourd with white stuff inside which the hyenas saw, and thought was fat.

"Where did you get that fat?" asked the hyenas. The crow answered: "In the sky, beyond the moon." "Take us there," said the hyenas, "and we will get some of the fat." "Very well," replied the crow. "Catch hold of my feet, and my neck, and my wings." The hyenas did so, and the crow took them up, up, up among the stars. "Can you see anything below?" asked the crow. "No, we can see nothing." "Very well." The crow gave a big kick and flapped his wings and all the hyenas fell off, and dropped to the ground and were killed. All except one. This was a female, and her legs were broken. She gave birth, and the *totos* were born with broken legs, and hyenas have limped ever since that day.

Someone suggested that Mr. Roos would be sure to know the best kind of trap, and to supervise its construction. Tilly had declared a week's holiday for me, because the time had come to graft the citrus trees now standing in glossy-leaved ranks near the house. Neither she nor Robin had ever done any grafting, but she had an illustrated book on the subject and was busy most of the day in the plantation with a knife and twine; so I was allowed to take a note over to Mr. Roos.

Although his farm was next to ours, to go there was like venturing into a foreign land. We seldom saw Mr. Roos—he came and went unpredictably, like an elephant—and his life was full of mystery. He scarcely had what we would call a house, it was a hut like the natives', only with a sort of veranda on one side and a fireplace made of scraps of corrugated iron on the other. A queer smell hung round his encampment, which perhaps originated from the slices of raw meat tied to a pole in a large cage to keep out flies. When this biltong was quite dry, it became as hard as timber, and did not smell unpleasant, but in its earlier stages it drenched the air with a vicious odour. It was strange to see a European's dwelling without a garden, not even a few salvias or daisies, or an attempt at a lawn. The tawny grass of Africa straggled all round the hut, and fat-tailed sheep grazed right up to the veranda on which there stood a bare table, a camp-chair and the white skull of an elephant. There was one touch of colour: a morning glory with its sky-blue flowers climbing up one side of the hut.

My elders considered Mr. Roos a dour and uncommunicative man but he was always friendly when I saw him, which was seldom enough. Sometimes he had a black, bristly beard, sometimes a rim of stubble giving him a saturnine look. His hat was even older, dirtier and more battered than Robin's, and instead of boots he wore sandals that he made himself from eland or kongoni hide. His face was creased like the bark of an olive tree, and almost as dark, but he had light-blue eyes that looked odd in such a setting, and a wide smile that deepened all his crinkles and exposed a few yellow, ill-assorted teeth. Most of these had been knocked out when he had been trampled by a buffalo, and he had a deep scar up the inside of one arm where it had gored him, and no doubt other and less visible injuries as well. I thought of him as carved out of wood, he was so hard and brown.

Mr. Roos was cutting skeys for his yokes with a bush-knife from branches of thorn. He put the note into his pocket without even glancing at it and said:

"Not often you come riding this way. Neighbours and strangers, eh? How you like it now I show you the nest of——" he added a word I have long since forgotten, which sounded something like *boomklop*, and of whose meaning I had no idea. I nodded nervously.

"You come with me."

Mr. Roos led the way round to the back of his hut and I followed, wondering what a *boomklop* was and whether I was really to see one, or whether Mr. Roos had some sinister motive in view. At home he was said to be "slim", and to trade with the natives for sheep and cattle in a manner described as sailing close to the wind. Perhaps the *boomklop* was only an excuse and he was going to capture me and sell me to someone, though I could not imagine to whom, and for what purpose. Or perhaps he would turn me into biltong, or dry my skin for sandals, or even feed me to the *boomklop*, which might be a large, angry beast with horns like a rhino and jaws like a crocodile.

I hung back, and suggested to Mr. Roos that he should read the note in his pocket.

"Plenty of time for that," he said. "You know what's down there inside, I bet?"

"It's about the leopard."

Mr. Roos stopped dead, and asked questions. His face never showed what he was thinking, but I felt that he was pleased.

Now that I was close to him, I could see little streaks of grime embedded in the crevasses of his leathery neck so deeply that obviously no one could remove them by ordinary washing. The air smelt sharply of hides and alum. Skins as hard and stiff as boards, their livid, sinewy undersides exposed to the sun, were pegged out on a flat space behind his hut, and skulls with horns attached, and flesh in various stages of decomposition, lay about in the grass attracting flies. It was all rather sinister. Pointing to a pegged-out skin, Mr. Roos remarked:

"You see that, man? Ten feet from nose to tail, a beauty. And what a trek, for three days he led me and he was the one was first tired. He got four legs, you see, and I got two, but that don't help him none."

"You must be good at walking," I said politely.

"Man, I walked from Bulawayo, and with an ox-whip in my hand."

"Is that farther than Nairobi?"

He laughed in a chuckling manner, tucking in his chin, and said that it was, and started downhill towards the river where the *boomklop* was. This creature was growing more and more alarming, and besides, might well be miles and miles away. So I managed to stammer out, feeling dishonourably craven, that I must take back an immediate answer and leave the *boomklop* for another day.

"You think I eat little girls?" Mr. Roos demanded, in a rather threatening voice.

As this appeared, in alliance with the *boomklop*, only too likely, I found myself tongue-tied. Mr. Roos relented and turned back, saying he would find another *boomklop* next time I came, and that I was to say he would be over later to fix a trap for the leopard. His tone had a definite edge of contempt for us poor *rooinek* incompetents who could not fix a trap, nor shoot so large a lion, nor walk from Bulawayo, and whose young even showed a disposition to be afraid of the *boomklop*.

When he came over, he scorned Hereward's trap. For one thing it had a live bait, whereas a hunk of high, stinking meat was what leopards really appreciated. They hoarded meat, Mr. Roos told us, in the branches of trees where hyenas and jackals could not reach it. Also they were clever, and when they came upon a live, tethered goat they suspected trickery. So Mr. Roos put some foetid meat in the fork of a tree, just out of reach, and concealed near the tree's foot a wicked steel gin with jagged, rusty teeth, which Hereward regarded with deep disapproval.

"Not at all a sporting sort of thing."

"You want sport, or you want your cattle alive?" Hereward of course wanted both, but Lettice was in such a state of mind about her dead Chang and threatened Zena that above all he wanted to see the dead leopard at his feet.

The trap was cleverly laid. It was in a patch of bush that invited the animal to approach the tree from one direction only, and so well concealed that, even when you knew it was there, you could not detect it.

For two nights nothing happened. Then we heard, first thing in the morning, that a leopard had been caught, but had escaped. Robin had no love for Mr. Roos, so was delighted with this proof of his fallibility.

"Never did think the fellow knew what he was talking about. Now he's landed us all with an infuriated wounded leopard. Well, it'll be up to him to finish it off. Always were a boastful lot, these Dutchmen. . . ."

It was Twinkle's safety that worried me. If the leopard would take Chang off a veranda, Twinkle roaming about the farm and garden invited tragedy. She slept in a lean-to shed next to the store, but in the daytime she had taken to wandering off goodness knows where. (Sometimes we did know, however: once she walked to a bed of young coffee trees and nipped off all their heads, and on another occasion demolished our entire bean crop.) When Randall Swift arrived to pay a call she bounded out from behind a bush and tumbled him off his bicycle. She had taken to playing hide-and-seek with the dogs, but Robin's favourite, a spaniel growing old and fat and called Bancroft (after the actor, to whom Robin had seen a resemblance when young), refused to play and slunk off into corners in a state of mournful gloom whenever Twinkle put her black, quivering nose round the door. Twinkle teased him unmercifully, while he glared at her with a pathetic mixture of supplication and loathing. So both Robin and Tilly were against Twinkle and wanted to get rid of her, although they did not want the leopard to do it for them. No one could quite escape Twinkle's charm, and anyway she had entrusted herself to our protection.

Chapter Eighteen

NOW that the leopard was wounded, things were serious; knowing himself doomed, with nothing to lose, he might well try to bring a valedictory revenge down upon his enemies. So a leopard-hunt was swiftly organized.

I rode with Robin and Tilly to the scene of the escape, where a lot of people had already assembled. The leopard had not dragged the trap away, as we had supposed. There it was, on the end of its chain, with a lot of fur and blood on it. Where it had been concealed, the bush was trampled and uprooted, grass carried the rusty stains of blood, and bits of yellow fur clung to thorns. There had been a terrific lashing about, a scene of turmoil, rage and agony, until the beast had freed himself by the most desperate expedient imaginable. He had evidently bitten off his own torn, bleeding foot to gain his freedom.

Even Mr. Roos shook his head. "Never known it happen before. Man, he's a *kali* one, this is." *Kali* was another word we made much use of, it meant fierce or bold, savage or bad-tempered, and on the whole it was a term of respect.

Most of the Palmers' Kikuyu labour had turned back into warriors, simply by abandoning their pangas, bringing out their long-bladed spears and wearing their vermilion-sheathed swords, and they were standing about excitedly talking, or else without words, as tense as coiled springs, staring into the bush with eyes brightened by anticipation, and all the old dreams of warriors' glory flooding back into their hearts.

Hereward and Alec Wilson, also, had a new urgency and vigour about their movements and voices, and looked pleased and purposeful. Even Robin was thoroughly awake, and grinning broadly. Only Mr. Roos seemed quite unaltered, but then the hunt was his normal element. The leopard had been tracked to a patch of thick bush and boulders on the bank of the river a mile or two upstream, and there he was no doubt angrily lying.

"I don't know what you fellows think," Hereward remarked, indicating that he had at any rate decided what they were to do. "Country's too thick to beat through—wouldn't be fair on the beaters. I'll go in and walk him up with the four-fifty; that'll settle the beggar's hash if he tries any nonsense. You three go ahead to cut off his retreat and bag him if he breaks back towards the reserve. Alec, you see that bluff above the bit of bush he's lying up in? That's your stand. Robin, will you go down by the river near that patch of reeds? And Roos, will you cross the river and get up by that big tree where you'll be able to command the bank opposite, and pick him off if he gets past the others?"

Although Hereward put his orders in the form of questions, these were not intended to be answered; the hunt was taking place on his land, so he had the right to direct it. But Mr. Roos was not a directable man. When Robin and Alec strode off obediently to take up their allotted places, Mr. Roos, squatting on his heels like a Kikuyu (a most useful position to master), continued to unravel the trap and its chain without paying any attention to the plan of campaign.

Hereward slid back his forehead in his peculiar manner, which could presage a smile or a display of icy displeasure, and pointed out that he could not proceed until Mr. Roos had taken up his forward position.

"You go ahead, man, finish him, the skin is yours."

"Good God! Is that all you're thinking of, the brute's hide?"

Hereward glared at Mr. Roos's back as if at some robber of the poor-box caught in the act, and walked off without another word. When he spoke to Tilly his tone was usually mellow and ingratiating, but now he was so offended that he positively barked at her, telling her to take me back at once to the safety of the house, and to succour Lettice.

"If you'll lend me a rifle I'll take Mr. Roos's place," Tilly suggested. Nothing caused her more distress than to be left out of anything that promised interest and novelty. As for fear, she was without it, at least so far as it concerned the animal kingdom; she was sometimes nervous in the presence of machinery.

"Have you gone out of your mind?" Hereward demanded, quite unkindly. "I'm not going to have a woman under my protection exposed to danger from a wounded beast."

"It seems to be very much outnumbered," Tilly remarked. "At any rate I shall watch the hunt, and you can't say I'm not protected here, with all these heavily armed warriors."

Hereward visibly disapproved, but did not like to order her away in case, like Mr. Roos, she should reveal herself as a rebel.

"And then they say these Dutchmen are all born hunters," he muttered. "Hunters my foot! Damned box-wallahs, that's all. Only interested in what they get for the pelt. Not an atom of sportsmanship in 'em. . . ."

The Kikuyu were not avid hunters like the Masai, who made a martial exercise of it, and dressed up in splendid finery to ring a lion with spears, goad him to the charge and then impale him. Nevertheless they enjoyed a hunt, and their spears had been lying a long time unused, thrust into the thatch of their huts; now they had brought them out in high spirits, and hoped perhaps to be brushed by the golden wings of glory and fanned by the hot breath of danger, and to have a topic for the harvest songs, and for lighting in the hearts of the young women a little flame of worship for the splendour and courage of the young men.

It was sad for them to stand about on the hillside, all dressed up and nowhere to go, because of Hereward's edict. Of course Hereward was only acting like a good officer who does not risk the lives of his men if it can be avoided, and puts himself in the position of greatest danger. A wounded leopard is (as he would have put it) a nasty customer, and a spearman no match for him. No doubt Hereward was acting correctly, but the young men were left baulked and silent on the hillside, like guests asked to a banquet, and anticipating golden wine in crystal goblets, stuffed quails and peacocks' tongues and perhaps rose-bud-breasted dancing girls, only to be offered ham sandwiches and weak, lukewarm tea on the trestle tables and hard benches of an institute hall.

When you read descriptions of hunts, it all seems very clear and sensible, everyone concerned knows what he is about; but when you watch one there is little to be seen, and events do not follow one another with logical coherence.

On this occasion nothing happened for a long time and I soon grew bored; even Moyale had cropped all the grass he wanted and stood half asleep, swishing his tail and twitching his ears to keep in circulation some of the innumerable flies. I fell into a conversation with Njombo but Tilly hushed me, in case our voices should disturb the hunt. Mr. Roos had disappeared. We did not see him go; the bush, or long brown grass, or reedy river-bed, had swallowed him. In his nondescript, untidy and unmended khaki clothing he blended immediately into his surroundings like an antelope or lion. Somehow I did not think that he intended to be left out of the hunt. We could not see Alec, but in the distance Robin's hat could be discerned protruding from behind a rock.

Once or twice we caught a glimpse of Hereward's head and shoulders advancing at a slow pace through the green patch of bush about half-way up the bank. He was following the leopard's spoor, and it must have been a jumpy business, for he could see ahead no more than two or three yards, and might well find himself upon it before he had the time to raise his rifle. His gunbearer, who carried a second weapon, was said to have been in his youth an askari attached to one of the trading expeditions that used to trudge from the coast to Uganda and back again, and therefore to be reliable and iron-nerved, but no one had seen him in action, or knew whether his claim was true. Alec and Robin were too far off to be of any help to Hereward if the wounded leopard were to pounce.

When the silence was at last broken, everything was confused. There was a very loud shot, no doubt from Hereward's enormous ·450 (which kicked like an ostrich), and then another almost at once, and a sound like the sudden rip of calico, and a shout, all mixed up. The warriors beside us emitted short, sharp sounds like barks, and in the distance Robin's hat appeared above the rocks, waving in the air. Then came an outbreak of other sounds: a shout, a rifle shot but not so loud, a crashing in the bush, a hubbub from the warriors. Tilly had a pair of binoculars and I heard her cry suddenly in a stiff voice: "Look out!" and then expel her breath in a moaning gasp. The control that had held back the Kikuyu snapped: they poured down the slope shouting and waving their spears, too late to use them, but taut as violin strings, musky with excitement and leaping with long strides like reedbuck from hummock to boulder and through the tufted grass. I tried to follow on Moyale, but Tilly seized the reins.

"Wait," she ordered. "Something went wrong, there was another leopard, I don't know . . ."

But she caught sight of Hereward's hat just before the warriors closed in, and we picked our way down the hill.

The tension in the air had affected our ponies and even Moyale jiggled and pranced, perhaps reminded by the shots and by smells whose impact was too light for our blunted senses to record—smells of cordite and blood and exhalations of fear and anxiety—of his youth upon the plains of Ogaden where he had chased giraffe or even lions, stung by the long spurs of his hard-sinewed, spear-hurling riders. The warriors had already started their thumping step around a circle, knees bent, buttocks out, swaying from side to side like running ostriches. They were chanting in short, sharp, open-throated bursts which would soon coalesce into an almost endless paean, links in a chain of throbbing sound. They made way for our ponies and we pushed through to the group in the centre where Hereward, like a stork, over-topped the others and glowed with gratified pride.

There were indeed two leopards, lying perhaps fifteen yards apart, half-hidden in grass of the same buff-yellow as their coats. One had a red-mangled stump for a leg and the flies were buzzing round it quite oblivious of people, intent only on slaking their greed; its fur was stained and matted, its blue, rubbery lips drawn back to reveal sharp, yellow incisors and to impart to its round, cat-like face a most ferocious expression, the embodiment of savagery. And indeed with its mangled leg, its hunted end, it had every reason to be savage, but Hereward's rifle had deprived it even of the final satisfaction of revenge.

The other leopard lay stretched out as if asleep, and I could at first see no injury, and for a moment drew back fearing it might not really be dead. It was a perfect animal; the soft skin with its barbaric markings lay like velvet over the stilled muscles and you felt that, should you touch a wiry whisker, the beast would leap up as if you had released a spring, and vanish like a rocket.

Nervously, I touched the leopard; the flesh was warm, it seemed impossible that anything so splendid, so magnificently made and so instinct with life should be lying there drained and empty. I fingered one of its great pads, large as a plate, rough as sandstone and yet springy and yielding, and ran a hand down the great sweep of its flank, built for speed like the flank of a race-horse; I could feel hard sinews under a silk-soft skin and sense perfection of design, not a single wasted molecule of tissue, nothing in excess, nothing lacking, nothing ugly or misshapen, the whole thing moulded by its purpose into a miraculous yellow engine of speed, ferocity and skill. Why did it have to be dead and useless, the agents of putrefaction at work already in its clotting blood? I knew the answer that satisfied my elders—it had failed to respect their property, their goats and calves and dogs, but it was a beast so much finer than the miserable goats it preyed upon—finer even than poor Chang—that for a moment, as I touched the leopard, that answer seemed ridiculous; rather one would have offered goats as tributes to a creature so imperial.

Mr. Roos, with a torn shirt-sleeve, was bending down to stroke the pelt as I had done, but with a different purpose. He, like Hereward, looked satisfied.

Hereward had already thanked Mr. Roos, not I expect with the best of grace, for saving his life. For Hereward had shot the wounded leopard successfully, and was bending over its corpse, when its mate, whose presence he had not suspected, came at him from the bush without a sound. Mr. Roos, who had almost miraculously been in the right position, dropped her just as she was about to leap on top of Hereward and demolish him. He swung round in time to see her topple over, dead.

"I can't think how the devil you managed to be in the right place," Hereward said, rather grumpily. "If it was luck, it seems incredible."

Mr. Roos shook his head and chuckled. "Not luck, man. Where you find one *chui*, you look for two, the mate."

"I still don't see how you looked just *there*."

The steep bank was full of little rocky bluffs and heaps of boulders poking through the shrubs. Mr. Roos pointed to one ahead of us.

"There is a likely place, those rocks. I think to myself: that is where the mate will be. I will look: if she is there, I shoot her; if she is not, I do no harm. She is there, she come, and so I shoot her."

It sounded as easy as making a pot of tea, and perhaps it was to Mr. Roos, whose own wildness had not quite been bred away, and who used a rifle as if it were an extra limb.

"I keep the skin, eh?"

"Of course, my dear fellow." Hereward glanced down at it

and realized, with a slight frown, that it was by far the better pelt of the two. "Worth a bit, I daresay," he added.

Mr. Roos gripped a fold in his fingers and let it go. "A few rupees, maybe," he agreed cautiously, unable to suppress a tinge of complacency.

"He didn't care two hoots about my life," Hereward remarked later. "All he was after was a good skin."

"It was lucky that he saved yours in the process," Tilly replied. "He must have known there was another leopard all the time, and never said a word to anyone."

"Afraid one of us would bag it and claim the skin. Never mind if someone gets killed. . . . Not an ounce of sportsmanship, just as I said."

To have his life saved by a man with no sporting instincts, and a Boer at that, must have been a great trial for Hereward; he would perhaps have rather received a mauling and strangled the creature with his bare hands, as people were reputed to have done.

"I sometimes wonder whether Lettice cares any more than that Dutchman if I get a mauling," he remarked gloomily as we rode along.

"How can you, Hereward!"

"Of course, I wouldn't say this to anyone but you. You're an understanding woman, Tilly. . . . I think she'd pay more attention to me if I was a dog."

"Well, you would need it then. Dogs have to be de-ticked every day, besides expecting constant reassurance that everyone loves them."

"Men need that too," Hereward said heavily, as if about to reach painfully for his martyr's crown.

Lettice did not in the least justify Hereward's gloom. She was delighted to see us all return safely, horrified to hear of Hereward's adventures and apparently thankful for his delivery.

"You must be careful, Hereward, you must be careful," she cried, "although of course that is a silly thing to say to any man; no man likes to be careful and, if he does, no woman trusts him, it betrays a finicky, suspicious nature, the sort of man who would set traps—not for leopards, I mean, but perhaps for wives. . . . And the poor leopard, I'm glad it was put out of its pain, but the mate, how tragic, and how faithful—faithful unto death without a lot of public vows. How much nicer animals are than we are, when we get to know them!"

"The leopard wasn't going to be nice to Hereward," Tilly pointed out.

"*Le léopard est un méchant animal; quand l'on attaque, il se défend.* Well, I suppose we are all like that, though not so graceful as the leopard, and we kill our food before we eat it, which perhaps is kinder—though not in the case of oysters, if you come to think of it. . . . Where is Mr. Roos? If he saved your life, Hereward, oughtn't we to offer him a cup of coffee?"

"He's got the best pelt," Hereward replied sourly, but he did invite Mr. Roos, who sat on the veranda twiddling between his knees his old hat, with a strip of leopard-skin round it in place of a band, and talking of the animals he had killed in different places—lions and elephants, buffaloes and rhinos; and discussing with Hereward the merits of different kinds of rifle, large and small. When at last he left he grinned at me and said: "You come soon again to visit me, and see the *boomklop*, eh?"

I had been worrying about the *boomklop* on and off all through the leopard hunt, for in retrospect I seemed to have been absurdly timid, indeed cowardly, about a creature that was probably a mere bird; and in any case, whatever it was, Mr. Roos would obviously have it strictly under control. In fact I was by now thoroughly ashamed of my behaviour and blushed, not wanting the others to know.

"May I come soon?" I asked, anxious to redeem my shame as quickly as possible.

"Any time, man. Jump on your pony and come."

I saw at once from Tilly's expression that she was displeased.

"What is a *boomklop*?" she inquired, when Mr. Roos had gone.

"I don't know," I truthfully answered.

"Of course you know. It seems to be something Mr. Roos showed you."

"He didn't show me, because . . ."

"Because what?"

This was becoming horrible. I could not reply, "Because I was frightened." So I said lamely: "Well, someone came . . ."

"Is this a thing he can only show you in *private*?" Tilly inquired, now looking quite alarmed.

"Surely he would hardly . . ." Lettice said, in tones equally perturbed.

"One never knows, with these . . ." Tilly suggested darkly.

"Of course, living alone . . ."

"Unless it's true about the native girl . . ."

No one seemed able to finish a sentence, and I felt that some dreadful penalty was in the wind for no crime at all—a situation that often seemed about to arise, and sometimes did so, although I suppose there could be room for disagreement on the definition of a crime.

"The *boomklop* has a nest," I said firmly.

"A *what*?" Tilly asked, as if she could not believe her ears.

"Well, Mr. Roos said so. Of course he didn't have time . . ."

"Whatever happens, you are *not* to ride over there alone again. And if Mr. Roos ever offers to show you a *boomklop* you are to refuse at once, do you understand?"

"Perhaps it would be a good thing to give her a whistle, and if she finds herself in trouble she could blow for help," Lettice suggested.

"But would anyone come?"

"That is a difficulty," Lettice agreed. "The nearest policemen are nearly forty miles away and probably they aren't trained to whistles. Perhaps Hereward was right after all about Hugh."

"I shall simply have to be more careful in future not to let her out of my sight."

It now looked as if I had been right about the *boomklop*; it seemed to be a most ferocious creature, not one to be trifled with. I pictured a nest the size of a thorn-bush, eggs like those of ostriches and a sort of dragon with fire coming out of its nose. Even so, I felt that Mr. Roos would have its measure and, now that I was expressly forbidden to see it, I made up my mind to ride over to Mr. Roos's at the first opportunity and ask him to show me the nest.

Chang was avenged: but Zena was lonely, and had no heart for the short walks with Lettice she had previously enjoyed so much. Tilly was already in correspondence with Roger Stilbeck, who knew someone who bred Pekinese. They were very expensive, and Tilly discovered that she would have to sell most of her turkeys, not merely a pair, to pay for a single puppy.

"You'd be mad to do it," Robin advised, for once playing the part of the cautious, level-headed male. "Think what they'll be worth at Christmas. Besides, the Palmers can perfectly well afford a dozen Pekes if they want them. They are much richer than us."

"Money's beside the point; Lettice is miserable, and I want to do what little I can to cheer her up."

"Surely there must be some cheaper way," Robin suggested.

"When the puppy grows up, Lettice can breed from Zena, and I'm sure she'll give me one of the litter; and then we can sell it, and get our money back."

"I suppose that's all right, if you can get rid of the things."

"Get *rid* of them? This friend of Roger Stilbeck's has a waiting list two years long. In fact, we might do better to buy another Peke, when we get a puppy from Lettice, and do some breeding ourselves. There's going to be money in pedigree dogs, just like horses; and if we could get in on the ground floor . . ."

Before the turkeys could be sold, Tilly received a birthday present from her sister, who had come into a windfall—whether a rising share, a lucky bet or an inheritance I cannot remember; anyway, she sent Tilly £25. This was looked on as an act of God; Tilly went into Nairobi and bought Lettice a Pekinese puppy for £10, a new saddle and a second-hand ram which Robin wanted to install to pump our water from the river, and save the oxen a steep, slippery climb.

The puppy came out with the rupees on Robin's next monthly trip to Nairobi: a small, cream-coloured ball of fluff with a bright pink tongue, two beady eyes and a tremendous fund of energy. Lettice was delighted with it, and called it Puffball.

Chapter Nineteen

ROBIN decided that he was too busy to go on the safari Ian Crawfurd had arranged, and Tilly said she would not go without him; but he urged her so earnestly to seize the chance, and Hereward implored her so convincingly to keep Lettice company, that she gave way, and the bustle of a coming departure stirred the life of the farm. Ian was collecting porters, equipment and stores in Nairobi, but Tilly wanted to contribute, and for some days there was a great roasting of chickens, a boiling of marmalade and a concocting of lotions according to a most valuable formula, handed down by a member of the family who had lived in India, which infallibly healed bites, alleviated sunburn and prevented the festering of sores.

Ian marched the safari out from Nairobi and camped at Thika, and Tilly and the Palmers rode down to meet him there accompanied by Robin and myself, who were to breakfast with them at the Blue Posts and see them leave for their long journey.

As we descended the last bit of hill above the Blue Posts, we saw the safari passing just below. The porters were marching smartly with their morning strength and chanting a vigorous song. Their loads were of all shapes and sizes: long tent-poles which, though jointed, poked out such a distance fore and aft that to manœuvre them through bush must have presented appalling difficulty; a tin bath full of lanterns; folding chairs and tables; rolls of bedding; chop-boxes of food; everything you could think of. It was a miniature army on the march, guarded by three or four askaris looking fierce and superior with nothing to carry but their rifles and water-bottles. The porters wore all sorts of nondescript clothing—tattered shorts, vests consisting mostly of holes, football stockings, discarded great-coats, red blankets. This was a working safari, not one of the de luxe affairs equipped by the firm of Newland, Tarlton & Co., whose porters marched forth in long blue jerseys, like those worn by police askaris, with the letters "N & T" stitched on in red. It was a rule or custom, I do not know which, among safari outfitters to present each porter with a pair of boots—much too good a pair to spoil by wearing, which in any case cramped and distorted the feet; so every man set forth with a pair of boots tied round his neck.

As the porters swung by with their bobbing loads, their song of challenge rose among the rocks, a dusty halo hung about the backs of the rear-guard askaris, two men left behind with slipping loads half-walked, half-ran after them, and the column wound out of sight along the wagon-road that dipped to cross the river by a log bridge. They were gone, marching to far romantic places beyond the last farm, the ultimate shamba, where the wild game of Africa had their wide plains and secret reeded water-holes all to themselves, and when you camped among the thorns beside a dry sand-river, and dug for moisture in the hot sand, it might be that you were treading where no man, white or black, had ever set his foot before. It was a moment to lift the heart, but also to fill the mind with anguish because the others were going, and I was left behind, and would never see these far imagination-torturing places, or taste the solitudes where nature keeps her pure and intricate balance free from the crass destructiveness of man.

"You shall come on a safari when you're older," Tilly promised, noticing my state of mind.

"I shall never be older," I said gloomily.

"You will be older tomorrow. You will even be a bit older when you get back to the farm."

"How wonderfully lucky you are," Lettice added, "to be glad of that, and not sorry!"

"Children are always being told they are lucky to have things they hate," said Robin, "like plenty of time ahead of them, and expensive educations, and healthy food, and considerate parents. It must be very annoying."

"Perhaps it's as bad to feel one isn't getting old fast enough, as to know that one is getting old too fast," Lettice agreed. "We are always trying to make time go at a different pace, as if it were an obstinate pony. Perhaps we should do better to let it amble along as it wishes, without taking much notice of it."

"That is what the natives do," Tilly said.

"And perhaps that is why they seem happier. Perhaps it is all a mistake, our trying to change them, and introduce new worries, like Time's wingéd chariot hurrying near. And yet, those awful sores, and bloated spleens. . . . It will be a nice change to get away from them into the wilds, like a visit to the Garden of Eden before Adam's tiresome curiosity started all our trouble. And here is Ian, managing to look urbane in spite of his bushman's outfit; and I hope he has ordered a good breakfast, the last we shall have in civilization (if the Blue Posts is that) for I wonder how long?"

They were to travel first across the plains below the Kikuyu highlands, alive with game and infested with ticks, to Meru on the northern slopes of Mount Kenya, the last place where they could buy food. From Meru they were to head northwards, beyond the Guaso Nyiro river, to Archers' Post, where the shooting was excellent and water plentiful. After that, they would see. To the north lay four hundred miles of desert and then the Abyssinian mountains; to the west, more desert, great ranges of kudu-sheltering hills and that strange, remote, enormous lake, set in a waste of sand and lava, discovered only some twenty years before by the German von Höhnel and called after Prince Rudolph of Austria; to the east, more desert still, and then the death of the Guaso Nyiro in the marshes of the Lorian swamp. All around them would lie mystery and harshness, where nature was filed down to the bone, where every drop of water was hoarded by some animal or plant, and birds managed with a mist of dew that only sometimes brushed the wiry grasses which crept in ropes along the ground to search for nourishment; where beasts grew elongated necks to pluck shoots from tree-tops, and spiky thorns gave birth to flowers or leaves at different seasons, not both at once, and for half the year looked as black and dead as old iron.

It was as well that Ian knew this country, for it had no tracks or settlements, and if you ran out of water you would die within a few days. Ian had been across it several times to Abyssinia on the business of the Boma Trading Company, which had been started by three or four enthusiastic young men with a thousand pounds between them, a charter from the Emperor Menelik and the blessings of the Foreign Office, to open up a trade between the Ethiopians and the Protectorate. So far the trade had consisted mainly of tough little Somali ponies which the Ethiopians were reluctant to part with, and the superior cattle of the Boran.

The moving spirit was Jack Riddell, a friend of Ian's, a young soldier who had quitted the Army to seek adventure in Africa. Where he could not find adventure, he created it; in Nairobi he would ride his pony into the bar of the Norfolk hotel or shoot out the street lamps along Government Road; in Abyssinia he would gallop his ponies across the terrain of a hostile baron pursued by swordsmen, drink *taj* and boast of his prowess with more friendly rulers all night, and he was reputed to conduct a flourishing illicit trade in ivory. There was a story that the Governor, having vowed to catch him, and mounted a guard over every water-hole on the route from the frontier, was prophesying, at a garden party, that this time the villain would be laid by the heels, when Jack Riddell walked up, bowed respectfully and shook hands.

At the Blue Posts we ate a large breakfast, and sat in the veranda while Hereward busied himself checking girths and bridles, and once more examining the armoury, helped with an air of lofty disdain by Ahmed, clad now in a khaki suit but with a green shawl loosely wrapped round a proud, small head held on a slender neck as erect as a tulip—a little like the gerenuks and giraffe soon to be his companions. Ahmed was headed for his own land, his own people, and there was a suggestion of eagerness and tension in his bearing.

"I would entrust my life to him a dozen times over," Ian said, "but if an unarmed, harmless youth annoyed him, he'd be as likely to stick a knife into him as to hold my stirrup when I mount, and think no more of it either." And he told us more of Ahmed's people: of the constant fights between the tribes, the deeds of bravery, the feats of endurance in this desert world so different from our own and existing side by side with ours, absorbed in its own life and struggles, and quite oblivious of us and of all our complications and intentions.

"They wear white robes, and gaily coloured skirts, and turbans as bright as jewels," Ian said, "and shawls thrown over their shoulders, and swords at their belts, and they can ride any pony born, and walk for three days across the lava rock without water or the camels' milk they live on, which makes them lean and strong and gives a healthy bloom to their skins. When the time comes for them to move on, they strap their dismantled dwellings, made of sticks and mats, on to the backs of their camels, with the big leather water-bags and all their household goods, and trek away to other wells and pans that hold the water on which all life depends. They worship Allah, and think no man fit to take a wife who hasn't killed an enemy; but they respect cunning, and if they can outwit you and take you unarmed, so much the better. They do not fear death as we do; it will come to all, and cannot be avoided, like storm or famine, so must be taken as it comes."

The time came for their departure; I cried, and so did Tilly, when she said good-bye; and we watched them mount their mules and jog away along the dusty road, and turn to wave at the corner, and disappear round a bend of the road.

It was tame and sad to ride back to the farm, which seemed dead and empty in spite of its usual activities, and to go on with ordinary living. Robin had desired with all his heart to go with the others, but the still he was putting up to make essential oils had reached a critical condition, and someone had to look after the farms, both ours and Hereward's. I was delivered like a parcel to Mrs. Nimmo, together with instructions that I was to weave a receptacle for dead-heads (Tilly had taken up basket-work from a book), memorize the Kings of England and the *Lady of Shalott*, learn the multiplication tables (which had somehow got overlooked) and the life-cycle of the liver-fluke, and draw the signs of the Zodiac. I was to have an examination when they returned and if I was successful I would get another saddle for Moyale (his was almost in pieces), whereas if I failed I should have to go to bed early for a week.

Twinkle was the main reason why I did not want to go to Mrs. Nimmo's. Not only did I hate parting from her, but I was afraid that she would meet with some disaster. At night she was safe in her hut, but by day she wandered sometimes to the river and had been seen to drink from the pool beside our coffee nursery, just below the waterfall, where the python lived. In some ways he was a harmless reptile—he did not emerge from the pool to threaten people working in the nursery—but if anything was rash enough to venture into the water, or to stand on its edge, he satisfied his hunger.

Robin had resolved to kill the python, but it was cunning and elusive; after swallowing its prey it disappeared, perhaps into a cave behind the waterfall, and he had never been able to get a shot at it. I had seen it once or twice—a glistening black and speckled coil on a black rock, its body thick as a man's thigh, like a wicked elemental shape spewed up from the ocean's caverns. I was haunted by the fear of Twinkle being sucked, still breathing, down the great black tunnel of its body, to be digested alive.

When I expressed these fears to Njombo he said, perhaps half mockingly:

"Why do you not get a charm to protect her from the python?"

I asked him where one could be got.

"From the *mundu-mugo*; he has charms for everything, and certainly one against a snake."

Mundu-mugos were the good witch-doctors, the anti-sorcerers, and it seemed that several lived close at hand, either on our farm or on those of our neighbours.

"Would it be expensive?" I inquired.

"No, because you are a child. If you gave him one rupee . . ."

"But I haven't got a rupee."

Njombo laughed to reassure me. "Perhaps he will do it just to help you. I will see."

The *mundu-mugo* turned out to be a thin, light-coloured man with a narrow nose and sharp eyes who worked for Alec Wilson and belonged, in some complicated manner, to Kupanya's family. Mrs. Nimmo allowed me to ride over to tea with Robin several times a week, provided I was escorted by Njombo, who was by this time accepted as a trustworthy chaperon. So we left early, and Njombo took me to the *mundu-mugo's* dwelling, which lay across a log bridge just above the waterfall, and we sat down in the shade of a tree. Njombo had told me to bring a few hairs from Twinkle's coat; I had snipped them off and carried them in a match-box, and I also brought a pencil for a present, and a packet of needles.

The *mundu-mugo* carried with him on his business two or three long gourds with stoppers made of cows' tails, and some smaller gourds, the size of snuff-bottles, containing all sorts of powders and medicines, hanging by fine chains from his neck. He scooped a little depression in the earth and laid in it a banana leaf, like a dish, and poured some brown liquid into it from an old whisky bottle. It was a great relief to me that we did not have to sacrifice a goat and use the undigested contents of its stomach, the basis of so many Kikuyu potions and magics. After he had added various powders from his gourds, Twinkle's hairs, one or two feathers and some ground chalk, and stirred it all into a paste, he built round it a little *boma* of twigs from a particular shrub, and uttered a number of incantations, at the same time smearing paste on his neck, wrists and ankles. Then he wrapped the remaining paste neatly in a leaf and presented it to me with the air of a marshal proffering the crown on a velvet cushion.

"You are to rub this on the head and legs of the animal," he told me, "and put a little on his tongue, and then he will be able to go to the river and the snake will leave him alone."

I thanked the *mundu-mugo* warmly but he refused both my presents. "It is not because he does not like them," Njombo explained, "but he does not want to take anything, he will help you because he is your friend."

I carried the folded leaf carefully home in my pocket, where it exuded a very peculiar odour, and managed to smear some of the paste on Twinkle's head, but she evidently liked the smell no better than I did and bounded away whenever I advanced towards her. With Njombo and two helpers clinging on to her, I managed to rub it on to her legs, but her tongue seemed impossible, and she struggled so frantically that we let her go.

Resorting to guile, we fetched some rock-salt from the store and put it down in front of her. Like all antelopes, Twinkle relished salt, and soon she sniffed her way up to it and rasped her tongue along its glistening surface. I picked it up and proffered it in my hand. At first she shook her head with an impatient gesture, flicked her ears, minced away and had a little frolic round, kicking up her heels; then she cautiously returned, sniffed gently at the rock-salt with her blue-black nose and gave it an exploratory lick. Reassured, she licked more vigorously while I scratched her neck behind the ears and, having lulled her, basely held out a piece of salt with a little of the paste on it. She took one sniff and then recoiled, wrinkled her nose and bounded off with her neck stretched out before her.

"She did not eat it," I said.

"If the medicine touched her tongue, that was sufficient. This it did: why else should she run away?"

I was not really satisfied; she might have been put off merely by the smell. However, Njombo was confident and he knew more than I did about charms and smells, so I hoped that Twinkle was now fully protected against the python. All the same, I thought, it would be better for the python to be shot. But Njombo said:

"It would be very bad to shoot the python. Then we should not get any rain."

"What has the python to do with rain?"

"Have you not seen the big snake of many colours that lies across the sky when the rain falls? That is the snake who lives in the waterfall. If you look down into the waterfall you can see him there sometimes. His colours are many, like the flowers your mother grows."

"But the python is black," I objected.

"When he goes into the waterfall he puts on his bright clothes. They are so bright that they shine up into the sky. If you kill the snake there will be no colours and no rain."

Robin, I recalled, had said that he would give the python's skin to Tilly, and she could have shoes and bags made from it. I was glad that I would be able to warn him, as we needed rain for the young coffee, and if Tilly wore shoes made from such a magical creature she might disappear.

Chapter Twenty

MRS. NIMMO was much stricter about hours than Tilly. At half past eight she rang a hand-bell and I had to keep at my lessons until ten, when I had a break for cocoa; then lessons again until twelve. Mrs. Nimmo herself presided over the multiplication tables and the Kings of England, and not only that but she added the Kings of Scotland, who were most confusing, and far too numerous. And she added Bible readings too. On the other hand she made delicious cakes and scones, and read me "The Lady of the Lake" and *Marmion*, and when I next rode over to see Robin the words, "Charge, Chester, charge: On, Stanley, on," were ringing in my head.

They were quenched by the news I had so long half-dreaded, and which now came down like a flood. Twinkle had gone. She had vanished the day before. That night her *boma* had been left open, but she had not returned. Because I had sometimes imagined this disaster, it was not any easier to bear.

"Twinkle will be safe, did you not get a charm to protect her?" Njombo said. "Perhaps she has gone to find a bwana of her own."

"Come with me and look at the still," Robin suggested. "It is nearly finished, and has several improvements no one has thought of before. If they work as well as I expect, I shall take out a patent."

The still appeared to be an incoherent mass of pipes, cylinders, coils and drums without the least rhyme or reason, and although I tried to look intelligent, I could not understand a word of his explanation. But I do not think he noticed this, the still was his child and, if it had faults, he would overlook them. The only one it seemed to have at the moment was that it did not actually work, but this would very soon be remedied.

We walked home by the river, and a sudden commotion from the direction of the nursery arrested us.

"Perhaps a child has fallen into the river," Robin said. "We had better go and see."

A small crowd had collected beside the pool under the waterfall, looking at something on the other side. Among them was a woman who wailed and gabbled in a high-pitched voice and appeared to be on the edge of hysteria. I knew at once it was the python, and so it was, although at first I could not see it; the reptile was lying in the shadow of some rocks, in a shallow cave. I saw it only when it moved a little, as if to make itself more comfortable. One of the Kikuyu pointed with his herding-spear and exclaimed:

"Look, can't you see, it has eaten something big and now it is lying there with a full belly like a man gorged on meat, or a woman with child."

And indeed, as its outlines disengaged themselves from the darkness of the wet rock, a large bulge could be seen distinctly in the snake's coils.

A horrible conviction swept over me, and I seized Robin's arm. "It has swallowed Twinkle," I cried, and burst into tears.

"Nonsense, it's probably just the way it's lying, unless . . . What is the matter with that woman, I wonder?"

His inquiries met a barrage of cries and lamentations in Kikuyu. The woman was distraught, the men excited, the python menacing.

"I was afraid so," Robin said gravely. "It has taken her *toto*. . . . Be quiet, or you will frighten it; stay silent while I fetch the gun."

I waited in a place he indicated, a little way back from the river. It was wrong, of course, but I could not help feeling thankful that Twinkle had not been the victim, although still not entirely convinced. Robin returned at the head of a posse of young men with spears and the long, thin swords of the Kikuyu. They walked softly, restraining their battle cries, and some vanished above the waterfall, perhaps to cut off the snake's retreat.

The python had moved back a little, but he was still on his rock. I had never seen him before so close and so bold. Usually all one could see was a gleam of oily motion as he slipped into the water so quietly one would think it must have opened to receive him, as the Red Sea divided before the children of Israel.

Robin's first shot boomed out loudly among the rocks and the python's great head, broad as a soup-plate, reared up and seemed to hang for a moment in mid-air, searching for its attacker. That pause was fatal to it; Robin's second shot was true. The head collapsed, the huge body writhed and lashed and threshed on the rocks, like some dark cauldron boiling over, like a monstrous worm of corruption spewed up from the caverns of the earth. The Kikuyu flung off their blankets and rushed naked into the stream to save it from falling into the river, but they did not touch it until the slithering coils lay still. Then they dragged it up the bank and stretched it out: and there in the middle, sure enough, was an enormous bulge, like a great bead strung upon a cord.

The Kikuyu began to slice the python up its pale under-side, as if they were filleting a fish. How neat and handsome were the little horny scales, each fitting so tightly with its neighbour to make a perfect coat of chain mail! The snake shuddered as its insides parted, just as if it were alive. The black and silver skin was drawn so tightly over the bulge that you could scarcely believe it could stretch so far without bursting. A swift slash of the knife freed the object within. I saw something black and that was all, people crowded in front of me; the leg of a child, or had it not been a black hoof, a slender dark-haired ankle? I turned away, feeling sick, smothered by the long-drawn-out ee-ee-ee-ees and ay-ay-ay-ays of the Kikuyu. Then I heard Robin exclaim:

"I'd never have believed if it I hadn't seen it with my own eyes!"

They had cut out a goat absolutely whole, not a scratch on it, or the least sign of damage, and if the python had been shot a little earlier I believe it would have got up and walked away. As it was, the poor goat was dead, presumably from suffocation, but it must have been alive, Robin said, after it had been swallowed, and struggled in the python's inside.

"You see, you mustn't worry about things that haven't happened," Robin advised. "Twinkle is probably quite safe somewhere, enjoying herself, and so presumably is that silly woman's child."

Three men were needed to carry the python up the hill, where the skin was peeled off and pegged out to dry. I was worried to think that Robin might have shot the rainbow, but when I asked Njombo whether the colours would never be seen again in the sky he said vaguely that this was not the only snake and perhaps everything would be as before. I asked:

"Why did that woman think the snake had eaten her *toto*? Is it safe?"

"She did not think so. She has a baby in her belly. When a woman like that sees a snake it is unlucky, the baby will belong to the snake who may come to fetch it away, and so she was crying."

I began to perceive that a third world lay beyond, inside and intermingled with the two worlds I already knew of, those of ourselves and of the Kikuyu: a world of snakes and rainbows, of ghosts and spirits, of monsters and charms, a world that had its own laws and for the most part led its own life, but now and again, like a rock jutting up through earth and vegetation, protruded into ours, and was there all the time under the surface. It was a world in which I was a foreigner, but the Kikuyu were at home.

Every night I prayed that Twinkle might be preserved. I had faith in the charm, if only I could have been certain that it had been properly applied. With charms, everything had to be done exactly right, and when they failed, it was because some detail of their application had been faulty.

Njombo came to me a few days later and said:

"I have news for you. There is a buck up there"—he pointed with his chin—"that perhaps is Twinkle. Will you go to see?"

Mrs. Nimmo did not allow rides into the reserve with Njombo, but I pleaded with Robin, and so, with some reluctance, he agreed to come too. We followed the twisting path up the ridge that led to Kupanya's, but when we had gone about half-way we diverged, and halted by a homestead whose occupants Njombo engaged for some time in conversation. At length an elderly man in a blanket led us through some shambas and up a hill to a large boulder, and, with a monkey's agility, clambered to the top. We followed. Evening shadows had already darkened the bottom of the valley but the boulder had the warmth of day stored in it, the warmth of life, as if it were the living flesh of the earth.

Our elder pointed across the river and spoke in Kikuyu, and Njombo translated. "He says that two buck come every evening to the river there."

"But why does he say that one of them is Twinkle?"

"The owners of the shambas have set traps, and these duikers walk round them. A man threw a spear, he was as close to it as that tree, and the spear turned aside."

This was just as I had feared: the enmity and wit of the Kikuyu were turned against Twinkle, no charm could be strong enough.

"They will kill her," I said miserably.

"This man says that the medicine is powerful."

We waited for perhaps half an hour while shadows crept like a stain up the hillside, killing the gold and chestnut and copper in which the tree-trunks and the shambas had been bathed, and drawing the parrot-green from the young maize and bean-growth as one might draw wine from a flask, leaving it dull and empty. Yet the umbered purple of the shadows gave the valley its own beauty. Women passed by almost invisible under huge loads of sweet-potato tops, on their way home to feed rams imprisoned in their smoky huts to be fattened under the wooden platforms the Kikuyu used for beds. At last the old man pointed across the stream and said softly: "Look."

In the pool of shade, two darker shapes were moving across a flat stretch of grass. They went jerkily, stopping often to look and listen, and now and then to crop a blade of grass, or the leaf of a shrub, as fastidiously as a queen plucking a flower for her lover. One of them wore two sharp points on his brow. Was the other Twinkle? How could I tell? Yet at that distance, in the dark shade, I felt that I recognized her, and the grace of her movements, and the proud lift of her head. As I watched her, she stood still, sniffed the air and, I could have sworn, looked straight at me, as if to say: I see you, I know you, but although I shall remember you I cannot come back, for I have returned to the freedom which is my heritage.

"I must go and call her," I said.

"She will run away," Njombo warned. "She belongs now to her bwana, not to the house any more."

Nevertheless I set off down the hill and when I plunged into a plantation of bananas near the river I could see them standing stock-still on the farther bank. The bananas blotted out the view, and then the stream had to be crossed by stepping-stones. At last I emerged on the other side, climbed a steep place and stood at the foot of the slope where the duikers had browsed. The hillside lay silent and lifeless, the duikers had vanished;

sunlight was withdrawing from the crest of the ridge and guinea-fowl were crying in the shambas.

I called to Twinkle, but my voice sounded alien and futile, a sound that belonged to nothing, that intruded on the valley's ancient secrecy—water whispering to stones, a soft hissing of banana fronds, goat-bells from a distance, a guinea-fowl's chatter, a francolin's call. I knew then it was no good trying to follow Twinkle, that the cord of trust had snapped for ever.

We rode back silently through the darkening landscape, Moyale jiggling, even prancing sometimes, in his anxiety to be back in his stable with his evening meal. I did not mention Twinkle again, and nor did Robin, but next time he went to Nairobi he brought me a new paintbox and a book about Buffalo Bill.

Njombo, too, not long afterwards proffered a basket covered with leaves, and inside were five little speckled furry balls with legs thinner than match-sticks and bright, pin's-head eyes. They were guinea-fowl chicks, warm and wriggling when you held them in your hand. Mrs. Nimmo put them under a broody hen in a wire-netting cage to shelter them from hawks.

"They will make good eating," she said, looking at those darting, grey-speckled little bright-eyed creatures with a mixture of affection and greed. At that moment I hated her. But she was kind, and had made me a dress, from material specially ordered from Nairobi, which she had worked at in the evenings by the light of a safari lamp so that it would be a surprise. There was painstaking embroidery on it, some little flowers, and drawn thread work, and altogether it was a fine dress.

"It's about time you were brought up to be a young lady, not a savage," Mrs. Nimmo said. I was pleased with the dress, and at the same time rather in awe of it; like Tilly's ear-rings, it was beautiful but not much use, and I remarked:

"I don't know when I shall wear it."

"That's just what I mean. This isn't the right place for a child. I expect when the coffee comes into bearing, your daddy will send you home."

I was thankful, even if Robin and Tilly were not, that many years would go by before the coffee was in full bearing, and everyone became rich.

Chapter Twenty-one

ALTHOUGH he had not been two years in the country, Alec Wilson seemed already to be an old hand, for he was hard-working, thorough, and did not rush with a burst of enthusiasm into every new project. Robin, for instance, had been launched upon geraniums by a fellow-Scot who in a single season had ploughed, prepared and planted a thousand acres of cuttings, and imported and erected a still capable of dealing with the resulting crop. At first this optimist's geraniums had thrived, but a few weeks before harvest some unknown disease had killed every one. Alec would never be caught like that. He tried everything first in an experimental plot, and did not expect to make his fortune for twenty years.

Now he took on a pupil, which was a profitable thing to do, for by custom pupils paid quite a large premium for the privilege of learning the trade. They were useless for about six months because they knew no Swahili, but after that they could become a valuable help on the farm.

Alec brought his pupil over to Mrs. Nimmo's one day. He was a tall, dark young man of about eighteen called Edward Rivett, with trusting brown eyes, high cheek-bones and a pink-and-white complexion not yet browned by the sun. This took some time to happen, because the hats everyone wore had such deep brims that the sun seldom penetrated as far as the face. In fact Edward Rivett asked permission, somewhat shyly, to keep his hat on during luncheon, because the house had a corrugated iron roof. He had already been a pupil with a farmer who had warned him never to remove his hat indoors unless the house had a ceiling, because galvanized sheets did not repel all the sun's rays.

He was a shy, polite, soft-voiced young man who did not speak unless he was spoken to, but replied to questions about his previous farm in a dry, concise way that made us laugh. His former masters had gone in for ostriches. As soon as he arrived, they sent him to a hilltop at daybreak with a pair of binoculars, and instructions to spot the ostrich cocks getting off their nests, soon after sunrise, on the plains below. Ostriches take it in turn to hatch their eggs, the hens by day and cocks by night—that is why cocks are black, and hens grey. At about eight o'clock he went down on the plain, found the nests he had spotted, and marked them with sticks. Later on, natives drove off the sitting hens to rob the nests, and the huge eggs (each of which would make an omelette big enough to feed twenty people) went into an incubator.

No one liked the ostriches much, they were testy and even vicious, and could break a man's bones when they kicked out with their bare, muscular, rugger-player's legs; but up until a year or so before, their feathers had been valuable. Then the price had collapsed, thanks to a sudden change in women's fashions resulting from the spread of motoring, which did not favour large, ostrich-plumed hats.

Alec got a bargain in Edward Rivett, because he already knew some Swahili and, Alec said, possessed a level head; so after he had settled in, Alec went off to Nairobi for a few days, leaving his pupil in charge. While he was away, trouble that had been brewing for some time between Mr. Roos and the Kikuyu came to a head.

Several of Mr. Roos's cattle had been stolen, and although he had complained, with some heat, to the District Commissioner at Fort Hall, no clue as to the culprits had been found. He had sacked his herd-boys and signed on others, but the thefts continued, and were so cunningly carried out that, although he had sat up throughout several nights, as he often watched for lions, he had caught no one. He tried offering a reward, but although several people claimed it their stories, when investigated, were found to be false.

The day after Alec went to Nairobi, five of Mr. Roos's best cows were taken from his *boma* during the night. Two guards had been supposedly watching, but both admitted they had been asleep. They were beaten and sacked, and Mr. Roos fell into a cold, determined, unrelenting fury. He rode up to see Kupanya, who disclaimed all knowledge of the affair, but he threatened the chief that, if the thieves were not produced before sunset next day, he would come and burn down all the huts that he could see in the reserve. Mr. Roos was the sort of man who carried out his threats and Robin, when he heard about it, said he was foolish to take the law into his own hands. A man called Russell Bowker, who had lost five hundred sheep without redress, had ridden into the Masai reserve and burnt down a *manyatta*, and he had been arrested and sentenced to imprisonment, which was later reduced to a fine.

"It is true that those who are paid to enforce the law fail to do so," Robin remarked, "but they refuse to let others do for them what they cannot do themselves. It's bitterly unfair, a crying scandal, but Roos will get himself into trouble if he doesn't look out."

That afternoon, while I was over at the farm with Robin, Mr. Roos arrived in a belligerent mood to say that he was not at all sure whether he had been right to blame the Kikuyu.

"Your Masai," he demanded, "how do you know they were sleeping in their huts last night? That headman, you let him boss you too much. Man, I don't trust him no farther than a mule can kick."

"Sammy has nothing whatever to do with it," Robin retorted, considerably huffed,

"You guard his hut, eh? He's a slim one, your Sammy. Big herds down in his own country, big pay here, friends with the Kikuyu, plenty places for hiding cattle—I don't trust him, man. Every Masai, when he sees a herd of cattle, he says to himself—'God give me all the cattle in the world and now I take them back from everyone else.' And as for law, I don't care that." He snapped his fingers and Robin promised to talk to Sammy, but added that he had never lost any cattle himself. He knew there was bad blood between the two of them, and thought that Roos was trying to get his own back.

"You ask that other Masai too, that cook," Mr. Roos added. "Once you get Masai in the place, man, you just as well have rats."

It was true that a Masai cell was forming itself on the farm. Some time ago, Juma the cook had decided to return to Nairobi. He had come to us largely as a favour, for he was a townsman really; nor could Tilly and Robin afford his wages, so they were relieved when he went. For a while the kitchen *toto* he had trained carried on very well, but then he had to go away to be circumcised, and there was a hiatus filled by various birds of passage, who scarcely knew how to boil an egg.

One day, when Tilly was riding through an uncleared part of the shamba, a large red Masai in pigtails, who Tilly said was stark naked—in actual fact he probably wore the little short cloak of the warriors, which fell short of the waist—a red Masai stepped out of the bushes and raised his travelling spear. Her pony stopped dead and snorted, and she stared at him in surprise. This was some way from Masai country and she had never before seen a warrior so far from his native plains. He seemed to be alone, not with a party of cattle-raiders, and gave the normal greeting, "Jambo!" in clear warrior tones.

She returned the greeting. "This is my bwana's shamba. What do you want?"

"I want to be your cook," the warrior replied.

Even Tilly was surprised at this. "Do you know how to cook?" she inquired.

"For two years I have looked after seven hundred goats."

At the time, she reported, this had struck her as an adequate reply. "It didn't seem much use to ask his form on cheese soufflés, or whether his puff pastry was really light. His repertoire will no doubt consist mainly of well-curdled milk and blood, served high, varied perhaps by a little ghee and raw steak, which I daresay is very healthy. At any rate he seemed quite resolved to come, and ran home behind the pony, his pigtails flying in the breeze."

He was not a good cook, but he had, it appeared, received a little training and he was willing, cheerful and anxious to learn. After a while he brought a wife, and a brother who looked after the oxen, and another relative who learnt to prune the citrus trees. Sammy's son had returned from hospital with one arm missing and a sadly-ravaged face and been provided with a job in the garden, so our little Masai colony grew. As a rule the Masai never worked for Europeans except to herd cattle, but I think all Sammy's relations had Kikuyu blood in them, and so were more adaptable.

Mr. Roos resolved to sit up every night to guard his cattle, and Edward Rivett volunteered to help, I suppose because he was of the age to enjoy any form of excitement.

There was a lot of feeling about stock thefts, at this time, between Government and farmers. The tiny, scattered police force could not possibly protect the farmers' property, yet when they protected it themselves, they were had up and condemned, like Russell Bowker, or like Galbraith Cole, who, after a succession of sheep thefts, had caught a man in the act and shot him as he ran away. He was tried for manslaughter, and, when a jury mainly composed of sympathetic fellow-farmers acquitted him, the Governor went above their heads and deported him from the country. All the farmers took his part, but this did not help him, even though he was said to be the finest stockman in East Africa, and Lord Delamere's brother-in-law. Robin warned Edward Rivett not to do the same thing, or he would get into the same kind of trouble.

For several nights nothing happened, as of course the robbers knew how close a guard was being kept. By day, Mr. Roos rode right down to the plains towards the Masai country to search for traces of cattle on the move, but his quest was hopeless; a hundred gulleys, dry river-beds and folds of ground offered shelter for a few cattle, or for a few hundred for that matter. Mr. Roos became red-eyed from lack of sleep and grew a bristly stubble, and Edward Rivett began to look quite pale instead of pink, and found the long nights anything but exciting. Mrs. Nimmo had taken a fancy to him, and made him sandwiches and cakes and a flask of hot soup to take every night to his place of concealment near Mr. Roos's cattle *boma*.

We had reached the time when, as the Kikuyu said, the moon died for three days before it was reborn as a slender maiden lying on her back, who would grow again to matronly fullness, only once more to wither away. The sky bristled with such innumerable stars, as close-packed as the quills on a porcupine, that a half-light resulted which, though stronger than in northern latitudes, was fickle, and as often tricked as served the eye.

Perhaps the thieves, like Edward Rivett, wanted excitement, or perhaps they felt contempt for the watching Europeans and a sly pleasure in challenging them. They must have stolen up to the *boma* and worked so quietly that they breached its thorns without alarming the cattle. Somehow they edged out three cows and drove them away. Mr. Roos and Edward Rivett were taking it in turns to watch and sleep. Edward Rivett was on duty, but he must have been dozing; when at last a sound disturbed him, he was just in time to see a dark shape vanish into the bush. As it disappeared he fired into the ground behind the shadow. He heard a sort of grunt or cry, and then pandemonium broke out, with people rushing about and shouting and the cattle trying to escape. He and Mr. Roos and the herds beat through the bush and searched for the rest of the night, but the robbers managed to slip away between them, and they had to wait for dawn to search for tracks.

When the light came they found blood on the grass. "You hit him, man," Mr. Roos said with satisfaction. "Now we can follow the spoor."

The blood went on for a little and then stopped. Although they searched all morning, they could not find the place where the cattle had crossed the stream in order to get down to the plains. Yet if the robbers and their booty had remained on our side of the river, they would have come by way of other farms to its junction with the Thika, near the Blue Posts, and found themselves travelling towards civilization instead of away from it.

Edward Rivett did not say much, but he was very worried, and repeated several times: "I hope I haven't done the fellow in. . . . I should have fired above his head. . . ."

Mrs. Nimmo, to whom he often came for meals while Alec was away, soothed him. If the robber had been killed, they would have found the body; as it was, he would not dare to make a complaint and prove himself a cattle-thief. Death was the native penalty for this, and always had been, and the tribesmen had not yet realized how light a view was taken by the new British law of a crime they all considered to be the worst that any man could perpetrate, except sorcery.

Next day Robin arrived at Mrs. Nimmo's with a grave face and called her outside. They spoke for a few moments and then Mrs. Nimmo bustled through the living-room saying that she would come at once and bring her first aid bag.

"Don't say anything," he warned her.

"Mum's the word, of course. Mind you, I'll not be a party to anything that isn't fair and above-board, but we don't know it's anything to do with . . . well, you know what. I'll be along in half a jiffy."

A week ago, I realized sadly, I should have feared for Twinkle, but now she had gone where nobody could help her if she was hurt, so I did not trouble to ask who had been injured.

Alec returned that day from Nairobi, and he and Edward Rivett came to supper. I was sent to bed, but not before I had gathered from their conversation the gist of the day's events. Mrs. Nimmo had gone over to attend to Andrew, our Masai cook, whose foot had been injured. He had lost a lot of blood, but they hoped he would survive, unless the foot was infected by gangrene.

"Perhaps I ought to report it," Edward Rivett suggested gloomily.

"Och, what would be the good of that?" cried Mrs. Nimmo. "They'd put you on your trial and turn everything upside-down. And Andrew would be put on *his* trial for cattle-thieving, and very likely Sammy dragged in, and everyone would finish up in jail or else be fined and made uncomfortable, and what would be the use of it all? Mr. Roos will never get his cattle back."

"I bet he will," Alec remarked. "He'll get them back if he has to go down to the Masai reserve and examine every cow between the German border and the Mara river."

"We must keep him from knowing," Mrs. Nimmo said. "If he hears of the injury he'll never keep it quiet, and then we shall all be in trouble."

"We had better have a good meal while we still can," Alec suggested. "I believe they play some good bridge in Mombasa jail."

Now I knew a secret of which Mr. Roos was ignorant, not to mention all the forces of authority; but it did not interest me a great deal. I kept it to myself, Andrew kept to his hut and Robin lived on tinned meat, bread like slabs of rock and tea tasting like Epsom salts, provided by the kitchen *toto*.

Mr. Roos went off to search for his cattle on the plains and up in the reserve; he cross-questioned Kupanya, he went to see the District Commissioner, he bullied the Italian Fathers, whom he suspected of harbouring the wounded thief in their rough-and-ready little hospital. It was all in vain.

Robin told Sammy he must quit the farm within a month. He could prove nothing, of course, and Sammy was a walking monument to injured innocence. He would no more take part in cattle stealing, he vowed, than he would blind his own eyes, or cut out Robin's heart, or forswear King George. He went about his duties with an air of patient courage under great affliction, and Robin mumbled at him sulkily. Robin had absolutely no wish to sack him, and Sammy did not in the least wish to leave, and probably both of them knew that in the end things would go on as they were.

Some weeks later, when Robin was at Thika, the Indian station-master handed him a paper to give to Mr. Roos. Robin did so when he next saw our neighbour, who glared at the paper and said: "I do not know what this is for."

"It's a way-bill from the railway," Robin replied, glancing at it, "for some cattle that you railed to Nairobi."

"I have sent no cattle to Nairobi!" Mr. Roos eyed the paper as though it had itself invented the lie.

"The railway think you have, but they make mistakes every day. You had better take it up with the station-master."

Mr. Roos evidently did so, for he rode over next day positively quivering with rage.

"Those cattle were loaded by a native," he exclaimed.

"What is wrong with that?"

Mr. Roos thrust two way-bills under Robin's face. "It is there, the dates, on those papers! I never loaded cattle! Those——" Mr. Roos swore. The dates on the way-bills corresponded to the dates of the days following the two stock thefts.

It was wrong of Robin, but he could not help it: he burst out laughing, he laughed and laughed. Mr. Roos very nearly knocked him down. It was surprising that he did not do so, but merely clenched his fists and ground his teeth (this he did literally, Robin said he had never heard the actual sound before, except when pigs had worms) and rode away.

That was not the end of it, of course. Sammy, Andrew (who gave out that he had sores on his instep), all our herdsmen, and many others were sent in batches to the station to parade before the Indian, in the hope that he could identify the culprits who had brought the cattle to be loaded. But in this the station-master failed.

If you came to think of it, the thieves had done the obvious thing. They had simply driven their booty to the station and loaded it in Mr. Roos's name, all open and above-board; and the one area Mr. Roos had never thought of searching was the township and the station holding-ground. At Nairobi station, someone had unloaded the stolen cattle and driven them, no doubt, into the Masai reserve, and down to some *manyatta* which, as Robin said, it was all Lombard Street to a china orange belonged to Sammy's clan.

What gave the final twist to the screw was that Mr. Roos was held responsible for the freight charge from Thika to Nairobi. The railway said there was no proof that the beasts had been stolen, when they were put on rail in his name.

Sammy went away for three months, and came back with a new wife from the reserve.

"I know I ought to send him packing," Robin admitted, "but he did have a score to pay against Roos. Besides, there wasn't a shred of proof that Sammy was mixed up in it."

"There never is any proof," said Alec.

Chapter Twenty-two

FROM the veranda of our grass hut we looked over the Kikuyu ridges to Mount Kenya, which could be seen only in the early mornings, and in the evenings, at certain times of the year. Unless you knew it was a mountain you would have thought it a persistent cloud, the shape of a breast, with the twin peaks, Mbatian and Nelion, blending at this distance into the semblance of a nipple. In colour it was a bluish-purple, like a grape, save for a white cap of ice and snow from which arose cold, clear little streams bringing life to the Kikuyu uplands that formed the shoulders of this great mountain, below the moorland and forest surrounding its peak.

The snow and glaciers were also the dwelling-place of God, according to Njombo, and if you wished to pray to God, you looked across towards the peaks and hoped that he would hear you; though this was only possible if you had offered a sacrifice. "Would you expect a chief, or any man of importance, to hear you unless you first gave him a present?" Njombo explained. "How then can God hear without a present?" No one had ever seen God, Njombo added; he dwelt by himself without a wife, or father and mother, but he had given land and sheep and goats to the first Kikuyu, and he watched over them so long as they obeyed his laws.

The twin peaks of Kenya, Nelion (the lesser) and Mbatian, were called after two great Masai *laibons*, or priests, the real rulers of the tribe. As to Nelion, no one seemed to know much about him, but when Sammy was a boy he had seen Mbatian, who had prophesied the great outbreak of smallpox twenty years earlier that had ravaged the Masai and Kikuyu tribes, and had foreseen also the coming of the white man in the head of a snake. He had told his people not to fight them, and that is why the Masai did not drive away the Europeans when they brought their snake, which was the railway, from the sea, and put an end to the greatness of the Masai people who had held the highlands with sword and spear and the prowess of their warriors.

Every morning the mountain floated in the sky as if sketched in lightly with a pencil, and I thought of Tilly and the safari, for it was somewhere beyond those peaks, to an unimaginable far country, that they had travelled. They would see the face of the mountain that was always turned away from us, and I wondered whether from that unknown angle they might catch a glimpse of something shining in the snow, a bit of God perhaps—a bead on his cloak, or the tip of his spear.

I thought also of Ian when I looked at the mountain, for I had heard him say that he was going to climb it, and drink a bottle of Tokay on the topmost peak on the feast of Stephen. Only two men in the world had ever reached the summit, Sir Halford Mackinder and his Swiss guide, who had scaled Mbatian fifteen years before. With them on this expedition was Mr. Campbell Hausberg, a partner of Randall Swift's, who had been to visit us on the farm, and had only one ear, the other having been torn off when a mule-buggy in which he was travelling overturned. He had given me some photographs taken among the glaciers, so that I felt a personal interest in Mount Kenya and could imagine what Ian would see when he stood on the top.

For I did not doubt that what he set out to do, Ian would achieve. Yet when an exploit was behind him, he seemed to take no further interest in it. Before he came to Africa, I had heard Lettice say, he had done many remarkable things; in the Rocky Mountains he had killed a ferocious bear by stabbing it, and won some great cowboy contest in Canada, for which the prize had been a pair of silver spurs. Once Lettice had asked him what, in his heart of hearts, he wanted most to do. After some thought, Ian had lit one of the small cheroots he smoked, no larger than short pencils, and replied that his true ambition was to be a lock-keeper on the Thames.

"There life would flow past you in an orderly manner, and you would stand among your snapdragons and phloxes and watch it go by," he had told her, "instead of going forth to seek it in the raw places, and perhaps being swept like a twig out to sea."

"That is an ambition it should be possible to satisfy," Lettice had said, "by the pulling of strings." Ian had replied that lock-keepers' posts were reserved for retired master mariners, so that to get one you must first serve thirty or forty years at sea.

At this time of year Mount Kenya seemed to move closer to us, the base became more purple, the outlines darker, the crest more white. By eight o'clock the peak had always disappeared behind a cloudy muffler. The cumulus clouds that drifted all day long across a sun-filled sky reminded me of huge swirls of whipped cream, but these clouds were heavier and denser, like bands of curd, and the colour of rosemary flowers. All this meant the approach of the rains, and the planting of many more coffee seedlings. In the shamba, big holes had been dug, at intervals of nine feet, to receive them. In Sammy's absence, the organization of the labour was in some confusion; the office work, Tilly's province, had been left largely to Kamau, and confusion was doubtless a mild word to describe the state it was in. In order to keep the household up to scratch—or so he hoped—Robin announced every morning that Tilly would be back next day, and the house was in a state of constant readiness, at least in theory; in fact, the Kikuyu had their own secret antennae to pick up the vibrations of coming events, and did no more than say: "Yes, bwana, we will get ready," and continue in their own ways undisturbed.

The long rains, which in those days were expected on 25th March exactly, arrived punctually at two o'clock in the afternoon. A deluge of enormous chilly drops beat with a noise of thunder on Mrs. Nimmo's iron roof, turned our surroundings into a mess like melted chocolate, poured in rivers down every slope, and swept through the unglazed windows of the rondavels on to sacks laid on the mud floor to absorb it. I could not ride over that day to the farm, but next morning was cold and drizzly, Mrs. Nimmo was busy supervising the repair of leaking roofs, and I was allowed to go.

Rain had stirred the people on the farm as it stirred the *siafu*, they too were scurrying about in a black stream, although not of course in such numbers. They carried on their heads boxes of bright-leaved young coffee trees, dumped them in the shamba and hurried back to the nurseries for more. The shamba-boys placed each seedling carefully in a hole and packed in the chocolate mud, which they pressed down with their naked feet. Most of them had discarded their blankets, and their bare satin skins glistened with moisture and made them look like seals. No African could perform any action of this kind for long without setting it to rhythm; some of them punched down the earth with a swaying motion, intoning a chant whose beat ended with a grunt as they threw their weight on to the foot whose toes were feeling round the infant tree to bed it in, as a mother might tuck in her child. Although they disliked the wet, they took an interest in this work, for they could see the plantation coming into existence before their eyes, and arising out of the labours of their bent backs and squeezing feet.

There was an art in planting young coffee, because if the little tap-root was not put in absolutely straight, if it had the least kink in it, the tree would die; so Robin hurried to and fro among the planters trying to ensure that every root was true. All the Kikuyu on the farm had been pressed into service, even Kamau, who had for the moment forgotten the cabalistic insignia of his art, the pens and digits and ruled papers, and was levering treelets gently from boxes with his fingers with a look of great concentration on his scraggy face. Njombo was there also, in the capacity of a self-appointed overseer, shouting encouragement and enjoying himself very much indeed.

"Now the rains have come and we will make a coffee shamba like a forest," he cried. "As big as a forest, with trees taller than the olive or the cedar, and their fruit will fill many, many wagons and our bwana will be richer than King George."

Robin would not let me plant any trees, I suppose because he did not trust me with the tap-roots; however, I was allowed to help scoop moist earth round the seedlings, and press it in with my fingers, which had all the delight of making mud pies with the added pleasure of utility; for children are bored with pointless things and, when they play, attempt by pretence to add the dimension of reality to their actions. Now there was no need to pretend, the mud pies had a purpose and so the making of them was delightful, at least until I grew tired.

"Memsabu will be back tomorrow," Njombo said. "The safari is not far away."

If this was so, it was time I came home; so when the planting was over, I asked Robin if I could stay, instead of riding back to Mrs. Nimmo's.

"Not until your mother returns."

"Njombo says she will be back tomorrow."

"Then Njombo knows a great deal more than I do," Robin replied. "I have heard nothing about it, and you must stay where you are."

When I got back to Mrs. Nimmo's, I could see at once that something unexpected had occurred. Several Africans I had never seen before were there, none of them Kikuyu, but blacker and fiercer, with a musky smell, large flat noses and big sandalled feet; and two strange mules were in the stable, and safari kit was lying around. When I reached the living-room, I heard a man's voice, not that of Alec, but deeper and gruffer. Two men, in fact, were there with Mrs. Nimmo, both brown and travel-stained. One had a shirt with little slots to hold cartridges above the pockets, and both wore hunting knives, boots and puttees; a big white bull-terrier with many scars lay by the fireplace, pricked his stubby ears and gave a faint growl.

"This is the bairn," Mrs. Nimmo cried, and she looked flustered and excited. "Come and say how do you do to Mr. Nimmo, dear. My goodness, whatever have you been doing now! Bringing all that dirt into my clean sitting-room! Mr. Nimmo will think I've got a savage in the house! Go and change at once, dear, and put on your nice new frock, and show Mr. Nimmo that he's got a little lady to welcome him, and not a Red Indian."

Although I liked the dress to look at, I did not in the least want to put it on. However, there was no avoiding it, and I returned feeling awkward and self-conscious, although cleaner, and curious to see in the flesh a person who had for so long been a myth, like my bearded grandfather in England, or King George V. It was some time before I discovered that Mr. Nimmo was the shorter of the two men, not so tall in fact as Mrs. Nimmo, but very solid, like hardwood, with broad shoulders, an unexpressive, pugnacious-looking, red but not unkindly face, and a hard blue eye with a suspicion in it of a wink or a twinkle. He spoke in a dry, pawky Scots voice, and looked about him in a quiet, appraising manner, and said several times to Mrs. Nimmo: "That's new since I was here", or: "You've treated yourself to a fine rug, when there's plenty of old sacks in the store", or, to his companion: "You see, Jim, what it's like to keep a wife in luxury while you're walking after elephants with your only pair of boots worn through. There's two knives on the table for each of us, and a spoon and fork, and a different plate for meat and pudding; next time I come perhaps there'll be wine-glasses and finger-bowls. If you marry a wife,

Jim, first she'll take one tusk for every elephant you kill and then she'll have them both off you, and you'll be left with what you can get for the tail."

Next morning, Mr. Nimmo seemed quietly to take charge of everything; the boys came to him for orders, and he was out early on his mule riding round the farm. At breakfast he found fault with a number of things on the grounds of extravagance, and Mrs. Nimmo took it all very meekly, which was unlike her, and did everything she could to please him, getting up to pour out his tea and herself making hot scones for him, and hoping that the eggs were done to his liking. In fact a great change had taken place in Mrs. Nimmo overnight and it was a surprise to me that Mr. Nimmo, who did not impress one much to look at, had been able to bring this about while he said little that was amiable, and never thanked her for her attentions, and might even have been making fun of her in a quiet, wooden, underground sort of way.

Mrs. Nimmo was delighted when I asked permission to ride over to the farm and see if there was any news of Tilly. And there was: Njombo had been right, although Robin could not imagine how, for he had only heard himself the night before when a syce sent to Thika to collect the mail had brought a telegram dispatched from Fort Hall. This said that Tilly was getting a lift by car for the last stage of the safari, and would be at the Blue Posts by lunch-time. So Robin and I rode down, leading Lucifer, and there she was, sitting on the veranda in her divided riding-skirt, her tight waist and a clean blouse for the occasion, a little thinner than when she went away, but with her bright hair shining over its wide frame, and her skin still rosy in spite of the deserts she had tramped over and the heat she had endured.

"Thank goodness you're safe," Robin said, beaming with pleasure, after they had embraced. "I have missed you. . . . I'm planting out the coffee and everyone is hard at it, and the office work has got chaotic, and Sammy is away."

"It's lovely to see you," Tilly responded. "And you look well. . . . Do you know I shot a lion: not a very large one, but definitely a lion: the skin is coming on with the safari, so we shan't need another rug in the living-room."

"I've got the still in working order, except for one or two

small details, and I think we shall be able to start on the geraniums in a week or two if this rain keeps on."

"In a way I didn't want to shoot it, but it sloped off into a *donga*, and when I saw something tawny moving in the grass I let fly and hit it in the leg."

"We've had a bit of bad luck with the oxen, one broke its leg, and another died of colic, probably a poisonous plant, I should say; and the boys broke the axle of the water-cart, but I've made a start on installing the ram."

Clearly it was more blessed, or at any rate more enjoyable, to give news than to receive it, and they continued in this independent vein for some time. Then Robin suddenly asked:

"But what has happened to Lettice and Hereward?"

"They've stayed behind at Nyeri—Hereward's had an accident, and must go down to Nairobi as soon as he can be moved."

When Robin asked what sort of accident, Tilly said a buffalo had charged him; and gave me her glass, telling me to get it refilled. We had lunch at the Blue Posts and rode back afterwards in the heat of the afternoon, which Tilly said was cool compared with the banks of the Guaso Nyiro river. They had shot many animals, it seemed; in fact it had been a successful safari except that a mysterious cloud had fallen over it towards the end.

"And Ian?" Robin inquired. "I suppose he is hardly sitting at Hereward's bedside, giving him ice-packs and enemas?"

"Ian is involved in a *shauri* about Ahmed."

"Ahmed! He's in trouble, I suppose."

"No, it's Ian who's in trouble, up to a point. Ahmed went back to his tribe in Somaliland, or wherever he comes from."

"Ian will miss him."

Tilly agreed, and added: "You must never breathe a word about all this."

Everyone was delighted to see Tilly. Andrew had returned, limping, to his duties, and we now had a Masai houseboy as well. These haughty, long-shanked young men had shaved their pigtails when they donned the *kanzu* of office, and looked noble and heraldic in their green sashes, like figures from Egyptian friezes. Tilly said she never grew entirely used to seeing them in the house, it was as if one were to come across a couple of panthers in the boudoir. She had dosed them heavily when they had arrived for several kinds of parasite, and dressed several kinds of sore. They trod softly and were delicate in their movements, and seldom broke things, as the heavier-handed Kikuyu were apt to do, and they dusted with the care of a woman; there was, indeed, something strangely effeminate about the warriors of this aggressive, battle-hungry tribe. They greeted Tilly with an upraised arm, as if a chieftain had resumed his kingdom, but with reserve; the Kikuyu were more demonstrative, and full of questions about the lands she had travelled in, the lions she had shot and the people she had encountered.

"You see, we have looked after bwana very well," they said, giving themselves a share in all this goodwill. "We have seen that he has not gone hungry and that his cattle and horses have not fallen sick, and that his shamba has thrived; and the *toto* also, we have looked after her."

It must have been about a week later that Lettice, heralded an hour or two before by a note in her large sloping hand on royal blue paper, came over to see us. Most people did not notice me when they arrived, but Lettice always did; she kissed me and said:

"You see, I was right: you have grown older since we've been away, and learnt many new things. But I am distressed to hear that you have had a great sorrow. It is just as sad for you to lose Twinkle, as it is for older people to lose their brothers or sisters or sons, and perhaps one's first great sorrow is the worst of the lot. But Twinkle may be happier, even if you are not; and Ian is bringing you a new pet, not perhaps so lively as Twinkle, but with a charm of his own. He wears a handsome black and yellow armour, and comes from the dry country in the north and can only speak Somali, so you must keep him warm and teach him English. He is called Mohammed, and eats grass."

Mohammed was a tortoise, and Ian would escort him to Thika in a few days.

"He very nearly brought you two small eagle chicks as well. Do you remember them, Tilly—how he clambered up among the rocks to find the nest after he had killed the eagle with a single shot into the sky?"

"Yes, it was a very fine shot," Tilly replied.

"Ian shoots as great pianists can play, each note is perfect, there is never any muffing or the least failure of touch; it is a sort of genius. But he didn't in the least want to shoot that eagle; he wouldn't have done so if Hereward hadn't challenged him in such a stupid way. 'It has a nest somewhere in those rocks,' he said, do you remember? 'Let it be.' Then Hereward sneered at him, and made it sound as if he had been boastful, which Ian never is, and so he put up his rifle almost without thinking, and the eagle fell among the rocks, and as it fell it gave a screech of rage, rather than pain. That cry made my blood run cold. I looked at Ian—he felt as I did, it was wanton and unlucky, he should have let the eagle be, and not allowed Hereward to provoke him. Ahmed was standing by, and I think that was when he first . . . Well, never mind, the eagle is dead and cannot be put together, and later Ian found two chicks in a nest he said was very smelly, and brought them down. Do you remember how they tried to peck and scratch even though they were so small, and the fierceness of their yellow eyes? Ian didn't think they would make good pets, especially as they would have needed mice and rats to eat, and even snakes and mongooses when they grew older; so he got you a tortoise instead."

Tilly sent me on an errand which I knew she had invented to get me out of the way, so I loitered in the veranda to listen, in case the mystery should be explained.

"I don't know what to do, Tilly," Lettice said when I had gone. "I am in great agony of mind. I must go back to Nairobi and there I shall meet Ian, and either we must say good-bye and he will leave the country or . . . How dreadful it is to drift into a position where whatever you do, somebody must get hurt."

"I suppose it is a question of who would get hurt the most, or recover the soonest."

"I know how you would decide that, and everyone else would think the same, but I believe you are wrong. Hereward has something to hold on to; he will always be a soldier fighting for his country, and sometimes he will suffer defeats and be betrayed, but that will not really twist the sinews of his heart, for soldiers are born to bear misfortune and take a pride in doing so. So Hereward would only be bloody but unbowed, whereas Ian . . . If he has looked for something all his life and at last found it, and cannot keep it, he will know there is nothing else to go on searching for, and that will be the end of him, like the eagle that fell down among the rocks."

"That is all rather too deep for me," Tilly replied. "Ian is tremendously attractive, and I can understand how you feel, and wish I could help you, but I don't see how I can."

"Yes, Ian is attractive, but so are other men; it is simply that I feel as if I had come to the end of a journey, and that often there is no need for words between us at all, and yet there is never any shortage of them; we are at ease together, and even when he is not there, all my thoughts are shaped to fit his mind, and I think his fit mine also without our intending it—a queer feeling, one I have never had before. And sometimes, when he isn't there, he seems more real to me than people who are with me, Hereward perhaps; I can see him there and almost touch and smell him, and I know that the same thoughts are in our minds. Well, there it is, and of course there is no doubt where my duty lies; but somehow, while that ought to solve the whole question, I'm afraid for me it doesn't solve anything."

"There is a practical side to it," Tilly suggested. "Ian doesn't seem to have any money to speak of, nor a farm here, nor anything at home, and he could hardly support a family by horse-trading in Abyssinia, or shooting elephants."

"He bought some land at an auction a year or two ago, and thinks he has enough capital to start developing it, so I suppose that he would settle down."

"If he is the settling-down type."

"I read a book the other day about pearl-fishers in the Persian Gulf; they dive without any apparatus, quite naked, and pick oysters off the floor of the sea; most of the oysters are useless, but now and again, very seldom, there will be a pearl, and always there is the belief that the very next oyster will have a stupendous pearl. I thought, Ian is like one of those divers, he won't case himself in armour, he is on his own, searching for pearls on the floor of the sea. . . . Most people enclose themselves in diving suits—they try to make fortunes or, if they have enough already, like Hereward, to win a big name, or to add a new bit to the Empire, something to make England mightier yet, like a bullfrog swelling out in a pond. Ian doesn't want to make a fortune, or a name, or even bits of Empire, he simply wants to live—though I shouldn't say simply, it is anything but that. You can't live, he says, if you are trying to grow richer or greater—only by fitting into the scheme of things, and not trying to alter it to fit you."

"That sounds rather Eastern," Tilly remarked with caution. "I can see he is a more interesting companion than Hereward, but not perhaps such a good provider."

"You are on Hereward's side," Lettice said sadly, "and of course you are right; there are no two ways about it; and there is also Hugh. It is easy to dress one's weakness up as courage, and selfishness as enterprise. To tell the truth I don't know which is which, and what is right and wrong, because while I know it in theory, when you look through a door into a garden that may be full of sorrow and remorse, and yet has been prepared for you, a force that seems stronger than you are—I suppose it is called temptation—tries to prevent you from shutting the door and turning back to what you now see is a prison, when you thought it was a home."

"I know what I should do if I were in your place," Tilly observed. "But that is not at all the same as knowing what *you* will do, as we are quite different people."

"You would do your duty," Lettice said regretfully.

"No, I should not; I should do what I wanted, and enjoy it, and eventually be sorry, and never admit that I was."

"You have buttered your bun, and now you must lie on it, as the babu said; and I expect that is the last word, if there ever is such a thing. At any rate Hereward is better; disaster was averted by a quarter of an inch. Poor Hereward, I hope that when he next loses his temper he will be careful that there are no Somalis near, and that he does not speak to them as he does to fellow-Englishmen with their cold, phlegmatic blood."

"I hope Ian will be able to keep it hushed up," Tilly remarked.

"I think he will; it is hardly worth sending a company of K.A.R. to look for Ahmed, and they would not find him if they did. Ian says Ahmed will come back some day, when it has all blown over, because he is a faithful henchman—too faithful, in a way—and because Ian owes him three months' wages. What a time we have had, Tilly! It's strange, but I feel now that I have passed the very peak and crown of my life. . . ."

They continued to talk, but my attention had long since wandered, and I went out to look for birds' nests in the reeds by the river. At tea-time Tilly remarked to Robin:

"Lettice has only just gone; she seemed very *exaltée*; I expect she will go off with Ian, but I can't see how it will work."

"Ian can sing and read Greek poetry, and Lettice can play and do *petit point*, and they are both fond of riding, and wine, and wild animals, and conversation. Perhaps it will be all right."

"When you are used to luxury, you think that you despise it, but when it disappears you realize that it has grown into your life, like one of those parasites that start as creepers and end up as trees. Or so I'm told; I can't speak from experience."

Robin looked a little guilty. "Yes, my aunt Dolly was like that. She created a scandal first of all by marrying a stockbroker —no one had ever done that before in Inverness—and then by leaving him for a sailor who hadn't a penny in the world; love in furnished rooms in Portsmouth was too much for her, she took up with a wine merchant from Bristol and ended in Jamaica with a rich old planter they said was a mulatto, but as she was past the age of child-bearing by then, I never could see that it mattered."

"How lucky she was to find a rich old planter," Tilly remarked. "We can only hope that you will become one, in the end."

Chapter Twenty-three

UNDETERRED by her losses, Tilly imported from England twelve more Speckled Sussex pullets and a cockerel to make a new start. We rode down to meet them at the station on a cool, wet day with low clouds, and an inclination to drizzle: we had weather like that sometimes in July and August, but it did not last.

We met several neighbours at the station and they all discussed the same topic, bad news from Europe, and the probability of war. Austria and Serbia were fighting, Belgrade was in flames, the Bank of England had closed its doors. All this came as a complete surprise to Tilly and Robin. People said the Army was mobilizing and that, if England went to war with Germany, we should at once invade German East Africa, and everyone would volunteer.

"I had better go to Nairobi and see what's happening," Robin said. Tilly replied:

"Let's get these pullets settled in first, for goodness' sake. I don't want to lose them all a second time."

Both my parents were rather silent on the ride home. There was a lot to think about. What would happen to the farm? To Tilly and me? To the crops and plans?

"It won't last long, that's certain," Robin remarked. "No country could afford it, for one thing."

Robin belonged to some kind of reserve force, having been in the Yeomanry, and began to fuss about getting back to his regiment. Next day he had a cable saying: "European war inevitable." So he packed his bag and rode off the following day to the station to catch a train to Nairobi. Tilly felt restless, worried and out of things. No one thought of lessons, she busied herself with looking after the new chickens and organizing the labour force.

"It's no good leaving me alone with your still," she had said to Robin. "You will have to come back and show me how to work it."

"It's very easy," Robin had assured her. "There are just

one or two little parts it needs. I can get them in Nairobi and bring them back when I come."

"What will Hereward do, I wonder?"

"Of course, he'll be recalled to his regiment, and I suppose go home by the next boat."

"I'm glad someone will be pleased about the war," Tilly had said.

Soon the district was almost deserted, with only Tilly, myself, Alec and Mrs. Nimmo left behind. Everyone else had gone to look for the war. Even Major Breeches had left the Blue Posts and was helping to organize rations for the volunteers who were pouring into Nairobi.

Robin returned in three or four days, full of news. People were arriving, he said, from all over the country, in trains, in carts, on mules, some of them with nothing but the clothes they stood up in and a rifle, anything from a light carbine to a double-barrelled elephant gun. On the Uasin Gishu plateau, miles and miles away, farmers who had assembled to discuss some agricultural matter had heard the news and travelled to Nairobi in a body to enlist just as they were, without even returning to their farms. As to what they were to enlist in, neither they nor the authorities had given the matter much thought. The K.A.R. did not want a sudden influx of quite untrained Europeans, so the more forceful of the volunteers proceeded to form their own units, appoint their own officers and n.c.o.s and drill their followers.

Thus there came spontaneously into being Wilson's Scouts, Arnoldi's Scouts (composed of Dutchmen from the plateau) and Bowker's Horse. Robin had a narrow escape from this last body. A man, he said, as large and broad as a piano, with a whole leopard's head, complete with bared fangs, snarling down from his slouch hat, practically shanghaied him on the steps of Nairobi House, which had become the headquarters of these home-made regiments. This was Russell Bowker, the South African who had lost five hundred sheep and set fire to the Masai *manyatta*.

Narrowly avoiding Bowker's Horse, Robin got himself a job to do with Intelligence. He was delighted with it, and even more delighted to delve into a tin trunk in the store and extract his kilt and its accoutrements. Whether it was needed for Intelligence I do not know, but he took it off to Nairobi, and that was the last we saw of him for some time. It was decided that Tilly was not to stay by herself on the farm, but was to take part in Nairobi in the starting of a military hospital. Alec Wilson offered to look after the farm; later on, he also took over the Palmers', and led a more strenuous life than many people did who had joined the Army. There remained my own future to be settled. Ian Crawfurd had an elder brother, Humphrey, with a farm up-country, and a wife. Tilly had met them both and liked them; and when Mrs. Crawfurd wrote to offer me a sanctuary she accepted gratefully, and threw in the Speckled Sussex pullets for good measure. I was not allowed to take George and Mary, the chameleons, nor Mohammed the tortoise, but Njombo promised to look after them as faithfully as if I had been there. To part with Moyale was the worst of all. It was a bitter moment when he ate his last lick of sugar from my hand, nuzzling me with his soft muzzle, and cocking one ear forward and one back. Moyale would look next day for his sugar, his carrots, his patting, his exercise, and I should not be there. Would Njombo keep his promises? Or would some *shauri* claim his interest and Moyale grow neglected and forlorn?

"We are not going for ever," Tilly said. "I expect we shall be back before Christmas, and meanwhile I shall come out at week-ends to see that things are all right."

"But I don't want to go!"

"Well, you must blame the Kaiser, he is the one. . . . Don't forget to clean your teeth, and try not to scratch your head so often, and when you ride for heaven's sake keep your toes straight and your heels down, and your elbows in, and don't look so much like a performing monkey."

With these parting instructions we left for Nairobi in the mule-buggy, with the crate of Speckled Sussex pullets, a basketful of vegetables for the hospital, and many other miscellaneous things. In theory, Tilly travelled light, but in practice the imminence of her departure acted like a summer thunderstorm on a mushroom field, and parcels, baskets, and mysterious objects in odd-shaped packages sprang up on all sides.

Nairobi was full of khaki men with rifles. They had no settled uniform, but most of them wore breeches and puttees, bush shirts and felt hats, with gay bandana handkerchiefs round their necks. While we were shopping in the town a platoon rode by carrying native spears adorned with red and yellow pennants; Tilly said they had turned themselves into Lancers, and were called Monica's Own, after the Governor's daughter.

In the evening Tilly put me on the train in charge of the guard, with a good deal of luggage, and some last-minute presents for Mrs. Crawfurd such as a box of little trees, a sack of seed potatoes, a preserving pan, an egg timer, and two new blouses and some material that had arrived in the last boat before the war began. "They will bring nothing now but beer and bullets, I expect," Tilly remarked gloomily, "so we had better get what we can." The guard said he would put the Speckled Sussex in the van.

When I got off the train next morning everything smelt quite different, fresh and cold. An ox-cart met me at the station with a young Dutchman who said his name was Dirk, and that he would take me to the Crawfurds' farm.

At Molo everything was much bigger than at Thika—hills, trees, distances, even sky and clouds. The trees were black and clumped, the grass naked and tufty, and bent over on one side, and you felt as if you had reached the very top of the world. The air was sharp and clean as iced lemon juice, and a wind blew, and spikes of pink and bronze wild gladioli grew among the buff sedgy grass. We passed no round huts, no goats, no shambas, no valleys with banana trees; everything was empty and cold.

I was silent on the journey, and so was Dirk, and we jolted along with very few words. Dirk walked with a limp, and told me he had broken his leg.

At the end of the track, I told myself, would be Mr. Crawfurd, and he would be just like Ian only rather larger, because he was the elder of the two. But Humphrey Crawfurd was another surprise. He was not like Ian at all, in fact I did not believe that they were brothers. Humphrey was certainly much larger, but dark instead of fair, with a heavy moustache and big thick hands; indeed he was heavy all over, bulky, silent, he did not sparkle at all. It was only in the eyes that I could see a resemblance, both pairs were proud and smoky blue; and a little in the smile, perhaps, which made Humphrey look younger and less preoccupied.

What I remember most about him was his ability to embalm himself so deeply in thought that flies could crawl about his face, even into his ears, without his making any sign. This gave him a monumental quality which impressed itself deeply on my mind. He did not flap and twitch like ordinary people, or like cows. He must, one felt, be sunk in some tremendous wisdom or philosophy. In fact, he was a man who held to one passion at a time, and at the moment his thoughts were concentrated upon water, and on ways of getting it about. He had a large farm, a ranch really, and it needed a great many pipes, channels and flumes.

Mrs. Crawfurd was as lavish with words as he was sparing. They bubbled out like water from one of his sluice-gates, and like the water they were fresh, bright, gay and occasionally a little monotonous. She had the knack of uncovering drama in every event, significance in every situation and importance in every human being. In fact monotonous is the wrong word, just as it would not be the right expression to use of a dappled, busy, flashing mountain stream. Such streams can lull you into a half-drowsy, half-dreaming state where every now and then you catch the intonation of a little waterfall, the whisper of a rock pool. That may have been how Humphrey Crawfurd felt. She did not expect him to listen to every word of hers, for she enjoyed talking, nor did he expect an over-lively interest in his water schemes. They gave and took. They had two children, a girl called Althea who was in Scotland, and a boy of about two years old who was with them, called Bay; and a baby was expected quite soon.

After my retinue of packages had been unloaded and sorted out, and Mrs. Crawfurd had exclaimed on Tilly's generosity, she added:

"And it was angelic of your darling mother to send such a splendid *kikapu* of vegetables, they are quite magnificent, but they are perhaps the one thing we could have done without. Now we are going to have so much water everywhere I shall be able to irrigate a garden, and meanwhile we grow splendid vegetables from English seed, that is one of the things we *can* do on our mountain tops."

This gave a jolt to my memory. The Speckled Sussex! They had not been in the ox-cart. Had they been left behind?

They were not at Molo station, and Mrs. Crawfurd wrote to break the news of their disappearance to Tilly. A week or two later, we heard their fate. Tilly had received a note from the matron of the hospital, thanking her warmly for her handsome gift of a dozen young hens. "The patients have enjoyed them, such a welcome change. . . ." Poor Speckled Sussex, it was sad for them to travel five thousand miles, so much cosseted and cherished, and destined to found a new colony of hens, only to be confused with a basket of vegetables and end up in the roasting pan.

A few days after I arrived, Mr. Crawfurd opened a furrow that was to carry water from a spring in the forest to his house and farm. The trench was nearly two miles long and had taken over a year to dig and to line with a kind of clay that had been hauled by ox-carts, with frequent adventures in the mud.

We rode up to the forest with a picnic, men with spades having gone on before. Nothing could have made Mr. Crawfurd talkative, but you could feel that excitement was coiled up inside him like a spring. The labour on the farm had decided to make this into a holiday, and all the people living round about, attracted by the party as ants by sugar, had come to join in.

Molo was not like Thika; there was no native reserve; only about fifteen years before, no humans of any sort had been living there. Too bleak for cultivators, too high even for Masai cattle, these Molo downs had lain there as God made them, empty and unchanged, with wild animals in sole possession and able to do as they pleased.

After the Government had built a railway from the coast to Lake Victoria, they had offered blocks of this land for nothing beyond a very small annual rent, but they had not found any takers, not one. The land was beautiful, but people were not after beauty, they were after profit, or at any rate the chance to make a livelihood, and at Molo this could not be done. The land lay unwanted for a while, and then a few South Africans arrived, and scratched a living not by farming but by shooting the game and running transport from Londiani, the next station but one up the line, to the Uasin Gishu plateau, where Dutch settlers were growing maize, but had no railway to take it away.

It was from a South African that the Crawfurds had bought their ranch, of five thousand acres. There was nothing on it, just a few huts made of split logs and some *bomas* for sheep and cattle. There was not even a road or track to link the ranch with the station. Mr. Crawfurd's trouble, like most people's, was lack of capital, so he could only do a little bit at a time. Like the Dutchmen, he was slowly building up his flocks and herds, animal by animal, calf by calf. About the only crop for which there was a ready sale was maize, and Molo was too high for that. The Crawfurds did sell a little butter, which went down once a week in an ox-cart to the station, and then in small consignments to people they knew in Nairobi.

As no Africans were living on this great western wall of the Rift Valley, of which Molo was a part, the earliest farmers sent to fetch some either from the Kavirondo country, or from Kikuyuland, and small native settlements arose near the European homesteads, and in folds of the hills. And as everyone within ten miles or so had decided to attend the opening of the Crawfurds' furrow, we arrived to find quite a lot of people squatting round on their heels, or leaning on their spears.

The head of the furrow lay a little distance inside the forest, in one of the glades. This forest, like the rest of Molo, was quite different from anything I had seen in the Kikuyu reserve. Most of the trees were either olives, or cedars with black, bitter berries, which grew to great heights. Their trunks, fluted and twisted like enormous sticks of Edinburgh rock, had a special talent for catching the sunlight and giving out a red glow. Their foliage was hung with long, drooping beards of lichen, dry and brittle, of a peculiar, soft greenish-grey. This gave them a look of ancient giants, full of wisdom and mystery, turned into trees.

Their branches were often twisted and half-bare, so that one might have imagined an ecstatic dance of venerable but frenzied priests, frozen by divine command and so obliged to spend eternity in those odd, tortured and yet dignified positions. Inside the forest's darkness the sharp cedar-smell was always in your nostrils, dry twigs cracked and whispered under your feet, the rotting fallen trunks lay as deep in moss as Plantagenet monarchs in furs and velvets. The slow decay of leaves, and the spotted fungi, added a pungent tang to the cool sunless air. The undergrowth was thick and spiky and you could not traverse it without getting torn to bits, and perhaps not even then. But game paths went everywhere, and some of these had been widened into human paths by the Dorobo, those little hunters who dwelt, like bongos, only in the very deepest forest. One seldom saw a Dorobo, but they had game pits in the forest, down which one might tumble on to a nest of sharp stakes.

The pleasant feature of this forest was the open glades, like lakes of grass in the mountains of cedar. At one moment you would be walking along a dark tunnel, scrambling over logs, pushing through creepers and listening for the squawk of a monkey or the harsh, sudden cry, like the protest of a rusty hinge, of that queer bird the plantain-eater, with its awkward flight and crimson-banded wings. The next moment you would stand on the margin of a glade lying before you as open and inviting as a garden or park. No human beings had created these glades; how they had arisen, why trees would not grow in them, I never discovered. Each time you came to one, you had the feeling that you were the first human being ever to stand upon that verge and gaze across the tufted grasses, like Cortez and the Pacific, and that some extraordinary prehistoric animal would be browsing there.

The Crawfurds' furrow started in one of these open glades, and the things I principally remember were the scent of jasmine, and the butterflies. A strong-smelling species of jasmine grew in this forest, for the most part invisibly, but now and then you would see a cluster of tiny white stars gleaming from the dark, knotted undergrowth. Its scent blended in an exciting way with the musky, fat-and-ochre smell of the spectators, and in the background was the dry smell of wiry grass, with a faint undertone of aromatic cedar.

The sunlight drenched us all, the air was clean as ice and large, vivid butterflies, purple and gold, quivered on the bush while Mr. Crawfurd took a spade to dig away the last foot of furrow, and thus to link it with a little pool that had formed just below a spring. It was quite a small spring, but Mr. Crawfurd was satisfied that it would supply many thousands of gallons, I forget how many, every day.

"What a thrilling moment we are coming to!" Mrs. Crawfurd cried. "Humphrey, I'm sure you ought to be presented with a silver spade. We should have the date engraved on it with a motto, or quotation. . . . Perhaps we ought to have asked someone to come and open it, not the Governor exactly, possibly Lord Delamere, or the D.C."

"No, not the D.C."

"Surely he would have loved it, such a change from collecting taxes and sending natives to prison, and he's a great one for a party, is our D.C."

"Not one with so much water about."

Mrs. Crawfurd laughed, not in a dutiful wifely way but as if she really meant it, and musically, in a series of up-and-down trills.

"If only Althea were here! How she would enjoy it! Althea would take a spade and make a lot of lakes and rivers, and a pond for ornamental fish. Do you think we shall be able to keep goldfish, Humphrey? Would they live at this height?"

"No," Mr. Crawfurd said, digging away with his spade. When he was not listening he always said no, because it was safer. You could change to yes later, but not from yes to no.

"Never mind, think of the sweet peas and new potatoes and the strawberries. And water from a tap! It's *too* exciting. Do you think frogs will get into the pipe? Do you think the buffalo will use the furrow to wash in, Humphrey?"

"No."

"The water's going to rush through any minute! What a lot of people have come! Isn't it a good sign, that they're so interested! Do you think they'll all go away and tell their friends, and the friends will start to irrigate in the reserves?"

"No."

Mr. Crawfurd had now paused beside the last barrier of soil to fall before his spade. The water seemed to lean against it, awaiting its release. Under a cedar, a group of elders sat on their haunches taking snuff. They wore robes of stitched goat-skin—their own dress, not blankets—and looked watchful and wise. They were fascinated by the furrow and everything about it, for the Kikuyu, although so intelligent in many ways, had never thought of irrigation; yet other, smaller and much less successful tribes such as the Elgeyo and Njemps had worked out clever systems of their own.

"Perhaps they think that we are being sacrilegious," Mrs. Crawfurd said. "They think it wrong to cut down sacred trees; if spirits live in them, they believe, the spirits should not be disturbed. Perhaps it *is* wrong to move a stream, or in this case create a whole new one. Do you suppose we're being sacrilegious, Humphrey?"

"No." Mr. Crawfurd straightened his back and looked round before he knocked away the last barrier. Several of the old men now came forward and made a little speech which I could not understand, for it was in Kikuyu; their faces were animated, they moved their skinny arms in graceful gestures and their voices slid like a stream over smooth rocks, and gurgled into little pools.

"He is saying that he is very happy to see water coming down from the mountain," the headman translated. "He asks God to see that it is good, and to help us."

Mr. Crawfurd waited restively while the old men invoked blessings, which took some time, for each one had to speak in turn. No doubt they felt that this was the very least they could do on such an important occasion. Had it been their own furrow they were opening, they would certainly have held a long and solemn religious ceremony, and sacrificed a goat at least, and probably a bullock.

"He is saying that God will send much water to help the crops and cattle, and he hopes God will help the bwana as the bwana helps the Kikuyu. And he hopes the bwana will help the Kikuyu to get back the cattle that the Nandi stole and sent to Fort Ternan, for it is a bad thing that thieves should come to this farm."

The elder was referring to a long *shauri* about some cattle lost by the senior Kikuyu on the place. Mr. Crawfurd had engaged as cattle-herds one or two men from the Nandi tribe, who despised the Kikuyu in the manner of a baron despising an ignorant churl, while the Kikuyu, for their part, hated the Nandi in the manner of a Roman loathing a barbaric Goth or Vandal. Ever since the Nandi came there had been nothing but *shauris*, and now the Kikuyu had accused the Nandi of stealing their cows. If Mr. Crawfurd had not been there they might have slain the Nandi with poisoned arrows, or attacked them in their sleep with swords, and probably been massacred in return; as it was, they were frustrated to a terrible degree.

"Thank you, old man," said Mr. Crawfurd, who, although a believer, liked God to be confined to Sundays and not to interfere in the farm. "If you have proof it was the Nandi, you must bring a case before the D.C. Meanwhile you must remember what I told you about this new river. You may water your cattle at the tank but never, never, never in this furrow, and if you do I will fine you heavily and confiscate your cows."

"That we understand," the elder agreed, "but you must also ask God to keep away the buffaloes." So he had the last word, as befitted a Kikuyu. Nor could he resist sprinkling a little earth on the water as it trickled through and muttering an incantation, a blessing of some sort, I suppose.

Mr. Crawfurd struck away the last clod and stepped aside and down gushed the water, full of curiosity to explore this new path. It curled along like a snake with a creamy-yellow head, and flowed in great excitement down the clay bed. There was a murmur from the people, surprised perhaps that the water really did flow along the furrow, as Mr. Crawfurd had told them it would. This they did not regard as a certain consequence of digging; it was a happy conclusion, as when a boy is safely born; he might have been a girl, or been stillborn, or led to the death of his mother, but he had not; the prayers and magic had succeeded, the hoped-for result had been achieved. I do not suppose there was a single person there, except for the Crawfurds and Dirk, who did not believe that, had spirits frowned upon the enterprise, the water would have refused to flow along the clay bed.

Now that all was safely over there was a great deal of smiling and laughter and congratulation. There must always be magic in the birth of a river, especially, no doubt, one that you have made yourself. Perhaps Mr. Crawfurd felt as Moses felt when he struck the rock and water gushed forth into the desert.

I can remember still the smell of the jasmine, and the purple butterflies, and the elders' red goatskin robes, their long bead ear-rings and dangling snuff-horns, and the water singing down among the cedars, and Mrs. Crawfurd standing with her hand in Bay's, her face gay with pleasure, looking from the furrow to Mr. Crawfurd as though he had indeed performed a miracle. Bay disengaged himself and waddled like a duckling to the furrow, and began to fill it with twigs and clods of earth. He was retrieved, and his father made a paper boat for him to launch upon the water, now flowing calmly as if it had been there for a hundred years. Of course one boat was not enough, and soon a small fleet had been dispatched, carrying sailors in the shape of twigs.

We ate our sandwiches beside the pool and listened to the silence of the forest, and birds moving in the foliage, and the humming of a bumble-bee. The war they had talked of in Nairobi was a word without a meaning, and Humphrey Crawfurd munched his luncheon with a satisfied look in his eye. But before the meal was over he had spoken to his wife about another, longer furrow that he hoped to dig, to carry water to a more distant part of his farm.

Chapter Twenty-four

IN the Crawfurds' sitting-room there was a photograph of Ian, looking young and handsome in a kilt. I hoped that he would come to see his brother, but Mrs. Crawfurd said that he had gone to a district called the Trans Nzoia, wild and uninhabited, to take up land the Government had given out, and start a farm of his own.

"But of course he won't stay there when he hears about the war," she added. "He will go straight down to Nairobi to join up. But I don't know how the news will reach him, there are no posts, and he said he wasn't coming back until he'd built a house and planted a crop, what sort of crop I can't imagine, and it's really quite unlike Ian to stay in one place and be a farmer, he will probably go off into the blue as soon as he gets wind of a herd of elephants. Do you think he will ever make a farmer, Humphrey?"

"No."

"Although of course it may be a sign that he's wanting to settle down, and perhaps for the usual reason; it is high time that he was married, although I can't imagine him as a domesticated husband with a little woman fetching him his slippers, but I suppose it might not be like that, he might marry someone like Tilly who is so good with horses, or a rich widow, or one of those women explorers. Do you think that would be a good plan, Humphrey?"

"No."

A little while before I came to Molo, Dirk had broken a leg. He had flatly refused to be put on a train to reach a doctor, so one of the Kikuyu, who laid claim to some surgical skill, had set the bone and bound the leg in splints. By the time I arrived, he was able to ride and to walk short distances. It was because of this leg that Dirk had not been able to enlist in anybody's Horse or Scouts, and he was burning with impatience and frustrated zeal. Dutchmen like Dirk had nothing against the Germans, but they longed for a fight, and did not want to let a lot of *rooineks* get in ahead of them.

His home was on the plateau, and he was one of a family of nine. His father had a light carbine rifle, the perfect weapon to shoot Germans with, and Dirk's immediate wish was to go home and claim it before an elder brother did so; whoever enlisted first, he said, would be sure to get the rifle, but it was useless to go until his leg was sound. So he was fuming at the slowness of his recovery, and almost in despair about the carbine; his hope was that his elder brother was away on a transport job, or else had enlisted in Nairobi without returning to the plateau first.

The day after the furrow was opened, I followed up its course to see if I could find the paper boats; a path had been made and it was easy going, so it became my favourite walk, especially before breakfast when the air was fresh with the smell of dew and leaf-mould and cedar, and when the chestnut bushbuck, with their graceful, twisted horns and dappled spots, were still abroad, and would bound back into the forest at my approach with a short bark of alarm, and vanish as abruptly as if they had been dissolved.

One morning I surprised two dikdik in the glade, standing among grass that countless quivering cobwebs had silvered all over, each one—and each strand of every cobweb—beaded with dew. It was amazing to think of all the untold millions of cobwebs in all the forest glades, and all across the bush and plains of Africa, and of the number of spiders, more numerous even than the stars, patiently weaving their tents of filament to satisfy their appetites, and of all the even greater millions of flies and bees and butterflies that must go to nourish them; and for what end, no one could say.

In the middle of this field of silver splendour stood the two dikdiks with their tiny heads lifted, their nostrils dilated and their unwinking eyes, as bright as blackberries, looking straight into mine. I never ceased to marvel at the delicacy and brittleness of their legs, slender as reeds; it seemed impossible that the dikdiks should not break them as they bounded over tufts or hummocks, even with their leaf-light weight.

These dikdiks had the charm of the miniature. They were perfectly made, not a single hair or sinew less than immaculate; little engines of muscle and grace, more like spirits than creatures. One always saw them in pairs. So long as I stood still, so did the dikdiks; I wondered what would happen if I never moved at all. Would they stand and stare all day? Should we all be there at evening, still motionless? But it was hopeless to try to out-stare the dikdiks; after a while I took a step forward and, with a movement of superb ease and elegance, the little buck sprang away to melt into the trees.

I then became aware, as one so mysteriously does, that I was being watched. I looked round, saw nothing, and stepped forward to sit on a fallen log. A current of watching still trembled in the air. After a while I saw a stirring in the dark undergrowth, and a brown furry figure stepped forth into a shaft of sunlight, which awoke in his fur pelt a rich, rufous glow, and twinkled on his copper ornaments.

He was a small man: not a dwarf exactly, or a pygmy, but one who stood about half-way between a pygmy and an ordinary human. His limbs were light in colour and he wore a cloak of bushbuck skin, a little leather cap and ear-rings, and carried a long bow and a quiver of arrows. He stood stock-still and looked at me just as the dikdik had done, and I wondered whether he, too, would vanish if I moved.

"Jambo," I ventured.

His face crinkled into a smile. It was a different face from that of a Kikuyu, more pointed, lighter-skinned, finer-boned; it wore something of the watchful and defensive look of an animal, with an added humour and repose.

He stepped forward, raised his hand and returned my greeting.

"The news?" I asked, continuing the traditional form of greeting.

"Good."

"Where have you come from?"

He threw back his head to indicate the hills at his back.

"The forest."

"Where are you going?"

"To seek meat."

He came and stood by me, fingering his bow. We could not speak much, for he knew only about a score of Swahili words. From him came a strong, pungent smell, with a hint of rankness, like a waterbuck's; his skin was well greased with fat, his limbs wiry and without padding, like the dikdiks'. I knew him for a Dorobo, one of that race of hunters living in the forest on game they trapped or shot with poisoned arrows. They did not cultivate, they existed on meat and roots and wild honey, and were the relics of an old, old people who had once had sole possession of all these lands—the true aborigines. Then had come others like the Kikuyu and Masai, and the Dorobo had taken refuge in the forests. Now they lived in peace, or at least neutrality, with the herdsmen and cultivators, and sometimes bartered skins and honey for beads, and for spears and knives made by native smiths. They knew all the ways of the forest animals, even of the bongo, the shyest and most beautiful, and their greatest delight was to feast for three days upon a raw elephant.

I knew his arrows would be poisoned. He pulled one out and showed me the sticky black coating on the iron head. "This kills the elephant, the great pig, the buffalo."

"There are many buffaloes?" I asked, thinking of Humphrey's water-furrow, and the warning uttered by the Kikuyu elders.

"Come with me." He turned and walked towards the forest with loping, bent-kneed strides. Where the glade ended the undergrowth looked black and solid as a wall, but he slid into it, and I found that we were on a little path. That was too strong a word for it; it was rather a crack in the spiked solidity where other feet had trodden. The Dorobo stooped, I copied him, and we proceeded slowly like crouching animals, he silently, I treading on sticks and barging into roots and getting caught by creepers and scratched by thorns.

We came to a small glade sloping down towards a stream that could be heard whispering at the bottom, clouded with reeds and long grass. Near the glade's margin was a patch of bare, greyish earth.

"See!" exclaimed the Dorobo, pointing with satisfaction: and I looked in vain for a herd of buffaloes.

"I see nothing."

He loped forward again. When we halted on the edge of the bare patch, I could observe hoof-marks and cattle-droppings; the hint of a rank odour, faintly bovine, hung about the place. It was a salt-lick, tramped by the feet of many buffaloes.

"They come every night," the Dorobo said. "If the bwana brings a gun early in the morning, he will see many, many, just like cattle."

"Where are they now?"

He pointed with his chin to the slopes beyond. "There above. They sleep. They eat salt at night, and in the early morning they play."

We returned along the game-track. "Where is your house?" I asked.

"In the forest."

"You have no shamba?"

"The elephant is my shamba. These are my hoes." He touched the quiver at his side. "Have you tobacco?"

"No." I felt ungrateful, and I had no money either. "I will try to get some."

"Good. Bring it here, and I will take the bwana to the buffaloes." He smiled, half-raised his hand, twitched his bushbuck cloak more securely on his shoulder and loped off, leaving his ripe civet smell on the morning air.

I wanted to keep the Dorobo to myself, he belonged to the same world as the dikdik and jasmine and butterflies, but I did not know how to get hold of any tobacco; so I was forced to confide in Dirk. His eye gleamed when he heard about the salt-lick.

"That is how to get them, man," he said. "There will be many, big bulls and all. I will find that Kaffir, he will show me the spoor."

"You must take me with you."

Dirk merely laughed. "A *toto* like you?"

"But he's my Dorobo!"

Dirk said that Dorobo belonged to anyone who brought them tobacco, and rode up with some next morning to the furrow-head. Although we had made no appointment, the Dorobo appeared, this time with another, even thinner and smaller than himself. They departed carrying the tobacco, having promised to meet Dirk at the forest's edge next morning, before dawn, and guide him to the lick. As for me, I was to be left out, and resentment stung me like *siafu.* I had discovered the Dorobo, and now Dirk was going to have all the fun.

That night I thumped my head four times on the pillow, so as to wake at four o'clock. Probably it was the stir of Dirk's departure that really woke me, the lanterns moving in the darkness, the tapping on the door of his rondavel, and the pawing and snorting of the pony he was taking as far as the furrow-head, because of his leg. I dressed in the darkness, shivering, for these early mornings were chilly and the water in the jug stung the skin. I waited until the pony had gone and the lights vanished, then I crept out like a vole to follow on foot.

This was not nearly so simple as I had expected. Although a half-moon threw black shadows, the path developed all sorts of bumps, holes and obstacles unknown in daylight. The grass was soaking wet and bitterly cold, and the twinkling guide-light soon disappeared, leaving me hemmed in by shapes that leant towards me with a crouching menace: leopards, buffaloes, hyenas, even elephants might be within a few feet, gloating at the prospect of a meal. I wished very much that I had stayed in bed, and with every step decided to retreat, but obstinacy drove my reluctant feet forward. Only the furrow hummed a friendly note with its gentle swishing; at least I could not lose the way, so long as I followed it.

As I approached my glade I could hear Dirk's pony cropping grass, and the movement of humans; he and the syce were waiting for the Dorobo. I waited also, frightened to reveal myself, shivering, and getting hungry; a rumbling stomach threatened to betray me, and I wanted to sneeze.

Many hours seemed to pass before the Dorobos' arrival. At last I heard low voices, the jingle of a bridle, an order given, and then silence, save for the noises of the pony, who was to be left behind with the syce while Dirk proceeded, limp and all, on foot.

The syce, a Kikuyu named Karoli, was to some extent an ally, and I decided to ask him to help me follow Dirk into the forest. When I appeared he was at first alarmed, then incredulous and finally discouraging.

"The bwana told me to stay here," he said. "I do not wish to be eaten by leopards and trampled by buffaloes. Are you not a *toto*? And should not all *totos* be in bed?"

"I shall wait here until he shoots a buffalo."

"It is too cold, and the bwana will be angry."

"I want to stay."

"Haven't you heard about the savage monster that lives in the forest and eats horses? When it smells one, out it comes. It is bigger than a forest pig, it has teeth like swords and five arms like a monkey's, and seven eyes. It will eat you up in one mouthful, like a stork eating a locust."

"You are telling lies."

All the same, I could not help thinking of the monster, with big pointed teeth and burning eyes, and wondering if there might not be a grain of truth in Karoli's tale. I hugged the pony's neck for warmth, convinced by now that bed would, after all, be a much nicer place.

"Why do you not go back to Thika, to your mother and father?" Karoli asked. "Thika is a better place than this. The maize grows tall, and there are sweet potatoes, and the land is fat."

"Is Thika your home, also?"

"Very close to Thika; and Kupanya is the chief of my people. But my family will think I have died in this cold place, for my bwana will not let me go home."

We talked of Thika while the darkness thinned slowly and the stars faded, and the sky glowed with a deep, rich, royal blue. The air was steel-keen, a film of dew lay over everything and a breath of frost passed over the glade, leaving no traces. A rain-bird called; its haunting downward cadence was like a little waterfall, melodious and melancholy.

The gun shot could not now be long delayed. Night was fading so fast that we could see tree-shapes thirty or forty paces distant. Something moved just down the furrow; I watched it fiercely: a leopard on the prowl, a homing forest pig? No, only a bush-buck, his pelt dark with dew, picking his way fastidiously along our glade, his nostrils a-quiver to receive the book of scents from which he could read with certainty the news of the morning.

The crash came and shook the trees: another after it, then a third. These three explosions united to form a hollow echo from the hills, and made the pony plunge and whinny. The sound rolled away into a watchful silence. The bushbuck had vanished, the rain-bird was stilled, only the furrow whispered to itself unchanged. Then from the forest came movement, a muffled crashing, the snap of branches, a thumping of hooves.

"They come towards us," said Karoli.

The sounds were indeed growing louder as the buffaloes, obsessed by panic, stampeded downhill, abandoning all caution in a frantic flight. At such times their big-bossed horns were used like battering-rams to thrust a way through thickets; in their panic they would plunge ahead with no regard for any object in their way.

"To that tree, quickly!" cried Karoli, tugging at the reins and trying to pull the pony after him; it smelt the buffaloes, threw up its head and bolted. I ran to the big cedar where Karoli cowered; he was sweating and rolling his eyes. The buffaloes went by as if a mass of great black boulders had detached themselves from the hillside and come hurtling down upon us at such a speed that they were gone before I had time even to realize what they were; their hoof-beats made the ground quiver under my feet as if it were a hollow gourd. The boulders vanished, the drumming faded, in a moment only the rank smell remained. Karoli rubbed his head and made chattering sounds. We both sat down on a log to rest our weak knees.

"These buffaloes are bad, bad, bad," said Karoli. "They will crush you with their feet as a man steps upon a beetle. Eee—eee, there were a hundred buffaloes, a thousand, more than the cattle of the Masai; they were angry, they were bad." He went on talking to himself in this vein.

By now the sky in the direction taken by the buffaloes was banded with rose and lemon and the colour of flamingo wings: the path was ready, the sun was on his way. From the forest came three figures led by my Dorobo, whose face was eager as a dog's. Dirk was the last, hampered by his leg. When he saw me he was furious, but had no time for more than swearing; he had wounded a buffalo, and had to find the spoor. Two bulls lay dead near the salt-lick, where he had lain in wait until dawn.

The Dorobo ranged through the glade like hounds casting for a scent, and soon one of them stood rigid and gave a low call. On a leaf-blade was a little crimson bead, which Dirk and the Dorobo bent to examine. By its colour they could tell whether the buffalo had been hit in the body, or in the heart or lungs.

My Dorobo took the lead with his head down and his eyes on the ground, bow in hand. Dirk followed with the rifle. The sun came up proud as a lancer, hurling long golden spears over the dew-white grass and silver cobwebs; a red flame sprang up the trunks of the cedars, the birds fluted, the whole world came alive. Karoli went over to the pool and sluiced his head in the cold upland water.

"Now we must go back with an angry buffalo on the path," he grumbled. "If it sees us it will trample on us, perhaps it is waiting for us now."

Nevertheless we encountered nothing more ferocious than a pair of dikdiks, a distant glimpse of waterbuck and some francolins. I had entertained a hope of sneaking off to my rondavel unobserved, but this was quickly dispelled. The pony had arrived, and a relief expedition under Mr. Crawfurd was about to set forth. He glared at me with an anger all the more alarming for its cold suppression, and told me in icy tones that I deserved to be kept in bed for a week on bread and water. But Kate Crawfurd, although she scolded, was too relieved to be severe, which in any case was not in her nature, and I enjoyed an excellent breakfast, and later in the day went with a party sent to skin and cut up the two dead buffaloes.

Dirk's shots had brought forth from the forest's recesses a little posse of Dorobo who could hardly restrain their excitement as hides were stripped from carcasses to reveal beneath the dark red flesh with its wonderful network of veins and arteries, the viscous blue coiled intestines, the purple liver, and the bright, spongy lungs. As the knives sliced away, a murmur of joy and eagerness arose. At a word from the chief skinner they fell upon the raw meat and hacked hunks off with swords and knives, smearing faces and chests with blood and mucus as they dug in their teeth like worrying hounds. The Kikuyu stepped back and looked on with contempt. They ate meat only, as a rule, on ceremonial occasions and, while they relished a fat ram or bullock, they tackled these decorously, old men eating before the young, men before women, each age-grade in its turn.

"They are like hyenas," Karoli said. "If they had no buffaloes or elephants, they would eat men."

But the Dorobo were sublimely happy, immersed in pleasure as a bather in the sea, and holding nothing back. They had no fear, as hyenas must have, of being driven off by stronger creatures; they simply gave way to their appetites, belching to make room for more. After a while their stomachs began to swell up like puffballs, the pace grew slower, and some of them wrapped slabs of meat in leaves to carry home.

Meanwhile, Dirk had not reappeared. Both the Crawfurds

began to get anxious; with a stiff leg he would lack agility, a quality indispensable to trackers of game. Buffaloes were said to double back on their tracks and take their hunter in the rear when they were wounded; a good many people had been killed that way.

"Poor boy, I do hope nothing's happened," Kate Crawfurd exclaimed. "I don't know what I would say to his parents; if it comes to that, I don't know who his parents are, or their address or Christian names or anything; perhaps they haven't got an address but are living in a wagon somewhere, or a laager, whatever that is (apart from a kind of beer); we never ought to have let him go after the buffalo."

"We didn't," Humphrey pointed out.

"Well, that's quite true, though I don't suppose his mother would believe us; perhaps he has just got tired and is coming back very slowly; don't you think we ought to send out a relief expedition, Humphrey, to search for him, with some brandy in case he's hurt, and a stretcher, in case he's quite exhausted?"

"No," Humphrey said.

And he was right: Dirk turned up a few hours later safe and sound, but angry and morose, because the buffalo had eluded him. He and the Dorobo had tracked it for miles, and the buffalo had not doubled back at all but gone very quickly; after a while the blood spoor had petered out.

"It can't be very badly wounded if it's gone so far," Kate said soothingly. "And now you must really go and lie down, Dirk, and rest your leg, goodness knows how you managed to go all that way, I hope you haven't strained it. You mustn't go and hunt buffaloes again until your leg has absolutely recovered."

"The hide was worth at least a hundred and fifty rupees," Dirk grumbled. Humphrey was equally put out to know that a wounded buffalo was at large and might at any moment attack one of his labour force, or indeed attack him.

"The Dorobo will finish it off and gobble it up," Kate Crawfurd said. "How very carnivorous they are! But I suppose we are just as bad, only we cook it first, which makes everything a little more restrained, but doesn't affect the principle, that we all live on dead animals, like hyenas and lions. I used to think that vegetarians were cranks, but now I wonder; perhaps they have climbed a rung higher on the ladder of civilization.

Perhaps it is more *spiritual* to live on beans and spinach, with possibly an egg now and then. Do you think we ought to try it, Humphrey, and give up being carnivores?"

"No."

We ate the buffaloes' liver and enjoyed it, in spite of Kate's doubts; but since then I have often wondered whether she was right.

Chapter Twenty-five

SOON after the buffaloes were shot I rode with Dirk to Londiani, which was then railhead for the Uasin Gishu plateau and all the country beyond—the Trans Nzoia, the far and fabulous Mount Elgon, and great valleys and escarpments only visited by hunters, and by very few of them.

The Crawfurds had not wanted me to go with Dirk, whose object was to get some cartridges, but Kate Crawfurd was unwell, Mr. Crawfurd was busy and I insistent, and so they gave way. Dirk had not wanted me either, but he had little choice; I mounted the pony the Crawfurds had lent me, a white one called Snowball, and set out at his side. On the whole he was a good-natured young man, and used to children. He had grey eyes and a skin that, although sunburned, was so fine-grained as to look almost transparent. Years later, I saw a pumpkin hollowed out for Hallowe'en with a lighted candle inside. The pumpkin's flesh shone with a deep golden glow that suddenly reminded me of Dirk's complexion as I had noticed it on this long ride.

Dirk had come to the country, as a boy, seven years earlier, with a party of Boers conducted from the Transvaal by a patriarch called Mr. van Rensburg, a modern Joshua leading his people to the Promised Land on the last of all the treks of the Afrikaner people. As we rode along, Dirk told me how Mr. van Rensburg had chartered a ship in South Africa and filled it with his followers—forty-seven families, all tired of life in the Transvaal and excited by dreams of the freedom, emptiness and virgin land of this new part of Africa. They loaded all their wagons, trek-gear, ponies and possessions into the ship and came to Mombasa, and thence by train to Nairobi, which was not much in those days—a single street of Indian *dukas* made of mud-and-wattle or of corrugated iron, and Government offices on wooden piles of the same harsh material, which used to creak and crack, like a man pulling his finger-joints, in the hot sun. The Boers arrived in a wet July; the streets were deep in mud, and wagons sometimes stuck between the station and the Norfolk. Women walked with their long skirts gathered up, showing thick black boots underneath, and perhaps thick black stockings, but even so the hems of their dresses must always have been bedraggled and dirty. They camped in the garden of a parson's bungalow—Tentfontein, people called it—until Mr. van Rensburg led them on, once more by train, to the small up-country township of Nakuru.

While they were camped near Nakuru, the D.C. arranged a sale of raw native oxen. Everyone bought at least one span of beasts, for about fifteen rupees each, and some men bought two spans, and then everyone settled down for several weeks to train these oxen, which had never even seen a yoke before, to pull the half-tented wagons they had brought with them.

I should have liked to have seen the cavalcade of nearly fifty wagons and teams setting off from Nakuru; but although I was born then, I was only about a year old, so would not have seen much. While most of the Boers had been training oxen, a few others had gone ahead on horseback to spy out the land. They had climbed three thousand feet, using elephant tracks through the forest, and had stood at last upon a rock (so Dirk's brother, who was one of them, had told him) silent with wonder, so noble did their promised land appear, teeming with animals who lacked the fear of man. Herds of kongoni, he said, browsed on the sweet green grasses, he saw wildebeeste and zebra by the thousand, and oribi wandering about wagging their tails, and the loping giraffe, like tiger-lilies bending with dignity before a gusty breeze, and the big biscuit-coloured eland with their drooping dewlaps and striped withers, and the red, nimble-footed impala walking in single file. And many birds: spurfowl, francolin and guinea-fowl, as well as pigeons cooing in the trees; and smaller animals like reedbuck and duiker, all feeding together without enmity or fear. Even the lions excited no alarm unless actually hunting, and were ignored, and sunned themselves peaceably. A man had no need to stalk and crawl, he had only to stand still and shoot and something would fall.

Years later, I saw a picture of the Garden of Eden, with all the beasts consorting together in a park of great beauty, painted with meticulous richness and care. I thought at once of this vision of the Uasin Gishu plateau as the Dutch first saw it, and as no one was ever to see it again. The difference was that in the picture, Adam and Eve walked at peace with the animal creation; but that was only a vision. The artist should have painted Adam setting a trap, and Eve chewing a morsel of liver. The Dutch, of course, had rifles, and fingers that itched to press the triggers. This they did as soon as they had recovered from their astonishment. They shot a kongoni, and had a good meal.

The scouts returned to say the promised land was all and more than they had hoped for, but the way to it was hard. There was not even a track. With their raw oxen, they would have to get the wagons up a mountain steeper than the Drakensberg. The ground was wet and treacherous, there was danger from elephants and buffaloes, and also from lions. These were just facts to be reckoned with, that was all. Having come so far, there was no retreat.

Their method was to trek for three or four days and then rest for two, partly for the sake of the oxen, partly to let the women wash the children's clothes and bake bread. They would scoop a hole, sometimes in an ant-heap, sometimes in a river bank, and in it light a fire, rake out the ashes and deposit a big iron pot containing dough. The smell of fresh bread, Dirk said, would draw him, and all the children, as if it were a kill and they were young lions, and they would stand with their mouths watering until their mother called them to the meal and broke the bread. But they must wait for the whole family to gather round and for their father to ask the blessing of God. Their father had the first helping, then they could eat. Biltong, bread and lard was their food, and fresh meat when it could be shot. And coffee, black and strong, and very bitter, because it was partly made of roots and herbs. When Dirk's father shot a buck, his mother would melt down the fat to use for cooking, and also to rub into the hide, which was dried, treated with alum and then cut into strips to make thongs.

Beyond Eldama Ravine, everyone waited while the men cut a track through the forest clothing the steep western wall of the Rift Valley. The ground was moist, and the narrow wagon wheels cut in so deeply, and so roughly churned the path, that those in the rear stuck fast again and again. Then a span would be unhitched from another wagon and sixteen pairs of oxen, panting and straining, would heave at the yokes; the forest would be startled by a great cracking of whips and by hoarse shouts of encouragement, women and children would trudge up the muddy track to lighten the load, and at last the wheels would edge painfully forward, inch by inch. A few yards farther on, the whole thing might start again. It took the wagons at the tail of the column four long days to cover the first seven miles.

Then they came to bamboos, and then to hidden swamps so treacherous that the oxen sank up to their bellies before their drivers saw the danger. The men chopped down bamboos to make a causeway, built it up with earth and leaves, and coaxed the teams across. When one of the wagons slid off, Dirk said, the men of the party spent a whole day extricating it. One of the oxen gashed itself so badly that it had to be shot, and several others were injured by the terrible strain. The air was damp and clammy, a Scotch mist came down, the sun vanished and the folk were silent, wondering how they could find good country right away on the roof of the world.

Gradually they drew away from the bamboos and into more open country, but still they climbed. The grass grew in thick, tufty patches which made oxen slip and wagons jolt and sway. A great fire had ravaged the forest, and charred stumps stood round them, Dirk said, like ant-heaps made of ebony. In the midst of this unearthly, haunted landscape they came upon Sugar Vlei, so named because its tall, green reeds reminded the Boers of the Natal plantations. They built another causeway, and this time fifteen wagons sank in up to the rails, with only the tops of their wheels showing. The women, their small children huddled round them, watched dumbly, fearing the loss of all they possessed in the world, while men, boys and oxen together called out the utmost effort from every muscle and nerve. Three teams, in all forty-eight oxen, were hitched to each wagon and, in the end, almost by force of willpower, they got the wagons over Sugar Vlei.

More swamps lay ahead, more causeways, more stuck wagons; oxen were beginning to fail, children to sicken, women to wonder whether their men had been deceived. Food was scarce, for forest-dwelling game kept out of sight. One day Dirk's father shot a waterbuck. Its flesh was sour, but his mother roasted the bones and they feasted on the marrow. Nights were bitter cold, hyenas' eyes, red as embers, ringed their camp and the oxen huddled together, hungry and afraid.

At last the day came when the ground was firmer and the wagons moved more easily. Now distant hills appeared ahead, the land levelled out, the sun shone in their faces and their hearts were lifted by the sense of freedom that belongs to the plains. Here at last was highveld, and they felt at home.

Next day they camped beside a river, the Sosiani, and shot guinea-fowl, and ate well. Their talk was all of where they would go, where they would settle. Each man could pick his own land. They trekked on to the great rock of Sergoit which stands above the plain, where they saw lions, and camped beyond it at a place they called Rooidrift, from the colour of the stream. There the column broke up, each family choosing for itself the direction it would take.

Dirk's father went on until they reached a gulley with a rocky bank, and trees, near a stream, and here they outspanned. Next morning, Dirk's father and his eldest son began to quarry stone for a house, and to fell trees. For nails, they used wooden pegs cut from olives. They made a harrow, Dirk said, from acacia logs and spikes of olive wood, bound with kongoni thongs.

"We are not rich like the English, to buy everything in a *duka*," Dirk said. "If we want something, we make it. If it is a house, we build it ourselves."

Dirk told me a lot more about his life on the plateau, and how his father cleared and ploughed land, and bought a few cows from the Nandi in exchange for tobacco, and now was slowly building up their farm. They lived on the maize they grew and ground themselves in a small hand-mill, on meat they shot, on milk from the little native cows. All they had to buy for cash was salt, paraffin, coffee and tobacco. Even the paraffin could be done without, at a pinch; the Boer women could make candles out of boiled-down eland fat.

After a while the Boer settlers began to make the few rupees they needed by trading with the Nandi, by transport to the railway, by shooting game for hides and, if they were young men like Dirk, by working for the British. However poor a British farmer thought himself, the Dutch looked upon him as a sort of Croesus.

What had become, I asked Dirk, of Mr. van Rensburg? He was still there, a respected man who owned a black coat and took a leading part in church affairs. For already these few Dutch families, who had brought two Predikants with them, had divided into factions for the worship of their God. As soon as a town was established, two rival little churches went up, each built by its congregations, without any pay.

When the farms occupied by the Dutch were surveyed and numbered by the Government, one was set aside to become a township. This was number sixty-four. The first man to live there was a Scotsman, MacNab Mundell, who opened a little store. This became the post office, mainly by virtue of a safe provided for the takings. Dirk said that when the Postmaster-General, Mr. Gosling, arrived one day to inspect his post office, and opened the safe, a lot of I O Us fell out, and that was all he found; for Mr. Mundell was a great one for poker. Later on, a bank was opened, and this also consisted of a safe, so large and heavy that when it was pushed off the back of the wagon, no one could shift it again, and the bank had to be built round it. This bank had two rooms, one for the manager, Mr. J. C. Shaw, and one for the safe and a counter. As Mr. Shaw's room was cramped, he took his morning bath behind the counter, where customers would sometimes find him (for he was not an early riser) wrapped in a towel. This did not embarrass him; he would put on a brightly-coloured dressing-gown and walk next door to Eddie's Bar to have a quick one before the start of the day's work. Most people, Dirk included, called the township Sixty-Four, but by now it had received an official name, and was becoming known as Eldoret.

By the time Dirk had finished telling me all this, and much else besides, we had reached Londiani, or at least seen the roofs, which shone like a pool of water in a fold of the downs. The corrugated iron threw back the sunlight and we seemed to be arriving at a city of splendour and glory, like the ancient capitals of Lanka that were copper-domed.

Londiani shrank, however, on our approach, as if it had drunk from the bottle Alice found at the bottom of the rabbit-hole; it shrank, withered and turned into a single rutted street with a few *dukas*, some sheds beside the railway, a *dak* bungalow, and a D.C.'s office with a flag-pole.

"Is that all there is?" I asked.

Dirk laughed. "What are you expecting?"

Whatever it had been, Londiani did not possess it. I was by then tired, sore and hungry, despite a sandwich and some roasted mealies Dirk had shared with me as we rode along.

"Now what shall I do with you?" Dirk wondered. Had I been a pony, he would have turned me out to graze.

"I'm hungry."

"We had better go to the D.C."

"Will he have some breakfast?"

"Certain to."

District Commissioners were accustomed to deal with any situation that might arise, and I do not remember that this one showed any great surprise at being handed over a stray child. He passed me on to his wife, who gave me a feast. On farms, the bread was made with yeast brewed from bananas or potatoes and imported dried hops, and was nearly always sour, and hard as old boots, so that one of the luxuries farmers most enjoyed when they visited a town, even a little one like Londiani, was baker's bread. Mrs. Pascoe's toast was pliant and delicious, and she even had apples and sausages, the rarest of treats. Nothing in the world tastes better than a crisp and spicy sausage, steaming from the pan, after a long ride on a sunny morning.

Mrs. Pascoe was a kind-hearted woman with a well-developed sense of duty; these two attributes, had made her into a dumping-ground for other people's pets, and a soft option for the locals, who caught birds and animals in the forest to bring to her for the sixpence she would generally pay to rescue them from their misery, and so the house was full of small beasts like bush babies and mongooses, and larger ones occupied pens outside.

Mr. Pascoe soon appeared looking rather harassed, and no wonder; the war had upset everything, and this was mail-train day, so his office was full of citizens with *shauris* needing immediate attention. No one expected to be kept waiting, and everyone felt that his turn ought to come first.

"What are we going to do with this child?" Mr. Pascoe demanded. "We can't keep her here, like those infernal mongooses."

"I'm going back with Dirk," I said.

"That young Dutchman? What makes you think he's going back to the Crawfurds?"

"He came to get some cartridges."

"Cartridges my foot. He's probably on the way to the plateau by now, or else to Nairobi to join the party."

"But he's got Mr. Crawfurd's pony."

Mr. Pascoe only laughed. "*That* won't bother him."

"I don't think we've any right to jump to conclusions," Mrs. Pascoe said. "He is probably quite an honest young man."

"Not if he's a Dutchman," Mr. Pascoe said ferociously. "They're in my office all day long. Permits to move cattle that turn out to be pinched from the Nandi—cases against each other that turn out to be faked—beacons moved about in the night—slippery as eels, the whole blessed lot of them. Now, what are we going to do about this brat?"

"I can go home by myself," I said.

"You certainly can't. Perhaps there'll be someone on the train who can take you to Molo, and then the Crawfurds can collect you there. As if I hadn't enough to do without playing nursemaid to a stray female brat!"

He was not really a savage man, just a little gruff and disconcerted; and in the end he called for Snowball, who had also breakfasted, and allowed me to ride with him to the *dak* bungalow to find out if anyone had seen Dirk.

The bungalow, a railway rest house, was full of bearded, dust-stained Dutchmen who fell silent as Mr. Pascoe approached; when he spoke they greeted him politely but with a wary, almost shifty look, behaving a little like wildebeeste that smell a lion about; they do not panic and gallop off, but tend rather to huddle together, stop grazing and stand ready for action, although uncertain what to do. Mr. Pascoe addressed a man who looked exactly like a leathery, bearded Boer, but spoke with the accents of Scotland.

"You're wearing your boots today, Sandy."

"Aye, my feet are looking after them. It's necessary, in a thieving crowd like this."

Sandy was one of the few transport-riders who was not a Boer. He was said to keep his boots in a knapsack and to walk barefoot beside his oxen in order to save the leather, and to have travelled back to Scotland on a third-class railway ticket from Londiani to Nakuru. Another story was that he once rode on muleback for three days into the Kavirondo country to retrieve a stolen pair of socks; but others said this was untrue, because he had never owned any socks.

When Mr. Pascoe inquired about Dirk, Sandy said:

"Och, he'll have gone after his brother, up to Sixty-Four. The brother came through by the last mail, to fetch his gun before he went for a soldier."

"You mean he took the pony?" Mr. Pascoe said.

Sandy looked astonished. "You don't think there's a Dutchman living who'd pay for transport when he could get his legs across a nag?"

In spite of Sandy's certainty and Mr. Pascoe's smile, I felt sure that Dirk would return the pony. Although Mr. Crawfurd would no doubt regard his present action as a theft, to a Dutchman or to an African it would appear merely as a rather long borrow.

Chapter Twenty-six

THE wagon-track from Sixty-Four ended outside the *dak* bungalow, and from its veranda, where travellers waited for the mail, someone called attention to a puff of dust rolling towards us with unusual speed. A high, old-fashioned buck-board came into view, drawn by four oxen who shambled along at a splay-footed jog-trot and drew up with obvious relief beside the bungalow. This was Whitelock's stage-coach, propelled by oxen trained to trot (if not very swiftly), and changed every fifteen miles between Sixty-Four and Londiani.

By these means, and by keeping his teams going all through the night, Whitelock had reduced the journey from five or six days—and anything up to three weeks in the rains—to twenty-four hours.

One of the passengers who stepped stiffly down from the buck-board was a man of six feet three or four, of massive bulk, but not fat by any means—solid muscle. Everything about him was large—nose, hands and feet, thick dark moustache, heavy shoulders. He seized Mr. Pascoe's hand and pumped it, and explained that he was on his way to join the war; from what he said, it was high time that someone put a little punch into it. In spite, no doubt, of Robin's efforts, the Germans kept on blowing up the railway line between Nairobi and Mombasa, and the arrival of troops from India had not made the difference everyone had expected. The local volunteers, who had coalesced into the East African Mounted Rifles, had been whisked up to Kisumu to man a boat on Lake Victoria, and had won a naval victory over a similar German vessel. But there still seemed plenty of scope for Mr. Pascoe's acquaintance, whose name was Dick Montagu.

"Oh, this is my wife," he added as an afterthought. Mrs. Montagu had been standing quite still, looking bewildered and nervous. She was as small and light as he was large and heavy; like some hesitant bird, bright-eyed and fine-limbed, she seemed to have alighted on the veranda, rather than to have climbed the steps. Her waist was so slim that her husband could surely have encircled it with his two hands. Dick Montagu ignored her while he got his baggage assembled, and told Mr. Pascoe that he would have to spend the night at Londiani in order to wait for the bulk of his kit, which was following by wagon in charge of his Abyssinian servant.

"It should be here tomorrow, and you can put us on a goods," he said. "I was caught in the Congo when the show started, and I don't want to miss any more of the fun."

Mr. Pascoe looked displeased, but said: "You'd better bring your wife over to our bungalow for the night, this place is full."

"Thanks, old man," Dick Montagu replied in a perfunctory manner.

Mrs. Montagu behaved as if the Pascoes' bungalow was a palace, entered after a long sojourn in a swineherd's hut. And, indeed, that may have been her situation. Her father was one of those rich Americans who had come to shoot big game after Theodore Roosevelt had made the pastime fashionable; and Dick Montagu had arranged his safari. The hunter had bagged not only a lot of large animals, but the daughter as well. She was barely eighteen, and her father forbade the match. After Dick Montagu carried her off to the Belgian Congo in a romantic elopement, her father had returned to Philadelphia to cut her out of his life and his will. Dick, who was twenty years older than his bride, boasted that the old man was sure to come round, but over a year had passed, debts had gathered and the old man was still in Philadelphia refusing to answer letters and as close as a clam.

"My, you have flowers and real nice furniture, even *books*," Lois exclaimed.

"Surely you need books all the more on the plateau," Mrs. Pascoe suggested, in a voice that sounded faintly accusing. "I mean, being so isolated."

"We have two books, Mrs. Pascoe: I have a Bible, and Dick has Rowland Ward's *Records of Big Game*."

"Well, I expect you would like a nice wash." A little soap and water, Mrs. Pascoe seemed to indicate, would soon put matters right.

When Lois Montagu reappeared she tried to talk to me, an uphill task for most people. Close cross-questioning revealed

Tilly's interest in a hospital, and this made Lois taut with hope; her fervent wish was to nurse wounded soldiers, but Dick had refused his permission because she was too young and inexperienced.

"Maybe if I get to know your mother, she'll kind of sponsor me," Lois said. "Then Dick will think it's quite respectable, and let me train to be a nurse. I'm pretty strong really, although I'm little, and I guess I can look after myself, as well as the poor wounded men."

"He's afraid the wounded men will look after Lois," I heard Mr. Pascoe say to his wife later. "He still thinks her old man will cave in."

Mr. Pascoe had decided that I was to stay the night and accompany the Montagus to Nakuru next day, where the Crawfurds would meet me. He had sent a syce to Molo on Snowball with a note to this effect. I knew that Mrs. Crawfurd would be worried and Mr. Crawfurd angry, and wanted to ride back on Snowball myself, but Mr. Pascoe would not allow it, and there was nothing to be done. However, when we boarded the train it appeared that we were to travel in the guard's van, and this redeemed the disappointment.

Even the Uganda Mail, which ran three times a week, was not a very fast train, and our goods made no pretences. Several steepish gradients so much exhausted our little locomotive that it paused a long time to regain strength, while its boilers cooled and the logs that it devoured were re-stacked. Once or twice it failed altogether at the first attempt, retreated, and took a longer run, while some of the passengers got out and walked, as if to help it. At every station it drank prodigious quantities of water while the crew, and various attendants who had attached themselves to it, got off to bargain with vendors of bananas, cooked maize, chickens, eggs, gruel, oranges and the many other comestibles on offer at every halt. In fact our train made something of a triumphal progress, with long pauses to allow the people to admire at close quarters a creature so strange and inexplicable, that brought to remote places a flavour of adventure, a whiff of the mystery of unknown lands.

We arrived in Nakuru latish in the evening, and made our way to the hotel. I was sent to bed in a cubby-hole too noisy to permit easy sleep. The kitchen quarters were nearby, in the public rooms people stumped about on bare boards and in the bar a sing-song developed, interrupted by shouts and laughter, and once by the smashing of glass. The hotel belonged to Lord Delamere and sometimes, when he felt the need of a rough-house, he would drive into Nakuru in a buggy and start to break up his own property.

Now he was away at the war, but the hotel was filled beyond its capacity. Somehow a war seems always to create more people than it destroys. Although armies of young men march away to battle-fronts, all the towns and centres become fuller, busier, more bustling than before. Where all these people, drawn forth as rain brings *siafu*, had been before, was a mystery.

Sometime in the night, a commotion arose. The station was very close, and I awoke to hear an engine panting and grinding, bells clanging, whistles blowing, shouts and cries. Had the Germans captured Nakuru, were we all to be lined up and shot? As I did not wish to be shot in my pyjamas, I dressed and went out to investigate.

A train was in, the platform was alive with khaki men, like giant ants whose nest has been disturbed. But Germans would be grim, orderly and helmeted; these men wore slouch hats or no hats at all, and even in the hard, shadowy light looked young and gay. I saw Lois Montagu standing by herself, and went up to her.

"It's the Mounted Rifles on their way back from Kisumu, they've won a great victory," she said, after the expected exclamations of distress at my truancy. "Why, they're heroes! Look at them, honey—next time you see them maybe they'll be marching through Nairobi in a victory parade!"

At the moment, food was what they wanted, and the Indian station-master, hemmed in by large foraging men, made helpless gestures and looked like bursting into tears. Hot food at one o'clock in the morning was hardly a thing he could be expected to summon with a blast of his whistle, and he must have felt as if an enormous pride of hungry lions had got loose in his station.

Lois stood with her lips parted and her eyes bright, clasping my hand. "If I was only a painter, what a picture this would be! All these fine young fellows going off to fight for king and country without a care in the world!"

They had this quite important care, however, about nourishment, which no one seemed able to provide. And then a sort of miracle occurred. Without warning, in the dead of night, the station was quietly invaded by the succulent odour of freshly-baked bread. A kind of mass hallucination? Had so great a volume of insistent thought somehow been turned into smell?

An amazed hush fell upon the men; they stood still and sniffed the air. It was as if a magic ring had been turned and their wishes granted. Through the entrance came a torch-bearer carrying a safari lamp, then a hand-cart piled high with baskets and finally a small, quick-striding figure that I recognized. The light fell upon a nob of red hair, a high voice cried: "Well, boys, here's what you've been waiting for. Come and get it!" And a stampede followed towards baskets full of warm, delicious rolls, whose crusts crackled as they parted to surrender a creamy, soft and satisfying dough.

Whether Pioneer Mary had started her bakery before the war, or after it arrived with its new demands, I do not know, but a bakery she had, here in Nakuru; getting wind of the troop-train she had prepared for the hungry travellers. Soon the station took on a festive look, with groups of soldiers sitting on crates or sacks of bedding or the carriage steps munching the rolls, joking, once or twice breaking into snatches of song. Pioneer Mary was among them like a red flame flickering along the platform, leaving a trail of laughter, and boisterously greeted as the lady of the loaf.

She was not the only acquaintance there. I looked round to see Dick Montagu approaching with a slighter figure at his side on whose bare head the lamplight shone as on a new golden sovereign. Even Dick Montagu was mellowed, and introduced his companion to Lois without disparaging her. Already half moonstruck by the masculinity of these joking, feasting, migrant soldiers on their way to war, who would seem tomorrow creatures of dream and legend, she gazed as if bewitched at the thin and smiling face of Ian Crawfurd.

"Dick has spoken of you often," she said.

"I don't know how the devil you got yourself into uniform so quickly," Dick grumbled. "I heard you were somewhere out Mount Elgon way, picking out some land."

"I happened to have gone down to Nairobi, and to be there

when the show started. Otherwise I might have been out of it for months. I haven't even let Humphrey know yet."

"I'll never forgive you if you clear the Hun out of German East before I can join the party."

"I think there will still be plenty for you to do," Ian said.

For a while they discussed the war, which they did not think was being well conducted. Then Ian smiled at me and said:

"I saw your father in Nairobi. He had just come back from questioning some German prisoners."

"Did he shoot them?"

"Well, no; one is supposed to shoot them before they are captured, not after. He had been finding out why they had failed to blow up the bridge at Tsavo. It was really awfully bad luck. They had been given British maps because the Germans thought they'd be more accurate than their own, which showed the Tsavo river in quite a different place. When they got to where the bridge should have been, they ran out of water and had to give themselves up. If they'd stuck to the German maps they'd have got to the right place at the right time and destroyed the bridge."

"That was the hand of Providence," Lois said.

"We're told that God moves in a mysterious way his wonders to perform, and perhaps the inaccuracy of British maps is included in the mystery. . . . I hear you are staying with Kate and Humphrey; you must give them my love, and say that I shall write, and that I hope they are very well."

"All right. . . . Thank you very much for Mohammed," I said. "But I had to leave him at home."

"Yes, he would not at all enjoy Molo; you would have had to make a coat for him from a blanket, with a hole to push his head through."

"I didn't want to leave him at Thika, but . . ."

Above all I wanted to hold Ian's attention, not to lose him, and to find some thread to lead me on to all the questions I longed to burst out with. But it was no use, they jammed my tongue. The moment passed, Ian turned away to speak again to the Montagus. Dick was asking him about the land he had taken up, but Ian only smiled and was vague.

"It hardly looks as though I'll need it, after all."

"Don't make any mistake, old man. That land will be worth

a lot of money when we've thrashed the Hun. Things will go ahead, we'll see land values really come into their own. Look after the development clauses, don't let it slip through your hands."

"I'll remember," Ian said. "And now I must go. I'm a corporal, and have a dozen men to look after who've never heard of discipline. But two or three are good bridge players, one plays the clarinet and another is an excellent conjurer, so we're never dull. I expect we shall meet somewhere on the border, Dick, and perhaps we shall ride together in triumph through Tabora, dragging von Lettow at our heels."

He took my hand for a moment to say good-bye.

"Did Ahmed come back?" I managed to eject one of the questions, even if it was a minor one, out on the perimeter.

"Funny you should mention that. He did, and he's joined a troop of Somali scouts and has a pony and a rifle, and glorious dreams of war and loot. So he's all right. Give my love to Tilly when you see her, and to everyone else. . . ."

He stood for a moment as still as a fish-eagle above a swirling, muddy stream, looking down at me, his hat in one hand and the other resting lightly on his belt. I thought he looked thinner even than before, older perhaps. The name in both our minds lay unspoken between us like a barrier, and yet uniting us, for this fleeting instant, like fish caught in the same net. So strong was this impression that I thought I heard through the chatter a clear musical voice and sensed among the stale platform odours, and the lingering reminder of bread, the sunny scent of heliotrope.

Ian hesitated; perhaps he, too, did not want to put to flight the ghosts of happiness whose presence there beside us turned all the khaki men of flesh and blood into puffs of vapour. Then he slipped from one wrist a little bracelet he wore—such things were then in fashion—of plaited hair pulled from a lion's tail.

"He had courage: some people eat the heart, but I doubt if that's necessary."

I took it without finding anything to say, but I knew in my own heart that it was not for me. He smiled at us, waved a hand and vanished into the throng and bustle of the train, which was now preparing for departure. The men began to sing the jingle that was then so popular—"Marching to Tabora"; and the shouts and cheers, the whistles, the hissing and chugging of the engine, filled the station as a kettle fills with steam. Everything seemed to bubble over; men waved from windows; Dick gave a hunting cry; the red hair of Pioneer Mary flared under a lamp; the guard jumped into his moving van; and we watched the rear light of the last coach vanish, and heard the chugging die away. A plume of sparks, a long coil of dancing fireflies, spread across the black, ancient shoulder of the crater Menengai; and gradually the vast digesting dark of Africa swallowed up all traces of that audacious grub, the hurrying train.

Chapter Twenty-seven

A COUPLE of days later I, too, found myself in the train and bound in the same direction, although not for the war. The Crawfurds, who came down from Molo together, had decided not to keep me any longer. Humphrey said he was tired of my disappearing act, and that Kate had other things to think about; and they had heard from Tilly, who had done all she could for the time being at the hospital, and was returning to Thika, that she would like me back again.

Lois Montagu offered with enthusiasm to deliver me to Tilly, but Dick did not seem pleased. I suppose I was a kind of protection for Lois, without realizing it; also, through me she would meet Tilly, who might help to get her into the hospital. Dick was resolved to hustle her through Nairobi, which he seemed to regard as a kind of Sodom and Gomorrah, and deposit her with friends who would keep her out of mischief. She did not seem mischievous, but of course I did not know her very well.

In the train Dick did not speak much to Lois, and ordered her about in the same sort of tone, only sharper, that he used to a cocker spaniel who lay at his feet in a position where everyone tripped over him. Lois insisted on pointing out to me from the window things I had spotted long before she had—herds of waterbuck and impala, a great many black-banded Thomson's gazelle and their larger cousins, the Grantii, and plenty of giraffe. Dick grumbled a great deal at the slowness of the train, and appeared to hold the Indian station-masters at every stopping-place personally responsible for the delays.

Tilly was at Nairobi station. She already knew Dick, but not Lois, who made the mistake of being effusive, and of praising me. Tilly knew that the favourable things she was saying about me could not possibly be true, and I could see that Lois was heading straight for the category of gushing fool, which was as bad as silly woman or stuck-up ass, and would not get her into the hospital. However, we all had tea together and Lois managed to manœuvre Tilly to one side and explain her wish.

"He is really very medieval," Tilly remarked, when Dick had taken her off. "If he had his way, he'd lock her in a chastity belt for the rest of the war."

Robin was still away somewhere on the railway, or perhaps on the German border, no one knew; the next day we took the train to Thika and once more rode out to the farm.

Several of the flame trees, now taller than I was, flanking the future drive, had burst into flower. The young coffee trees were looking healthy and had a few green berries on them, their first. I was thankful to discover Moyale in excellent health, too plump if anything. On the farm, Sammy reported, all was in order, save for a fight after a beer-drink in which two men had been injured, but not fatally, and the death of one of the oxen. When Tilly inquired into this she found that the Masai herd, wishing to hasten the ox, had prodded it up the backside with a sharp stake, puncturing its rectum, so that it had died in agony. She lost her temper with the herd and fined him, but it was obvious that everyone, including Sammy, thought it was the loss of wealth that had provoked her anger, and concern about the poor beast's feelings was something they simply failed to understand.

Here on the farm the war, except for Robin's absence, might not have existed at all. Some of the young Kikuyu were full of ardour and would shake their spears or sticks and cry:

"Show me these Germani! Where are they? Have they run away? I will kill them as we used to kill the Masai! Ho, ho! There will not be one left between here and Kilimanjaro!"

This bellicose atmosphere so infected me that one day Njombo came upon me chopping off the tops of old maize stalks with a hunting knife.

"What are you doing?" he asked.

"Cutting off the heads of the Germans!"

The attitude of the Kikuyu was put down to a gratifying, if not surprising, loyalty to the British, who had done so much to bring civilization, law and order to the savages. No other explanation occurred to anyone but Alec Wilson, who came over soon after we were back.

"It's the prospect of law and order being removed, not their introduction, that is so much exciting them," he said. "All the men in their thirties are pulling their spears out of the thatch where they've been hidden, and telling frightful whoppers to the newly-circumcised about the Masai, who in fact always beat them, while the young lads are saying: 'Those old has-beens had no more fight in them than a chicken. But *now* you'll see something!' I'm afraid they're going to be dreadfully disappointed."

"I daresay they like a scrap," Tilly conceded. "But theirs wasn't civilized warfare. The women and children were carried off or killed."

"From what I hear, the Kikuyu will be made into porters, and sent down to German East. I hope that when they're humping the troopers' bully and the Generals' champagne through the bush, which is stiff with tsetse, rhinos and malaria, they'll appreciate the advantages of civilized warfare. But I'm afraid it's not exactly what they're hoping for when they demonstrate their loyalty."

"You're a cynic, Alec, that's your trouble." Like most cynics, he was very kind, and frequently came over to offer Tilly help in running the farm. There was a lot to do: coffee to be weeded, citrus pruned, a stone store built, land ploughed, maize planted, seedlings nursed. I rode errands on Moyale, added to my collection of birds' eggs and started a scrapbook about the war, although there was not yet much to put into it.

A chit came one day from Lettice: she had returned, and invited Tilly over for the night. I went too, because there was no one to be left with, and for the same reason a syce carried over a woven-reed basket containing a pair of carrier pigeons Tilly had bought from a man who kept a *duka* in the farthest depths of the Masai reserve, and used a pigeon post to Nairobi. Tilly anticipated a need for carrier pigeons when our troops were pursuing Germans beyond Tabora and hoped, by breeding them, to make a small contribution to the war.

Lettice we found pale and tired; her eyes looked huge and dark, a peaty brown. She kept patting her hair and making other nervous gestures, and she had taken up smoking. The smell of heliotrope was still there, but almost overlaid by Turkish tobacco.

"Now I am being caught out, as I knew I would be eventually," she said, after she had greeted Tilly with affection. "None of the things I am good at are the least use in a war, and

I cannot even help Hereward by running the farm efficiently, as you help Robin. Hereward gave me a manual of instructions made out in duplicate, telling me what to do with each labour squad and ox-team and shamba, and I put it in a hat-box which I left behind in Nairobi."

"How is Hereward?" Tilly inquired.

"Getting impatient. This is just a side-show, he says, and he wants to get back to the real thing. But he isn't quite so worried now that it will all be over before he arrives."

"I would expect Hereward to be bellicose, but I must say I'm surprised at Robin. He is just the same, and all this sword-sharpening is out of character."

"One would have thought so, but I'm afraid their characters are all the same; once they get among the trumpets, they are bound to say Ha-ha. . . . Hereward expects to get a passage any time now, and I shall follow by the next ship I can get on to."

They fell silent, with an unspoken question lying heavily between them. Lettice had taken up her tapestry work, but she was only fiddling with it. She sat on a low stool of plaited thongs before the open fireplace, her head, with its chestnut hair loosely gathered up, bent over the neglected work, and Tilly was on the deep velvet sofa, frowning a little over her thoughts, which might have been of Lettice and her troubles, or of the pigeons and theirs, or of Robin, or of some new notion that was coming to birth. When she spoke to break the silence it was a matter on the outskirts of her mind.

"I met that girl Dick Montagu married for the money she turned out not to have. She's trying to escape, but he won't let her; people say because he still thinks she'll get the money, but I think he's fallen in love with her in his peculiar way."

"It must be rather like having a hippopotamus in love with one, or a gorilla."

"Matron gave her a job as a sort of bottle-washer and Dick came storming up in a black rage to carry her off. She locked herself in one of the empty private wards. Dick mounted guard and spent the night lying outside the door wrapped in a blanket. It was a great sensation. In the morning Matron had to call the military police to take him away."

Their laughter slackened the tension a little, and Lettice was able to say:

"I saw Ian in Nairobi."

"Yes. . . . May I try one of your cigarettes?" I had never seen Tilly smoke before. She puffed experimentally, blowing out the smoke in little jets.

"You know he took up some land at the back of beyond, near a mountain. He said it had caves full of bats, and wonderful butterflies. His nearest neighbour brought a house out from England in bits, carried for the last hundred miles or so by porters, and kept a cheetah chained to his veranda."

"I suppose this rotten war . . ."

"Ian is chasing Germans on the border, if they're not chasing him, and Hereward's heart is absolutely set on becoming a hero. . . . Oh, Tilly, what am I to do?"

Lettice had jumped to her feet and was prowling round the room, changing the position of an arum lily in a vase, patting out a cushion, winding up a little leather-coated clock on her writing table. Tilly frowned at her cigarette, which had made her eyes water, as if it were the cause of all these complexities.

"You know what I think," she observed.

"Yes, and of course you were right then; everything was settled, and it only remained to face up to Hereward. But now. . . . He would pay us out, I know, poor Hereward; his life is nothing to him, or at least it comes low down on the list of things he considers important. So he would think nothing of discarding it, and we should have it with us for the rest of our lives, whenever we opened a cupboard we should see its skeleton quietly standing there at attention. And Ian . . ."

"Yes, Ian! Hereward will be in his element, he'll be a General covered with tabs, you'll see. Surely it's Ian who needs to be considered. . . ."

"I consider little else. At home we used to keep bees; a billy goat got loose once and tipped over several hives; the bees were in a state of absolute hysteria, their whole routine gone west, they flew in all directions buzzing hopelessly, with no one to tell them what to do. And now that billy goat of a Kaiser. . . . Tilly, if I go home, will you look after Puffball and Zena?"

"Of course I will; but I suppose I shall have to go too, if Robin manages to get himself recalled."

"I don't suppose Maggy Nimmo will go, but she'd feed them

on porridge and oatcake which would make them much too fat, and sooner or later Mr. Nimmo would turn up with that dreadful bull-terrier, who'd gobble them up in two mouthfuls. Oh, dear, *everything* is difficult. . . ."

"Come and see my pigeons," Tilly suggested. "Do you know when the mating season occurs? They don't seem to take the slightest interest in each other."

"It would save a lot of trouble if we were the same, and only took an interest in each other at certain times of year. Then we could prepare for it, and if we had husbands like Dick Montagu they could keep us under lock and key."

"There doesn't seem to be any way of telling with pigeons. Or perhaps they are shy."

We rode back next morning with the pigeons, and a few days later Robin came home on leave, bringing me a present of a pair of German field-glasses, and a lot of news about the war, which was not going very well. However, the Mounted Rifles were patrolling the border and hoped to meet the Germans in a fair fight at any moment, and of course to win a victory. So far the enemy had avoided open battle in a typically Teutonic way; the bush was exceedingly thick, and more trouble had been caused by rhinos than by Germans; hyenas were so bold that, at night, the men made pillows of their saddles, and even then sometimes the leather was chewed. Malaria was the worst enemy. A secret force was said to be coming by sea from India to land on the German flank, and that would turn the balance, Robin believed.

"After that I shall be able to get home without any trouble, except that all the ships are full. There's a rumour that my battalion has gone to France already. It's maddening to be stuck out here."

It was indeed a surprise to find Robin, in his new martial spirit, no longer really interested in the still. He rode off to the station again in a few days, promising to send me a button from a German uniform.

I cannot remember how long it was after Robin's leave that I was down in the coffee nursery one evening, engaged in the construction of a little furrow to irrigate some orange pips I had planted, when Alec Wilson appeared, looking for Tilly. A couple of shamba-boys were repairing the banana-leaf thatch over beds of young coffee trees, and we could hear shouts and laughter from women washing their babies in the python pool. The shadows had fallen already on the river, all was peaceful and serene.

Alec looked dusty and smelt of pony, so I knew he had just returned from Nairobi. He nearly always went on horseback rather than by train, because it was cheaper. He asked me what I was doing.

"I'm going to have an orange shamba of my own."

"Splendid. When it's grown, you shall sit in the orange grove at dusk with humming-birds flying round your head, playing love-songs on a dulcimer, and I will come and lie at your feet and stroke the spotted fawns."

"I haven't got a dulcimer," I objected.

"I'll buy you one next time I go to Nairobi. And now I must find Tilly to tell her my news."

"Is the war over?" I asked.

"No. Less so than ever, in fact."

"Have the Germans run away?"

"No, they have fought a battle near a hill called Longido, and won it, I'm afraid. Now I should forget about it, and go on with your shamba."

I took his advice, but somehow I had lost interest in the oranges. I made a little mound to represent Longido, and stuck some twigs and leaves in it, and some stones to indicate soldiers. The ants that were crawling about made themselves into rhinos, lions and zebras.

One of the shamba-boys came up, adjusting his red blanket, and said:

"What is that you have made on the ground?"

"That is a hill with Germans on it."

"Germani? Eee, they are bad men."

"I am going to drown them with this water."

"Good. But if you drown them, you will also drown their cattle and horses. It would be better to shoot them. Haven't you any guns?"

"Yes, but they have run out of cartridges."

"In that case you must take your sword and rush upon them and slit their stomachs, and then they will all die like this."

He lifted a bare foot and stamped on the mound, twisting his foot so that it was flattened and scattered.

"There, you see," he said, "now there are no Germani. That is the way." He picked up his club, tucked it into a belt round his bare middle, shook out his blanket and set off up the hill, his day's work over, the enemy obliterated. It seemed a satisfactory conclusion, also, to me, and I clambered up to the house.

I found Tilly on the veranda, with Alec, having a late cup of tea. They both looked gloomy, and Tilly's eyes were red.

"Run along now and play with something," she said.

"With what?"

"Oh, never mind. Why don't you sit down and read a book?"

I went inside and looked at an atlas lying on the table, but I could hear them talking on the veranda.

"It would be best for you to tell her," Alec said.

"Yes, I shall have to; but it's late now to go over tonight."

"She will have the rest of her life to think about it, so you will do no harm by waiting till the morning."

"If it had been anyone else . . ." Tilly's voice was hoarse and muffled. After a pause Alec said:

"Those fools of doctors threw me out. They're idiots, I'm as sound as a bell. I shall have another shot, but meanwhile . . . Good night, Tilly, try not to fret. All the king's horses and all the king's men . . ."

Like the bees, our routine was upset. This was the time of our evening ride; instead, Tilly settled down on the veranda to do accounts. Then she laid them aside and returned to a scheme she was working out to supply fresh vegetables for the troops. It proved so successful on paper that she cheered up a little; when the present stung her, she sought her antidote in the future, which was as sure to hold achievement as the dying flower to hold the fruit when its petals wither.

But she was sombre and the evening sad, and I went to look for George and Mary and for Mohammed, who was kept from roaming by a long string tied to a hole in his shell. George was clinging to a twig, wearing his usual expression of immense self-satisfaction, like a politician (Robin had said) seeing his name in the Honours List—but it may have been Mary; although I pretended to know them apart, I could only guess.

I knew that someone was dead. People often died, animals and people; I had seen a dead body once, lying in the grass by the side of the road; a cloud of flies had risen from it, the ponies had shied, I had been hustled past it, and past the stench of putrefaction. It did not make any great impression. But none of that could be connected with Lettice, or with anyone I knew.

When I sat over my supper, and the lamps had been brought in, I asked Tilly if anything was wrong with Lettice.

"Nothing, so far as I know."

"Are you going to see her tomorrow?"

"Probably."

"Can I come too?"

"No, you have been neglecting your lessons; you must learn some French verbs."

"We should have lost Mohammed, if it hadn't been for the string; do you know, he dug himself a hole under the Cape gooseberries. Will Ian come back soon?"

"You must eat up the white as well as the yolk, it contains albumen, which is good for you. . . . No, Ian—well, if you must know, he has been killed. Now don't ask any more questions, and I'll read to you for twenty minutes before you go to bed."

This was a great treat—we were reading *Robbery Under Arms* at the time—and so I did not think any more then about Ian, but when I was in bed I remembered how I had seen him on the station platform, and how his hair had shone in the lamplight like a golden sovereign, and the bracelet he had given me made from a lion's tail. I had it wrapped in tissue paper and tucked safely into my scrapbook, too valuable to wear. It was hard to imagine a dead Ian, lying limply in the grass with blood on his face and flies buzzing over him, so hard in fact that I gave it up and thought of him as I had seen him when we had found the whydah birds dancing, and when he had lain under the fig-tree talking to Lettice, and when they had sung together after the piano had arrived. I had not seen Ian many times, but each time had been like a special treat, even though nothing unusual had happened; when he had been there it had seemed as if the sun had been shining, and I thought that he would never altogether disappear from my mind.

Even when I went to sleep I dreamed about him; we were

riding across a great plain to reach Lettice, and in the distance Germans moved about like grey lice; he had no rifle, but if only Dirk would come with the carbine, we should be safe. Dirk would not come, and then Ian was sailing boats on the furrow with Kate Crawfurd and Bay, and she told him that she had a flock of butterflies which carried messages. Even here, a danger threatened Ian; it grew closer and more ominous, something terrible and final that none of us could see. Ian only smiled and said that he must wait for Lettice, and then the sky turned dark, and a gigantic eagle spread its black wings overhead. We ran away, but Ian took a bow from the Dorobo and fired an arrow, and the eagle gave a screech; just as it fell upon us, Ian changed into a bushbuck and bounded away. I woke up struggling to escape from the enveloping eagle, which resolved itself into a blanket swathed round my head.

My dreams were always jumbled, and next morning I could remember only bits of this one, but the eagle stayed in my mind for some time. The Kikuyu believed that when a man died, his spirit could enter an animal, and it seemed quite likely that the spirit of Ian, who was so much a part of the wild and silent places, would choose a forest creature like a bushbuck for a habitation. As for his body, I knew it would be eaten by maggots and hyenas; but if in time its remnants turned to dust, as the funeral service said, his dust, I thought, would not be quite the same as other people's, but would shine like those little specks of brightness that sometimes glitter in the sand.

Chapter Twenty-eight

THE life of the farm continued as usual on the surface, but underneath there was a feeling of suspense and uncertainty. Our time at Thika was running out and everyone knew it, even though no word had been said.

Tilly was waiting for news of Robin, of the war, of our departure; and when news did come, it was never good. She hated, as she said, marking time, but could not forward march towards some major project like the vegetable scheme. Hearing of a meat shortage in Nairobi, she bought a dozen native ewes and wrote up-country for a pure-bred ram to make a good mutton cross. The ram duly arrived in an ox-cart, took one look at his scruffy little brown brides and fled into the coffee plantation, pursued by the entire labour force waving sticks and uttering cries. Before he was recaptured a number of coffee trees had been damaged, and could not be replanted until the next rains.

News came at last of Hereward; he had secured his passage and would sail at once, rejoicing, to rejoin his old regiment. Lettice came over to tell us and stayed the night, as she did sometimes when she was alone. In a way that I could not define she had changed; life seemed no longer to bubble up in her, but had died down. She was thinner and her arms looked brittle, her rings were loose, shadows had come into her face, and whereas before she had possessed the quality of repose, she fiddled now with things and did not pay attention, and moved in a curiously leaden way. I wanted to speak alone to Lettice, but could not say so, and fretted for an opportunity.

"So Hereward will be home before Robin," she said. "I hope that will not make Robin angry. What will happen to us, I wonder? Do you suppose we shall still be waiting for a passage when the war ends? Now that I know I must go, I should like to get it over quickly; this is like hanging about in purgatory, which I have never thought a very good invention, in spite of Dante; if God is merciful, he would hardly wish us to suffer any more than we already have on earth."

I asked what was to happen to Puffball and Zena. They sat now in our only comfortable arm-chair, one on her lap, one tucked into her side, snuffling—a comfortable sound, like a kettle boiling—and licking their black button noses, and sometimes hunted noisily for fleas. Lettice replied that she wanted to take them with her to England; no one here could look after Pekinese. I asked:

"And bring them back again?"

"If I come back."

"But you can't *not* come back!"

Lettice smiled. "Yes, I suppose it seems the centre of the world to you. But when you get home you will find it all looks different; as for myself, I don't belong here, it is a cruel country that will take the heart out of your breast and grind it into powder, powdered stone. And no one will mind, that is the worst of it. No one will mind."

I did not understand her meaning, and asked her what would happen to the farm, and the stone house they had built, and the ponies.

"Don't ask so many questions," Tilly said. "It is bad manners."

"But if I don't ask questions, how shall I find out things?"

"You are not supposed to be a private detective."

"All the same, that is quite an interesting point," Lettice remarked. "The best way to find out things, if you come to think of it, is not to ask questions at all. If you fire off a question, it is like firing off a gun; bang it goes, and everything takes flight and runs for shelter. But if you sit quite still and pretend not to be looking, all the little facts will come and peck round your feet, situations will venture forth from thickets and intentions will creep out and sun themselves on a stone; and if you are very patient, you will see and understand a great deal more than a man with a gun."

"Yes, I see."

"I don't suppose you do, but it doesn't matter; shall I come and say good night to you when you are in bed?"

This was a rare treat, so I had my supper and went off more willingly than usual. Lettice came later and sat on the edge of my camp-bed, and I noticed that the Turkish tobacco prevailed over the heliotrope. She told me a story, and talked about

Hugh; perhaps now that she would soon be seeing him, he was more often in her mind.

At last my opportunity came, and I said:

"I have got something for you."

"How nice! Is it a bird's egg, or a lizard that is indisposed? Or a particularly smelly Kikuyu charm?"

Lettice was on the verge of making fun of me, which was unlike her. It was in such small, subtle ways that she had changed, as perhaps she was bound to; if you fall into a fire your looks are altered, and if it is a fire that burns your spirit, that must be altered too.

"It is not mine really," I said. "It is something I was given."

"If it was given to you, then it is yours."

Now that I had come to the point, I had the greatest difficulty in passing it, as if I was swimming through a pool of treacle with weights tied to my limbs.

"I think it was really meant for you."

She would not help by asking who had given it to me, or what it was, and I knew that she was not really interested, so I put the little parcel on her lap without saying more. She unwrapped it and held it close to the safari lamp, and I said nervously:

"It's made of lion's hair, from the tail."

I felt her stiffen and go rigid; she sat for so long without a movement that I thought she had fallen into a sort of trance. Then I felt the bed shake a little; she was trembling, and the hand that held the bracelet quivered very slightly like the wing of a humming-bird.

"How did you . . .? When did . . .?"

"He gave it to me, but I think it was for you. A sort of charm."

She said nothing. Sometimes, in the garden in the early morning, I would find a snail moving forward, like a tiny ship with hunched brown sail, and would tickle it with a grass-blade to watch its grey questing horns quickly curl and vanish with the eyeless head, both sucked out of sight, and the whole snail became instantly becalmed. It was like that now with Lettice. I could not help prodding with my grass-blade.

"Do you want it?" Still she sat without a word. I searched for something to say that was not a question.

"One of the men he was in charge of was an excellent conjuror."

Lettice got to her feet and tried to speak, but her throat had dried up, as I imagined the throats of men who die of thirst must do. Her hand now shook so much that she could not hold the bracelet; at any rate, she dropped it on my bed, put the hand to her face and hurried away. I picked up the bracelet feeling dazed, as perhaps a beetle feels when, all but scorched against a burning lamp-glass, he tumbles out of range and lies there, half stunned, to recover.

Now the bracelet was really mine. It was black, neatly plaited, pliable. I slipped it on and thought about the lion; perhaps he had come charging from behind a rock to challenge Ian, perhaps he had been wounded and roared out, a mask of fury, for his revenge. Although the rifle had been too much for him, he had been brave, and Ian had respected him; and Ian had perhaps been killed in much the same way.

I put away the bracelet, and for a long time valued it. When I was away from Africa I would sometimes take it out and look at it, and think of the tawny lion crouching among wiry grasses and grey boulders, and the heat and aromatic smell, and dust and dryness, and the flat-topped acacias with their tightly clustering yellow sweet-smelling flowers, and the big clouds with their crowded sail throwing patterns on the furrowed hills, and the doves cooing, and the whistling thorns. But later still, in some move or other, the bracelet was mislaid. I did not notice its loss at first, and then I was sorry, but other things soon put it out of my mind.

Hereward came over to say good-bye a few days later, and not long after that we had a telegram from Robin; he had got his passage, and was coming on his final leave. He spent the time making plans for the shamba while we were away, for how long no one knew, and going round to say good-bye to those of our neighbours who were left on the ridge. Most of them had gone, and the rest were going, except perhaps for Alec; even Mr. Roos had vanished, though whether in pursuit of animals or of Germans there was no way of knowing. Edward Rivett had been wounded at Longido, a word that had a heavy sound for us all.

We found Mr. Nimmo at home on one of his visits, with the news, quite unexpected, that he, too, would soon be in uniform. Robin congratulated him, and asked what unit he had joined.

With his feet squarely planted, his head slightly on one side and a pugnacious look in his eye, Mr. Nimmo replied, vigorously rolling his r's:

"I've joined the Guar-r-r-ds."

This was a surprise; the Guards seemed a far cry from Thika and the Mounted Rifles, so Tilly inquired which regiment, Coldstream or Grenadiers, or perhaps the Scots Guards. Mr. Nimmo looked at her impassively and said:

"The railway Guar-r-r-ds." Mrs. Nimmo went off into shrieks of laughter.

The time came for Tilly and me to ride down to the station to see Robin depart, as Hereward had departed a few weeks before. His belongings had gone ahead in the ox-cart: his kilt and its embellishments, his sword, his surviving tweed suit that had been packed away in moth-balls in a tin trunk. He had been excited, but now the time had come upon us, we were all subdued. Things were not going as they should have, either in France or in Africa, where our troops had been routed at Tanga by Germans and bees; and submarines had started to prey upon shipping in seas that should have been indisputably ours.

"When I get back," Robin said, "we must start at once on the coffee factory. I think it will pay us to hull our own beans, rather than to send them off in parchment. I was working it out last night; in a decent year, once everything is planted up, and with this new system of pruning, we ought to get a hundred and fifty tons. . . ."

Robin's calculations went on; he had been busy with scraps of paper and our fortunes were as good as made. He had bought a steam plough, a race-horse and a Mercedes before we reached Thika, and was considering a new wing to the future house. All there was of it at present was a few foundations beyond a flame tree avenue planted soon after we had arrived.

Njombo was waiting at the station to ride the extra pony back to the farm. He shook Robin's hand and said:

"Good-bye, good-bye, bwana, and may God help you to kill many, many Germans; kill one for me, since I cannot go myself, and slit open his stomach and cut off his head! You will kill them all single-handed!"

"Perhaps not quite all," said Robin.

"Here is a charm that you must wear round your neck and it

will protect you from iron; it came from a very powerful *mundu mugo* near Mount Kenya and I have worn it since I was circumcised. It is a charm for warriors, and as I cannot be a warrior any longer I give it to you."

Robin was touched, and thanked him warmly, but in the mumble into which he always retreated when embarrassed by someone's good will; so Njombo could scarcely have heard. The charm was a little leather cylinder with ground-up powder of some sort inside—it was best not to inquire too closely about its origin, which in any case would not have been known to Njombo. It hung on a fine, light chain made by a Kikuyu smith. Robin slipped it into his pocket and looked more embarrassed than ever; he had intended to give Njombo some money as a parting present and now this would seem like paying for the charm. He felt in his pockets but found nothing suitable, and remarked ruefully: "I suppose he doesn't smoke cigars." Then the station-master was on us, bowing and smiling and wishing Robin luck in his babu English.

"You kill many Germans, please. You come back here to family safely and soundly. We praying for you, please."

The train snorted, the engine-driver shooed everyone inside, passengers hauled themselves up into high carriages, the guard waved a flag.

In retrospect, much of one's time in that early war seems to have been spent in seeing people off in trains, or else in travelling in them. A Kikuyu might have called it the war of the train; and its successor, the war of the aeroplane. Even in peacetime, there is in the departure of any train the faintest echo of the raven's croak; in times of war, trains are freighted heavily with fear and sorrow. This one, however, went off cheerfully, with many people waving from the windows, including Robin; and we mounted our ponies and rode away. At the Blue Posts we paused to pick up a parcel and saw Major Breeches, with florid look and spiritous smell.

"I've just heard splendid news, good people," he cried. "Splendid news. The enemy have been routed, our troops have crossed the Pangani river, they'll be in Tabora before the week is out. I think that calls for a little celebration, don't you?"

The trouble about Major Breeches was that you never knew whether, one day, he might relate a rumour that turned out to be true—although, up to now, we had never known it happen. So while Tilly was certain in her mind that he had made up this victory, her heart whispered that it might conceivably have occurred, and she went back a little bit comforted. About half-way she noticed that Njombo was wearing Robin's wrist-watch.

"Where did you get that?" she inquired.

"Bwana gave it to me at the station. When the engine shouted, he gave it, saying: 'This is for you, so that you will know the time when memsabu calls you to help her while I am away.' This is my baksheesh, I shall keep it as if it were my child, and it will bring me good fortune like a charm."

"I did not see him give it to you," Tilly objected.

"No, he did not wish you to, he thought you would be angry. He turned his back and put it into my hand as the train went away. Bwana is a good man, and God will help him in the war."

This sounded just like Robin, and I felt sure it was true. The watch was all that he could find to give Njombo and he gave it, and would buy another when he reached Nairobi, I supposed. But then, you never could be quite sure. Njombo with his open, cheerful, smiling face was packed with guile and an accomplished liar; he had long desired a watch, and Robin was often careless with his possessions. As with Major Breeches and his victories, there was always an element of doubt. Indeed in our double world there was very little we could be sure of. Tilly hankered after certainty, but never found it, and rode back in silence to the farm.

Chapter Twenty-nine

BERTHS were found for us at last in some kind of ship, a Greek cargo vessel; no one knew just when it would sail, and we were to wait for it at Mombasa.

To be torn up by the roots is a sad fate for any growing thing, and I did not want to leave Thika for the unknown. Especially I did not want to leave the animals and people of Thika, to leave Moyale and Mohammed, George and Mary, or Alec and Mrs. Nimmo, Njombo and Sammy and Andrew, or Kupanya and old Rohio, and even Kamau, and many others. Lettice had gone already, suddenly, in response to a telegram. Her belongings had been packed away, her furniture sheeted, Zena and Puffball had vanished with her, and the Palmers' farm had sunk into a haphazard lethargy jogged every few days by a visit from Alec. Despite his goading, weeds had begun already to gain the upper hand.

A painful moment came when Lucifer and his companion, Dorcas the chestnut mare, went away to join the war. They were to become remounts, mere units of transport in the hands of people who cared nothing for them, and we knew that we should never see them again. Moyale was spared. He was too fat and spoilt, and Tilly convinced herself that he would be useless to the war. Alec was to have him, and of course he could have had no better home.

Lucifer and Dorcas went off unsuspecting to be put into the train, and while this happened I took Moyale for a farewell ride in the reserve.

It was, as I remember, a cloudy day, with a sky of storms, low and threatening. Yet the sun threw long, triumphant shafts down the ridges to make huts and trees and goats look hard and solid, as if carved from wood, like objects in a toy farmyard. The green of the new grass was so intense and fierce that every hillside seemed afire with an emerald flame, rising to meet a sky of glutinous indigo. Moyale's progress was dignified; nothing would hurry him. We made our way up to Kupanya's to say good-bye. The chief emerged to greet me in a cloak fashioned, I was distressed to see, of many duiker skins, and with elaborate bead ornaments hanging from his ears.

"Have no fear, we will look after your father's shamba until all the Germans are killed," he said. "I will look after it myself and see that no harm is done by strangers and wild animals."

"When we return, will you still be here?"

"How should I not be here? I am too old to be taken for an askari. The Government has trusted me to look after the people, and to send them warriors."

The war had, indeed, enhanced the chief's powers and importance, not to mention his wealth, for it was understood that if a young man wished to avoid recruitment, and gave Kupanya a goat, or possibly two goats, he would not be sent to Fort Hall. And while a good fight with loot to crown it would have pleased the warriors, news had already got round that the young men, far from being given spears, much less rifles, and a prospect of booty, were expected to carry grievous loads in foreign countries and to eat poor food; as this was the work of women, not only uncongenial but insulting, no young man was going to volunteer to undertake it.

"The ponies have gone," I said, "except Moyale, who will stay with bwana dungbeetle."

"Good. When we see this white pony, we shall say: here is the *toto* of bwana bad hat, she will have this pony in her head as a man herds his cattle there, so we will think of you when we see him. Eee-ee-ee, but he is fat, and shiny, and strong; Njombo will feed him, when you return he will be as big and strong as a buffalo."

Several of Kupanya's wives, of whom he had by now at least a dozen, came up to wish me well. Coils of copper wire glinted on their seal-sleek skins, their loaded ear-lobes dangled on to mahogany shoulders. One of the wives, with wide cheek-bones, eyes like a moth's and an air of wisdom and sadness, spoke to me in Kikuyu and put into my hand a necklace of blue and white beads.

"These you must take to Europe and wear for us," Kupanya explained. "These beads will be like our people, the blue ones are men, the white ones are women and the children are the spaces in between, and the thread is the river that runs past your father's shamba. If you wear it always, you will come back safely to greet us again."

I thanked him, and looked for something to give in return, but my pockets yielded only a crumpled handkerchief, a knife, a few beans and bits of string. I thought perhaps the knife would do and offered it to Kupanya, but he shook his head.

"The traveller does not give a present to those who stay, it is those who remain who give presents to the traveller to help him on his journey, and bring about his safe return."

The women crowded round and several of them gave me presents also—a lump of dough wrapped in a leaf, an iron bangle, a roasted maize-cob, a dried gourd, a small *kiondo* (a woven bag used for carrying grain). It was difficult to manage these things on a pony, but I stowed them away in pockets, or tied them to the saddle, and rode away rather like the White Knight, festooned with objects whose use it would have been hard to define.

The day of our departure rushed towards us. Alec came over to fetch the tortoise, the chameleons, Bancroft the spaniel, and Moyale; he had become a universal dumping-ground.

"A tortoise lives a hundred years, they say," he remarked, "so with any luck Mohammed should be here to welcome your return; and George and Mary are planning a surprise already, there will be a row of little chameleons lined up on a branch to greet you, and nothing much will change while you are away."

The Kikuyu on the farm decided to hold a dance to celebrate our departure and bring destruction on the Germans, they said; in Tilly's opinion it was merely an excuse to extract from her a fat ram. Grudgingly, she agreed to provide one; and then on impulse decided that the flock of mutton ewes must go, Alec would not have time to bother with them, so she gave the two biggest to the dancers and the rest to Sammy, whose delight was scarcely to be expressed in words. Sammy was getting richer and richer, he had a bicycle, a wrist-watch, three wives and, in his own country, an ever-growing herd of cows; now we were going away and he was sorry, because something was ending, but glad, because the chances both to enrich himself, and to exert his superiority over the Kikuyu, would now become incalculable. With a charming speech about remembrance, he gave me a present of a Masai spear, the light kind used for daily herding, not the big long-bladed weapon of war, which he said would be too heavy to carry.

An immense amount of beer was brewed for the dance; big fat gourds bubbled for days in the huts by the fire that was never allowed to go out, night and day, from its lighting in the newly-built home, when the timbers were white and fresh, until the home's abandonment, when the rafters were encrusted with thick, black deposits of smoke. The young men came in full fig with white feathers in their hair, wooden rattles on their ankles, and patterns in chalk and red ochre all over their faces and their naked, glistening skins. The young women greased themselves from head to foot and put on all the ear-ornaments and wire coils they could muster, and their best leather aprons with beads sewn into the seams. They looked gay and festive, but not as decorative as the men.

Camp chairs were set for us to watch the dancing and feasting. Sammy stood beside us wearing an expression tinged with contempt for the caperings of such monkeys; had this been a Masai dance, his look implied what nobility, what strength, what splendour we should have witnessed! At the war-cry of the lion-maned warriors, all this Kikuyu trash would scatter like a flock of weaver-birds when the axe is laid to their tree. However, Sammy's manner suggested, the Europeans had elected to tolerate these people, and children must be expected to play, so he would do his best to conceal his feelings.

Andrew the cook did not watch the dance. He was offended with Tilly. When he had told her that he was going with her to Europe—this seemed to him a natural and, indeed, inevitable consequence of his attachment to her service—she had been obliged to refuse. Europe, she had told him, was distant and cold, but he had not minded that; would she not need a cook just as much in Europe as in Africa?

"There are other cooks in Europe," she had said.

"But *I* am your cook."

"The houses are different, the food, the customs. . . . Besides, where would you sleep?"

"Are there not kitchens in Europe?"

It was very difficult. Tilly had been compelled to say: "I have no house in Europe. Truly, you cannot come."

Andrew had picked up a clod of earth—they were standing in the garden—and dashed it to the ground.

"That is how you treat me. Because I am black."

Tilly was distressed, Andrew pierced to the core of his spirit, but no one could put matters right. So Andrew did not come to the dance. Once launched on its career it would have continued, had it been allowed to, all night and all next day as well. The feet and limbs of the Kikuyu, unlike mine or Tilly's, never seemed to tire.

When we awoke next morning it was grey and drizzly and the world appeared to share our sadness. The clanger sounded promptly at half past six, but the labour force was not responsive. People drifted in with downcast eyes, walking slowly, their stomachs queasy and their heads like drums full of heavy stones. Sammy stood by the store directing them with a quiet hauteur, speaking with patience even when they were particularly dense. Already he felt the potion of authority working in his blood and brain.

"Alec is going to have a packet of trouble," Tilly said, observing this as she gave Sammy her last instructions. There was no time to worry now. Everything was packed, and loaded into the mule-cart. I had said good-bye to Moyale and Njombo and to many others; I could not believe that in a few moments the house, the garden, the farm and everything in it would be out of sight and gone, as if on another planet; or that it was beyond my power, beyond anyone's, to freeze it, to catch it in a groove like an old gramophone record and keep repeating the same few minutes over and over, forever.

"Kiss each of the four walls of the living-room," Tilly said, "and you will come back for sure." I did so, and fingered Kupanya's bead necklace with the men, women and children in it, and felt better. This was only an interlude, like going to Molo, and everything would still be here to greet us when we returned after the war.

Chapter Thirty

WE went to Nairobi in the train, and then in a procession of three rickshaws from the station to the crowded hotel. The Norfolk was a great place for running into people; sooner or later, it was said, every up-country European climbed the steps of its veranda, or passed in front of it along the dusty avenue of gum-trees planted by John Ainsworth, the sub-Commissioner who had helped to lay out the town, towards the bridge called after him just out of sight down the road.

Tilly met many acquaintances, including Dick Montagu, who was standing everyone drinks and recounting, in his booming voice, his adventures while leading a patrol into German territory and wiping out a dangerous enemy post. But Randall Swift, whom we also encountered on his way to Europe, had a different story; according to his version, Dick Montagu had advanced upon a German mission, found the missionary at breakfast, shot him through the window and walked in to finish up his bacon and eggs.

We saw Humphrey Crawfurd, which was unexpected, and he looked older, and tired, and somehow dispirited, like a bird that is fished out of a tank. Perhaps he had run out of money to make water-furrows, and of course the death of Ian would have been a hard blow.

"Is Kate with you?" Tilly inquired.

A strange look came over Humphrey Crawfurd's face, like the despairing look of a cornered animal. He turned his head away and mumbled a sentence impossible to hear, and then looked back at Tilly in a puzzled way and said:

"You haven't heard. You see, Kate . . . Kate . . ."

That seemed to be all. He ducked his head and walked away, looking at the ground.

We stood there in confusion; Tilly frowned. "Perhaps it is the baby," she said. "Perhaps Kate has lost it. She ought to have come to Nairobi, instead of staying up there on the farm."

I imagined a baby lost in the forest; perhaps Kate had put it down and it had crawled into a hole and gone to sleep, and Kate had searched everywhere, calling vainly. I was sorry for Humphrey, who looked as if his spirit had been crushed by a python and lay inside him limp and shrunken, instead of filling his body as the sap fills a tree.

That night I could not get off to sleep because of the excitement of our coming journey, and the heat, and mosquitoes which pinged outside my net with a malignant obsession to find a chink. No sound concentrates so much spitefulness and malice into a very small volume as the pinging of mosquitoes, as if needles tipped with poison were vibrating in a persistent tattoo. Sometimes, from the Norfolk, you could hear lions grunting on the nearby plains, but that night they were still.

After a while Tilly came in. She turned up the safari lamp so that I could just see her sitting on the other bed, a dark shape against the soft, folded whiteness of the mosquito net which hung above her like ectoplasm in a spirit photograph. I asked sleepily:

"Has the baby been found?"

"What baby?"

"Mrs. Crawfurd's."

Tilly paused for so long before replying that I thought she had forgotten my question. But at last she said: "The baby's all right. It is Kate who is lost. If you see Mr. Crawfurd, you mustn't mention her. He is half off his head."

I was muzzy with sleep, and could not understand how Kate had got lost. She had never walked far, or wandered off alone. Perhaps the Dorobo had led her in search of something in the forest, and then deserted her.

"She needed a doctor," Tilly added, "and if he had got there in time, she might have been saved. If only she had gone to Nairobi, as Humphrey wanted her to. . . ."

If I had been there, I would have saddled the pony and galloped so fast to Nakuru that he would have fallen dead at the doctor's feet, his nostrils flecked with bloody foam, like the horse that brought the good news from Ghent to Aix; the doctor would have galloped through the night and reached Kate Crawfurd in the nick of time.

"It wasn't the doctor's fault," Tilly added. "He came as soon as he got the message. But the boy they sent with it spent four hours up a tree to escape a wounded buffalo."

The marks of its horns were on the tree-trunk, Tilly said, to confirm his story. And he had seen a half-healed wound on the buffalo's shoulder, suppurating and fly-devoured. So no one could blame the messenger, or even the buffalo.

"It was that Dutchman—that young brute who stole their pony and was always blazing off with his gun. He wounded the beast and let it get away. And then it did for Kate. I'd like to do for him. . . ."

"It wasn't Dirk's fault," I said. I remembered that wounded buffalo, and how Dirk had tracked it nearly all day, even with his stiff leg. It was the Dorobo who had found the buffalo, and I who had found the Dorobo, and it struck me suddenly that I was to blame for this disaster, in a roundabout way. If I had never told Dirk about the Dorobo, he would never have wounded the buffalo; and if I had not stood that morning in the forest looking at the dikdik and the butterflies, and wanted to get tobacco for the Dorobo, none of this would have come about. This sudden glimpse of a pattern of events in which one had a part without knowing it, in which some force beyond all comprehension moved one about like a counter on a board, was very frightening, and I lay still without saying anything more, and thinking that the deepest magic of the Kikuyu would be needed to keep one out of reach of these malignant powers that controlled a sequence starting with butterflies in a forest glade and ending with the death of Kate Crawfurd.

"Now Humphrey's got the baby on his hands," Tilly continued, talking more to herself than to me. "He can't find anyone to look after it, wounded soldiers are more in fashion now than babies; I offered to take it home with me, but he wants to keep it here. . . ."

That was just like Tilly; starting next morning for a voyage on a cargo-boat with an unknown destiny ahead of her, and no preparations, she was quite willing to include a new-born baby among her kit. Mrs. Pascoe had taken it in for the time being, and Bay as well, among her abandoned pets and salvaged animals, while Humphrey looked for someone in Nairobi to return with him to Molo. Kate's death had shattered him; he was like a tree whose taproot has been cut, or a broken-winged hawk. Even the water-furrows had been made for Kate, as other men would bring fine clothes or jewellery.

He came to see us off for Mombasa next day, and busied himself getting our luggage into place. Every corner of the train was occupied; so packed were the native coaches that you could hardly see the woodwork, people were like bunches of human bananas attached to a wooden stem. It seemed impossible that even one extra body could be squeezed in, but travellers kept arriving and somehow penetrating inside. We had our food with us in baskets, and bottles of soda-water for drinking and for cleaning our teeth.

"Will you be seeing Lettice," Humphrey asked, "when you get home?"

Tilly said that she would.

"Then give her this." Humphrey thrust a package into her hand. "It was Ian's. She might like something of his." It was his watch, as we saw later: a gold half-hunter, thinner than a penny-piece and engraved with his monogram. It was something she could treasure, if she felt so inclined. But it was a question whether Africans were not wiser to burn everything a dead person had owned and keep no memorial, nor try to cultivate seeds of immortality in a desert of time.

"Did Dirk send back the pony?" I asked Humphrey.

"No, he took it with him. But he sent a message to say he'd pay me back after the war."

Humphrey had a thin, brittle look, his eyes were sunken, and did not appear to be taking things in. He moved slowly, like a mechanical man. But he got our luggage on board and paid the ragged, self-appointed porters, and refused to accept Tilly's change.

"I think I have found someone for Bay and the baby," he said. "I think Lois Montagu will come."

"But is she giving up wounded soldiers?"

"The only soldiers she has nursed so far had d.t.s; and she wants to escape from Dick, who keeps turning up in Nairobi and trying to carry her off. She is too young and silly, but for the time being . . ."

"If it's any help, I'll take the baby, wherever I am."

"Thank you, Tilly, I'll remember that."

"Lois may turn out all right, once she has responsibility."

"Yes. . . ."

"The train's late in starting."

"There may have been some trouble down the line."

At last the whistle blew, flags waved and they shook hands through the window.

"My love to Robin."

"Write to us sometimes."

Humphrey nodded, and looked up at her as she peered down from the coach, and for the first time a twinge of life returned to his face. The engine chuffed, people shouted, smoke billowed, the carriage gave a jerk like a twitching muscle. All we could do was to wave at the upright figure standing stiffly on the crowded platform.

We saw him turn and walk away, but had no time to watch him out of sight. Our varied collection of packages had to be reorganized, with the aid of our fellow-passengers, who eyed it with misgiving, especially a bundle done up in sacking from which a pungent odour emerged. This contained home-cured sheepskins Tilly was taking with her to fashion into a warm waistcoat for Robin, a piece of work more suited, she thought, to a Greek cargo-boat in wartime than the bedspread she was embroidering with flowers and birds in fine Chinese silk, and which she had left in the bank, having heard that submarines were sinking ships all over the Mediterranean, and feeling reluctant to risk the loss of something that had cost her so much time and care.

"I wonder if those skins were properly cured," she remarked, inspecting the bundle. "If not, they will make their presence felt in the Red Sea."

I carried the *kiondo*, that soft woven basket Kupanya's wife had given me, with a number of treasures inside: the stuffed baby crocodile presented to me by Pioneer Mary, my bead necklace, a cardboard box of birds' eggs, several cocoons in matchboxes, some grenadillas—Kamau's parting present—from the vine partially covering our kitchen, and Njombo's gift, the little bead-edged cap made from a sheep's stomach that I had so much admired. Sammy's spear lay in the rack, together with a small native drum, a Kikuyu sword in its vermilion scabbard, a Dorobo bow and arrows and my favourite hippo-hide riding-whip. It was not until all our hand packages lay around us in the confined space of a railway carriage that Tilly quite realized their number and variety.

"Do you think," she inquired, "that you will really need all those weapons, as *well* as a drum?"

"Sammy said I was to kill Germans with the spear, and cut off their heads with the sword."

"There are no Germans at your aunt Mildred's in Porchester Terrace, where we shall stay: only a Belgian refugee."

I was surprised to see that when she looked out of the window at the retreating wooden shacks and tin roofs of Nairobi, her eyes were red. She delved into her bag, made by an Indian from the skin of the python Robin had shot.

"All this luggage," she remarked glumly, "and I seem to have left my hankies behind."

I was preoccupied with other troubles. A ripe pawpaw someone had given us for the journey had fallen from its basket on the rack into a large pith topee resting on the seat by its owner's side. He was a red-faced gentleman with bloodshot eyes, generous moustaches and a neat, compact and well-disciplined quota of hand luggage, including one of those leather cases, shaped like a coal-scuttle, used to transport top-hats and other headgear of a superior kind. The pawpaw had burst, releasing a cascade of squashy yellow pulp and slimy black seeds, like fish-roe only many times larger. The topee's owner, who had not yet noticed this accident, coughed and turned his head.

"Look at that funny animal," I cried, pointing out of the window. Everyone turned, but there was nothing to be seen except the plains, green with fresh growth, the tin sheds, a rusty siding, a knot of ragged gangers leaning on their picks, a few waggle-tailed Thomson's gazelle, a pair of ostriches and an Indian, obviously a Muslim, squatting with his back to the train.

I made a face at Tilly. She saw the pawpaw, and frowned; we were trapped, the train had no corridor. She did not hesitate; smiling with all her charm, she asked the red-faced gentleman to help her stow our soda-water bottles on the rack, and in five minutes he was eating out of her hand. I looked through the open window at the undulating purple ridge-back of the Ngong hills, a haunt of lions and buffaloes, and was glad that I had kissed the four walls of the grass hut at Thika, and was bound to return.